EFFECTIVE MANAGEMENT IN HUMAN SERVICES

Walter P. Christian
Gerald T. Hannah

Prentice-Hall, Inc., Englewood Cliffs, New Jersey 07632

Library of Congress Cataloging in Publication Data

CHRISTIAN, WALTER P.
    Effective management in human services

    Bibliography: p.
    Includes index.
    1. Social work administration.   I. Hannah, Gerald T.
II. Title.
HV41.C47   1983   361'.0068   82-18082
ISBN 0-13-244244-2

Editorial/production supervision by Richard Kilmartin and Fred Bernardi
Interior design by Richard Kilmartin
Cover design by Photo Plus Art
Manufacturing buyer: Ron Chapman

© 1983 by PRENTICE-HALL, INC., Englewood Cliffs, N.J. 07632

Printed in the United States of America

10 9 8 7 6 5 4 3 2 1

ISBN: 0-13-244244-2

PRENTICE-HALL INTERNATIONAL, INC., *London*
PRENTICE-HALL OF AUSTRALIA PTY. LIMITED, *Sydney*
EDITORA PRENTICE-HALL DO BRASIL, LTDA., *Rio de Janeiro*
PRENTICE-HALL CANADA INC., *Toronto*
PRENTICE-HALL OF INDIA PRIVATE LIMITED, *New Delhi*
PRENTICE-HALL OF JAPAN, INC., *Tokyo*
PRENTICE-HALL OF SOUTHEAST ASIA PTE. LTD., *Singapore*
WHITEHALL BOOKS LIMITED, *Wellington, New Zealand*

perience as human service managers. We would be remiss, however, if we did not acknowledge the extent to which this experience has been influenced by our colleagues. Our greatest debt is to Dr. Todd R. Risley for his support of our professional activities and for his constant encouragement to improve our management methods. Our approach to human service management has also been shaped by those who have been our managers in recent years, especially Drs. Joe Burnett, Richard Surles, and Robert Harder. Our editor at Prentice-Hall, Mr. Ted Jursek, has provided us with invaluable guidance throughout the course of this book's development. We also gratefully acknowledge the contributions of Marie Williams and Barbara Dyer, our superb secretaries, whose typing skill is exceeded only by their patience.

A final note of appreciation to our families whose patience, understanding, and support made this book possible—our wives, Barbara Christian and Jacki Hannah; and children, Katherine and Kent Christian, and Julie, Thomas, Emily, Michael, and Lindsey Hannah.

WALTER P. CHRISTIAN
GERALD T. HANNAH

1

Issues and Problems in Human Service Management

The human service system is composed of public health, mental health, and social and rehabilitation services. It is second only to national defense as the nation's biggest governmental industry. Human service programs include both governmental (federal, state, and local) agencies and private profit/non-profit organizations. For the most part, the human service system is not organized to provide services for profit, but rather must offer services either without charge, below their actual cost, or at cost. Its consumers may be reluctant and may even have to be forced to accept its services.

There may be no industry in greater need of effective management than the human service system. Escalating costs, increasing governmental regulation, and persistent consumer demand have created an industry that appears actively to resist direction and control. Our technology for developing service delivery systems has surpassed our technology for effectively managing them.

One reason for this discrepancy is the gulf that frequently exists between management theory and practice. Evidence of this problem can be found in an examination of the reference literature written for managers and administrators. The literature is dominated by theoretical approaches that resemble fads. The manager who turns to the literature for assistance is often encouraged completely to overhaul his or her administrative policy and procedure consistent with the philosophy of "matrix organization," "management by objective," "key factor analysis," and

1

so forth. Furthermore, theory is more often classroom-specific than situation-specific. The student of human service management may therefore learn a theory without learning how to adapt it successfully to his or her specific work situation.

This problem is further complicated by the fact that a new theoretical approach just might not work; indeed, it might create more problems for the manager. In fact, many of the models and theories so highly recommended in the management literature have not been adequately tested, that is, their applicability and effectiveness have not been experimentally verified. For example, a review of the literature on "management by objective" (MBO) reveals that, with few exceptions, performance measures have not been used to assess the effects of MBO. Instead, testimonials, anecdotal reports, position papers, satisfaction ratings, and/or attitudinal measures have been used.

Another reason for the frequent discrepancy between the technologies of program development and management is the complexity of the human service system. Human service delivery involves three major components: programs, providers, and consumers. Ideally, these components should operate and interact to produce a high quality of service and consumer satisfaction. In such an ideal scheme, programs would be well-organized, effective, financially solvent, and accountable. Providers would be willing and able to meet the needs of the consumer. Consumers would be cooperative with and supportive of the program and the service providers.

Unfortunately, the various components of the human service system rarely operate so effectively and harmoniously. The human service manager is constantly faced with major issues and problems that ultimately determine the nature of his or her job, and how effectively he or she gets the job done. A number of these major issues, or pressure points, will now be described.

COST EFFECTIVENESS

The United States human service system has become one of the largest industries in the world. Government expenditures for social welfare, including health care, have grown from $77.8 billion in 1970 to $289.9 billion or 11.6 percent of our gross national product in 1980 (U.S. Government, 1979, 1981). Meyer (1975), Williams (1981) and others have observed that these increasing costs may work to the detriment of human service delivery in the future, for example, by decreasing federal support of certain programs, increasing federal regulation in an attempt to cut costs, and so on.

Indeed, cost effectiveness has become everyone's concern. Cost effectiveness can be defined as the relationship between resources and outcomes. For example, we speak of a cost-effectiveness ratio of the amount of staff time spent with a client to the amount of improvement seen in a client's behavior. The "how-to" of cost-effectiveness analysis will be discussed in Chapters 6 and 7. In this section, we are concerned with issues related to cost effectiveness.

The bottom line seems to be that services must be cost-effective if funding and public and political support for them is to continue. However, the variables affecting cost effectiveness are much easier to understand than to control. They include factors as diverse as (1) the consumer's presenting problem and level of functioning; (2) the quality and quantity of direct service and administrative personnel; (3) management practices; and (4) program evaluation. Specifically, consumers with severe problems require staff in greater numbers and with greater expertise. In addition, low-functioning, dependent consumers require assistance to perform even the most basic of daily activities (for example, toileting, bathing), and thus are able to provide little assistance to staff. Cost effectiveness is difficult to achieve when the consumers who cost the most to serve are also those who are the most difficult to serve effectively.

Another issue concerns the choice of the appropriate unit of cost to ensure effective cost analysis. For example, Binner and Nassimbene (1980) have observed that while the *daily maintenance expenditure* (the average cost of a day of service to the consumer) has traditionally been used as the unit of cost for mental health services, it may not be appropriate for present-day mental health service delivery. They argue that, as active treatment and return to community living have become the primary goals of mental health services, the *episode of care expenditure* (the cost from admission to discharge for a single patient) may be a more appropriate unit of cost. The appropriate unit of cost is therefore dependent on the type of service delivered.

In addition, cost effectiveness requires a well-designed, ongoing system of program evaluation. Without close monitoring of service costs and outcomes, the administrator is not able to make the modifications necessary to offset undesirable trends in service costs and program effectiveness.

Finally, much of the literature on cost effectiveness is concerned with analysis and theory. It does not enable the beleaguered administrator to envision cost effectiveness as a function of consumers, staff, administrative practices, and program evaluation strategies, that is to say, in terms of specific aspects of his or her environment on which he or she can exert influence.

Cost effectiveness is further complicated by the unrelenting mixed message of the public and the courts: *increase* effectiveness, *decrease* costs.

FINANCING

A problem closely related to cost effectiveness is that of maintaining adequate financing for one's program. Human services are financed by (1) direct payment from the consumer; (2) payment through some form of private insurance; (3) payment through agencies of federal, state, and local governments (for example, federal block grants to the states, payments to private human service programs by local school districts and state social service agencies); and/or (4) funds received from private contributors (individuals and/or foundations).

However, as service costs continue to rise, each of these funding sources is showing signs of strain. For example, the changing political climate of the 1980s has resulted in significant cuts in federal support for human services, especially in areas concerned with research and program development (Williams, 1981). Since the double-digit inflation and decline in work productivity of the mid 1970s, private foundations have decreased their financial contributions in support of certain human service programs.

It is, therefore, becoming increasingly apparent that human service managers must implement effective procedures for increasing consumer fee collections and must explore new methods for increasing private contributions. If managers are to be successful in maintaining funding for their programs, they must also understand both the constraints and the opportunities contingent upon their interactions with various governmental agencies.

CONSUMER NEED

Another serious problem facing the human service manager is the frequent lack of correlation between the consumer's *needs* and the *services* the consumer actually receives. This problem is also difficult to remedy since it is the result of a large number of factors, including (1) the accuracy and appropriateness of diagnostic (need) assessment and service planning (goals, objectives, and criteria for success); (2) the advantages and limitations of the program's physical environment and available resources; (3) the quality and quantity of program personnel (for example, expertise of staff, staff-to-client ratio); (4) the extent of the consumer's understanding and participation (for example, informed consent); (5) the training, supervision, and evaluation provided for program personnel; (6) the effectiveness of program evaluation and accountability systems (for example, client progress reviews, client tracking systems); and (7) the effectiveness of regulatory agencies.

Breakdowns or deficiencies in any of these areas could threaten the need-service correlation and, thus, the legality of the program's service to the consumer. The consumer's *need,* as opposed to program policy and procedure, must determine the services he or she receives.

LEGAL POLICY

Reed Martin, a leading expert concerning the rights of clients and students, warned in 1975 of a "growing legal challenge to *all* public programs as courts begin to inquire into areas previously left to administrative discretion." Every human service manager is acutely aware of the accuracy of Martin's prediction.

Martin (1975) identified four sources of legal policy concerning the delivery of human services: (1) the due process clause of the Constitution; (2) the equal protection clause of the Constitution; (3) judicial precedent; and (4) the application of administrative guidelines. *Due process* requires that when services involve deprivation of an individual's liberty or property (for example, administering a drug which limits the patient's control of his or her behavior, withholding mail or personal belongings from institutionalized clients) there must be due process of law. Due process is understood to require a hearing before an impartial body, the opportunity to hear witnesses, and the opportunity to appeal the decision.

Equal protection of the law requires that a human service agency treat each consumer or consumer group in substantially the same way as other consumers or consumer groups entitled to the same treatment. Violations of the equal protection clause can be seen in the assignment of consumers to service programs and research projects on the basis of race; the refusal of a public school to educate a child on the basis of his or her race, religion, or handicapping condition; or the often arbitrary and capricious treatment of the institutionalized mentally ill and developmentally disabled.

The third source of legal policy affecting human services is common law—*court cases which build legal doctrine by precedent.* An understanding of these legal precedents is critical for the human service manager. These court decisions have not only determined standards for human service delivery and specified the rights of consumers, they have provided a valuable source of information for predicting the nature of legal challenges that may lie ahead.

The fourth and final source of legal policy concerns the *application of administrative guidelines by the courts.* This involves the government's use of funding contingencies to ensure that clients' rights are protected and that standards for human service delivery are met. Examples of these guidelines can be seen in the re quirements of P.L. 94–142 (for example, individualized education plans for handicapped children) and Titles XVIII and XIX of the Social Security Amendments of 1965 (for example, regulations concerning the use of seclusion and restraint in institutions eligible for funding under Titles XVIII and XIX).

The message for the human service manager is clear: provide a high quality of individualized, cost-effective services—but only within the limits of the consumer's rights as client and individual. Problems in this area are the result of the manager's lack of understanding concerning (1) the law and its implications for the human service consumer, and (2) the various procedures that can be employed to preserve the consumer's rights in service delivery. The manager's dilemma is further complicated by the lack of literature on protecting consumers' rights. (We will discuss strategies for safeguarding rights in Chapter 8.)

EXTERNAL REGULATION

Self-regulation is no longer the prerogative of the human service manager. External regulation has accompanied our increasing dependence on financial support from federal, state, and local governments. In short, when governments underwrite funds, they regulate expenditure. The more governments are asked to underwrite, the more they are likely to regulate. Thus, government dollars such as those available via Medicaid/Medicare carry a price tag in the form of required utilization reports, compliance with the requirements of Titles XVIII and XIX, and so on.

Increasing regulations, and the quantity and quality of effort necessary to comply with them, are a constant source of concern for the human service manager. Human service management in the 1980s requires a working knowledge of federal, state, and local governments and how they act individually, cooperatively, and/or competitively to regulate human service delivery. In addition, the manager must be knowledgeable concerning such diverse issues as eligibility criteria, utilization control, information systems, and regional planning.

It has also become imperative for the human service manager to be constantly aware of the status of his or her program vis-à-vis applicable regulations, that is, when the program is in compliance with or in violation of the regulations. This requires effective program evaluation and quality control procedures as well as the type of data-based, proactive (as opposed to reactive) approach to program management that will be presented in subsequent chapters of this book.

PERSONNEL MANAGEMENT

It is his or her work with others that is likely to be the source of both the greatest satisfaction and the greatest exasperation for the manager. Despite the multitude of theories and models concerning how to motivate and satisfy personnel, the manager typically finds the leap from theory to practice to be difficult if not impossible. Thus, while the manager might want to be consultive and participative, he or she may lack the interpersonal skills to do so. Similarly, the manager who attempts to implement a job enrichment program may lack the supervisory skills to keep personnel on-task.

Managing human service personnel is further complicated by the nature of the services they provide to the consumer. Human service consumers are likely to be ill, handicapped, or disadvantaged in some way, relative to the general population. Services are often remedial and may involve considerable risk to the consumer unless they are carefully and expertly provided. In addition, programs, services, and providers are subject to an unusual degree of scrutiny and regulation by the public. Common personnel problems, such as resistance to organizational policies, work slowdowns, sabotage, absenteeism, and turnover, take on special significance when they occur in human service programs.

Other personnel management problems concern the work force characteristic of most human service programs. Human service professionals come from a variety of disciplines, some of which may have a history of conflict with others (for example, psychology with psychiatry). In addition, each professional has his or her own perception of expertise, area of responsibility, and so on. Since human service consumers often require the attention of more than one professional and/or more than one discipline, overlap, conflict, and bruised egos are bound to occur. The manager must be adept at understanding and resolving these conflicts.

The human service work force is also characterized by a large number of para-professional, nonprofessional, and volunteer personnel. These personnel may require special orientation and training programs, on-the-job coaching, and close supervision.

ORGANIZATION

Numerous investigations, beginning with the classic Hawthorne studies of the 1930s (Parsons, 1974), have examined the effect of formal and informal organization on employee behavior. Research has shown that organizations, by definition, are characterized by rational planning, control, and coordination of members and activities. However, research also indicates that any given organizational strategy may, in some circumstances, result in employee dissatisfaction, apathy, frustration, and/or lack of productivity.

Thus, *how* people are organized effects their behavior. For example, if a particular organizational design features rigid adherence to rules, it may not be adaptable to the social, economical, political demands of the human service environment. On the other hand, if an organizational design is characterized by too much flexibility, role ambiguity and role conflict may result. It seems clear from the literature that unless the design of an organization is consistent with its size and function, problems are likely to develop. The manager must therefore understand the specific needs of his or her program as well as what can be expected from various organizational strategies.

PROGRAM EVALUATION

In the preceding sections of this chapter, we have described a number of problems that the effective human service manager should attempt to identify and remedy. However, problem identification requires program evaluation and feedback mechanisms that may be difficult for some managers to develop and implement. One source of concern is the *focus* of the evaluation activity: What aspects of the problem are to be the focus of evaluation efforts? What dependent variables are to be measured? Dependent measures frequently used in the evaluation of human service programs have included health status outcome, estimates concerning quality of service, quantity of service, consumer satisfaction, resource utilization, and cost (Roemer, 1968).

A second source of concern is the choice of the actual *evaluation model and strategies* to be employed. How will data be gathered? How will results be analyzed and interpreted? The choice of an evaluation model must be governed by the criteria of appropriateness, adequacy, effectiveness, and efficiency.

A third concern is *how feedback from program evaluation is assimilated by the program* and acted upon. Is feedback from program evaluation understood by those who need to act on it? How does one insure that program evaluation results in quality control and program improvement?

A final issue is one of *personnel management.* How does one recruit a competent program evaluator? How does one determine and schedule the activities of a program evaluator?

AUTHORITY

Another recurrent problem in human service management concerns the degree of control that the manager has over his or her program. Human service programs are characterized by the large amount of power vested in those responsible for delivery of services. In addition, considerable power is exercised by state governments (for state-administered programs), by the federal government (for federally funded programs), and by boards of trustees and boards of directors (for private, profit and non-profit programs).

Levey and Loomba (1973) and others have argued that the present status of human service management often does not afford the manager sufficient control over his or her program. They have recommended that "administrators . . .must be given the authority to formulate policies and *manage* them—not simply administer policies" (p. 11). But how is this done? How does the manager increase his or her degree of control over program policy and procedure? How can the manager work more effectively with state administrators and boards of trustees to ensure a cooperative rather than a competitive relationship?

THE MANAGER

The final source of problems in human service management concerns the behavior of the individual manager: his or her understanding of the job, competence to perform the job, and ability to interact successfully and work productively with others. Specifically, the effective manager must understand and perform (or successfully delegate) the functions of organization and planning; recruitment, training, supervision, and evaluation of personnel; program evaluation and quality control; management of material resources; financing; public relations; and client advocacy.

As previously discussed, the manager's academic training and professional experience are not always sufficient preparation for such a multifaceted role. This may be especially true of the *clinical manager*—the human service professional who has been promoted to an upper-level management position. Clinical managers may be at a disadvantage if they have not had adequate training and experience in such areas as accounting, financial management, and personnel management. On the other hand, the clinical manager may enjoy the advantage of understanding clients' needs and knowing the type of professional who must be employed to meet those needs. Evaluation and supervision of service personnel may also be facilitated when the manager has had experience as a service provider.

The *business manager* may have strengths in the very areas that the clinical manager has weaknesses (and vice versa). But whatever his or her background, training, and experience, the manager must work well with people—colleagues, program staff, consumers, supervising officials, and the general public. He or she must therefore possess the interpersonal skills necessary to communicate with others, to be assertive without being abrasive, and, in general, to initiate and maintain mutually reinforcing social interactions. In addition, the manager's "achievement motivation" (McClelland, 1965), "leader effectiveness" (Argyris, 1976), and "management style" (Vroom & Yelton, 1973) should be conducive to effective management. Finally, the manager must be able to respond to the many work-related problems that have been described in this chapter, while at the same time coping with the personal problems (physical or mental illness, marital problems, financial difficulties, and so on) that can effect his or her management performance.

The Reactive Manager

The issues and problems discussed in the previous section present a formidable challenge for the human service manager. Drucker (1974) has observed that "management has no choice but to anticipate the future, to attempt to mold it, and to balance short-range and long-term goals," but that "it is not given to mortals to do any of these things well." Indeed, managers tend to behave *reactively* (reacting to problems) rather than *proactively* (anticipating and preventing problems). This is understandable, since reactive management may appear to be the course of least effort—the "no news is good news" approach to management. In addition, managers may be tempted to adopt a packaged solution to a problem (a new administrative organization, or a philosophical approach) that itself is static, inflexible, and reactive. In choosing such a comprehensive solution, the manager may overreact and initiate changes that are neither time- nor cost-efficient.

Reactive management is characterized by ambiguous administrative structure, since the manager's organizational chart often has not been established through delegation of responsibility, communication, feedback, and supervision. Communication, when it does occur, is up-down and typically takes the form of negative administrative feedback in response to crisis, or of staff meetings where little long-term planning or proactive trouble-shooting occurs. Poor staff morale and decreased productivity are predictable in such situations.

Under reactive management, therefore, the problems that have been discussed in this chapter are more likely to be complicated than solved. The reason for this is that, by reacting, one does not learn to understand, predict, and control problems. Reactive management is therefore ineffective management.

The Effective Manager

Up to this point, we have focused on the many problems that face the present-day human service manager and on some of the reasons why he or she is often ineffective in attempts to understand, control, and predict them. What, then, is effective management? How does one learn to cope more effectively with the issues and problems of managing human services?

Manager effectiveness has been the subject of a great deal of theory and rhetoric. For example, we have learned that effective managers are characterized by supervisory ability, need for occupational achievement and for self-actualization, intelligence, self-assurance, and decisiveness (Ghiselli, 1971). In addition, effective managers reportedly possess high ''need-achievement,'' high ''socialized need-power,'' and low to moderate ''need-affiliation'' (McClelland, 1965). Some have argued that effective management is situation-specific—that directive, non-participatory management is effective in some situations while in others non-directive, participatory management is called for (Vroom & Yelton, 1973).

While these observations and theories can be informative, they tend to confuse the central issue: *effective management is essentially a performance measure.* As Drucker has observed, ''In the last analysis, management is practice. Its essence is not knowing, but doing. Its test is not logic, but results. Its only authority is performance'' (1974, p. xiii).

Manager performance can in turn be viewed as how the manager acts on the environment to produce some change or product. Beginning with the work of B.F. Skinner, research studies have demonstrated a number of ''laws of behavior''—the ways in which behavior is understood, controlled, and predicted. This literature differs from that more typically read by managers in that it is data-based: the laws of behavior have been empirically validated and replicated over a variety of behaving organisms, behaviors, and environments.

The fact of the matter is that we behave, perform, manage in ways that bring us some form of pleasure or pay-off from the environment. When our behavior or performance is rewarded, we are likely to engage in it again under similar circumstances. Our behavior has been *reinforced*. For example, if an employee submits a correct, timely, written report and is met with positive feedback and compliments from Supervisor A, he or she is likely to submit other correct, timely reports in the future. In this case, a desirable consequence (positive feedback) was made contingent upon a particular behavior (timely submission of a correct report) so that the probability of this behavior occurring again in the future has been increased.

However, our behavior is not always met with positive consequences. When a behavior results in some undesirable consequence we are less likely to engage in that behavior in the future. Our behavior in this case has been *punished*. For example, if the same employee submits the same report to Supervisor B and is met with petty criticisms and little in the way of positive feedback, he or she will be less likely to make the effort to submit a timely, correct report to Supervisor B. In this case, an undesirable consequence (negative feedback) was made contingent upon a particular behavior (timely submission of a correct report) so that the probability that this behavior will occur again in the future has been decreased.

In each of these cases, an employee's behavior has been influenced by his or her supervisor. However, the employee has also influenced the supervisor's behavior. The employee has "taught" Supervisor A that providing positive feedback is a way to increase his or her timely submission of correct reports. The employee has "taught" Supervisor B that his or her timely submission of correct reports will not be favorably influenced by negative feedback; hence, the *communication function* of behavior change.

Notice the powerful influence of the employee's environment on his or her behavior: the same individual exposed to the same situation is likely to respond in entirely different ways as a function of environmental consequences. Indeed, we know from the research literature on behavior change that Supervisor A in our example will come to occasion approach behavior (social interaction) by the employee, while Supervisor B will come to occasion avoidance behavior by the employee. This basic paradigm can be represented as follows:

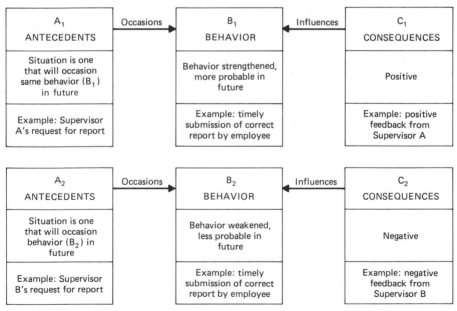

FIGURE 1-1   The ABC's of Behavior Change

The effective manager knows these ABC's and how to use them, that is, how to schedule antecedents and consequences to bring about and maintain a desired quantity and quality of performance. In short, the effective manager realizes that management is lawful—it follows the laws of human behavior.

Personnel management provides an excellent example of these ABC's in action. The effective manager develops a description of the tasks that the employee is to perform; provides orientation and training concerning how the job is to be done; and provides an environment conducive to task performance. In each of these cases, the manager has scheduled *antecedents* that he or she hopes will *occasion* a certain type of performance by the employee.

The effective manager also schedules environmental *consequences* for employee performance while the task is being performed, as well as at its completion. For example, the manager schedules feedback that helps the employee adjust or shape his or her ongoing performance to be consistent with the manager's criteria for successful task completion. At the completion of the task, the manager provides either positive consequences (for example, praise, a pay increase) for appropriate, timely and efficient task completion, or negative consequences (for example, criticism, a pay decrease, change of work) for inappropriate, untimely and inefficient task performance.

The effective manager can thus *predict* that rewarded performance will be strengthened and will become more probable in the future while punished or non-reinforced performance will be weakened and less probable. In other words, the job description provided by the manager can come to occasion either the performance of certain reinforced behaviors or the non-performance of certain non-reinforced or punished behaviors. The manager has therefore learned to manage behavior and has found it reinforcing—his or her managing got the job done. Both appropriate management and staff performance have been strengthened.

Given the logic of the preceding example, it is understandable that behavioral management is often dismissed as simplistic, although, relative to other management strategies, it is far less confusing, has been more thoroughly tested, and is more consistent with the real world of the manager. However, behavioral management is also *systematic* and requires that one attend to a sequence of operations. The operations ensure that management is responsive, effective and accountable, and that it is sufficiently task-analyzed to be understood and performed.

The operations involved in systematic behavioral management will be described in the next chapter. In subsequent chapters, they will be applied to some of the most serious problems facing the human service manager.

SUMMARY

The technology of human service management is in need of improvement. It is more theoretical than practical and lacks sufficient field-testing and empirical verification. As such, it is no match for the complex human service system and its incumbent issues and problems, the most serious of which are cost effectiveness, financing, consumer demand, legal pressure, external regulation, personnel management, organization, program evaluation, authority, and the strengths and weaknesses of the individual manager.

Ineffective managers react to problems; effective managers learn to understand, predict, and control them. Effective management is a performance measure, that is, the manager acts on his or her environment to produce change. Management is lawful: it follows laws of behavior that have been documented in a large number of well-controlled research studies. Specifically, behavior is strengthened by positive environmental consequences and weakened by negative consequences. The effective manager learns to use the antecedents and consequences in the human service environment to occasion and maintain an appropriate quantity and quality of staff performance.

2

Planning for Effective Management

The issues and problem discussed in the previous chapter suggest a cautious course for the human service manager. The manager must recognize the *goals* and *standards* to be achieved (for example, meeting consumer need, following legal policy, being in conformity with external regulation) and the *resources* that he or she can use in achieving them (for example, finances, personnel, his or her own skills and abilities). The manager must then take the necessary steps to *utilize resources* and *implement procedures* in order to meet objectives and achieve goals, for example, by organization, control, personnel management, and financial management. Finally, the manager must *evaluate* the success of the program relative to its mission, goals, and objectives, and must change aspects of his or her management strategy when it is evident that goals are not being met.

In short, the very nature of the manager's environment requires that he or she develop a strategic plan and follow it systematically. Such a plan provides a sequence of interdependent operations which help to orient, direct, and structure the day to day performance of the manager. An effective operational plan also provides the manager with a set of guidelines for identifying and correcting problems. Effective planning, therefore, specifies the task to be completed (*What?*), the person responsible for completing it (*Who?*), the time-lines for completion (*When?*), and the quantity and quality of performance (*How?*).

The acronym AIM provides a useful model for management planning. It

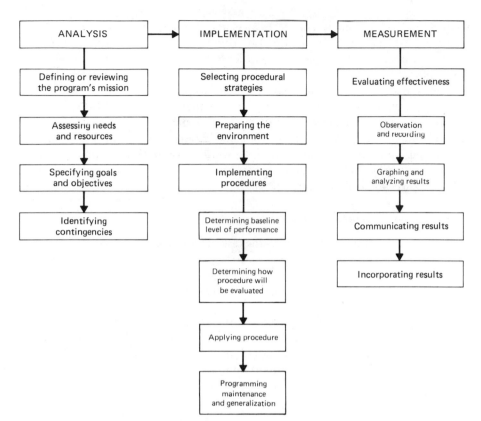

FIGURE 2-1   The AIM of Effective Management

represents three major components—*analysis, implementation,* and *measurement*—
each of which involves a sequence of operations for the manager.

ANALYSIS

Defining or Reviewing the Program's Mission

In general, the program's mission is to provide some form of service to some
population of consumers. A specific mission will be determined by (a) the needs of
the community in which the program is located; (b) the decisions of supervising officials and/or Boards of Trustees concerning the type of services to be offered, consumers to be served, and staff to be employed; and (c) the requirements of funding
and regulatory agencies, legal statutes, and so on.

The program's mission provides the manager with the ultimate criterion or
"bottom line" against which to assess his or her program's effectiveness. Does a
community mental health agency provide services effective in meeting the mental

health needs of the community? Does an acute-care hospital meet the needs of the acutely ill? The program's mission also provides a basis for determining specific goals and objectives for program operation, as well as the first indication of the types of resources that will be needed to meet those goals and objectives. Thus, a program mission "to provide residential and health care services for the elderly" serves to initiate the more detailed planning that must follow. Specifically, it denotes the population of consumers (the elderly); the nature of services to be provided (residential, health care); the types of facilities (housing, hospital or nursing care capability); and the kind of staff that will be required (residential care staff, nurses and nurses' aides, social workers, psychologists, physicians, housekeepers, maintenance workers, administrators).

Assessing Needs and Resources

Before the manager goes about the task of specifying goals and objectives for program operation, he or she must assess the present status of the program. This assessment must consider both the current status of the program relative to its mission, and the availability of resources necessary for program operation.

NEEDS. Assessing the current status of program operation. gives the manager a standard against which to judge the effectiveness of his or her management strategies and indicates priorities for the specification of goals and objectives for the program. Therefore, it is important that the manager utilize a wide variety of data sources in his or her needs assessment. For example, the human service manager might look at the status of program operation in each of the following areas:

Area		Sample Data	
1.	Administrative organization, policy and procedures	a.	Current organizational chart.
		b.	Satisfaction ratings from staff.
		c.	Satisfaction ratings from supervising officials.
		d.	Copy of current policy and procedures manual.
2.	Staffing	a.	Demographic data including number of personnel by department, educational level, etcetera.
		b.	Current staff-to-client ratio.
		c.	Staff turnover during past six months.
3.	Training	a.	Training sessions scheduled during past six months; number of staff involved.
		b.	Scores from post-training tests.
4.	Services	a.	Services provided.
		b.	Satisfaction ratings by consumers, referring agencies, etcetera.

5. Consumers	a. Mean operational capacity/number patients served during past six months.
	b. Demographic data.
	c. Sources of referral.
	d. Patients discharged during past year.
6. Rights	a. Rights violations during past six months.
	b. Satisfaction ratings from consumers (for example, informed consent given, confidentiality protected).
7. Evaluation	a. Description of evaluation activities regularly conducted.
	b. Results of outside evaluation and professional peer reviews.
8. Budgeting and accounting	a. Report of current status (for example, budget control form).
	b. Projected budget for next fiscal year.
	c. Cost-effectiveness analysis for last fiscal year.
9. Physical plant	a. Results of building inspection (needed repairs and their priorities).
	b. Schedule of proposed renovations.
10. Fund raising	a. List of local contributions during past year.
	b. Grant proposals submitted and funded during past year and projected for the present year.
11. Communication with Board of Trustees/state officials	a. Copies of correspondence, reports, etcetera, to and from supervising authorities during past year.
	b. Satisfaction ratings from supervising officials concerning their ongoing communication with program staff.

Data from each of these areas can be obtained by a number of methods. Written reports can be requested from program staff; questionnaires or satisfaction ratings can be completed and analyzed; videotape and photographic studies can be made of the physical plant; interviews with staff, consumers, referring agencies, and supervising authorities can be conducted; and reviews can be conducted of case records, performance evaluations, and internal and external correspondence. (More information on evaluation strategies is included in Chapter 7.)

Whatever the assessment method, it is important to get as much data as possible before implementing a new management strategy or procedure. If more managers collected data such as these before and after they attempted a new strategy, the literature in human service management would be based more on actual performance than on theory and rhetoric.

RESOURCES.   Before specific goals and objectives can be identified, the manager must assess the availability of the resources that he or she will need to achieve the program's mission. This is important since availability of resources will in large part determine what those goals and objectives will be and the feasibility of their being achieved.

FIGURE 2-2   Resource Inventory

Resource	Required*	Available	Needed

1. Consumers
    a.   need
    b.   number
    c. demand for services			

2. Funding
    a.   sources
    b.   amount
    c. cash flow			

3. Space
    a.   amount
    b.   furnishing
    c.   safety features
    d. utilization			

4. Staffing
    a.   staff-to-patient ratio
    b.   qualifications
    c.   sex, ethnic background
    d. function			

5. Materials and Equipment
    a.   educational
    b.   medical
    c.   clerical
    d. maintenance			

*As per legal guidelines and pertinent regulatory requirements			

For example, a nursing home program must have funding, space, and staffing adequate to meet pertinent federal, state, and local regulations. In addition, there must be a sufficient number of individuals in the community in need of nursing home services. Staff must be present in sufficient numbers and possess sufficient expertise to meet the needs of the consumer if the services are to be consistent with legal guidelines.

The manager must also learn how to increase his or her resources—how to obtain increases in funding, space, staffing, and so on. For example, the manager must be aware of all potential sources of funding for programs with a mission similar to his or her own (for example, federal funding such as Medicaid reimbursement, grants from federal agencies and private foundations). He or she must know about staffing available through affiliations with university practicum training and work-study programs, and space available through an association with the local housing authority.

Identification of resources includes planning for their availability in the future. The effective manager anticipates the needs of his or her program and initiates political lobbying, fund raising, grant writing, university affiliation, and so on, well in advance of the time that additional resources are actually needed. This type of proactive resource management ensures that the goals and objectives for program operation are practical and achievable since they are developed with a good understanding of the program's resources.

Specifying Goals and Objectives

Once the manager understands the program's mission and the resources available for program operation, he or she is ready to specify more precisely the task of human service management.

GOALS.   It is important that goals be understandable, practical, and achievable. Ideally, they should be defined in terms of observable, measurable components. Goals should also be consistent with the program's mission and must be realistic in terms of the resources and technology required to achieve them.

Mager (1972) recommends a procedure called "goal analysis" to ensure that goals meet the criteria specified above. In particular, Mager shares the authors' concern that if management is properly to be perceived as performance, the goals and objectives for program management must be performance-based, that is, they must call for some specific performance by the manager. Goal analysis consists of the following steps (Mager, 1972, p. 72):

1. Write down the goal, using whatever word best describes the intent.
2. Write down the performances that would cause you to agree the goal has been achieved, without regard for duplication.
3. Sorting
   a. Look over the list and cross out duplications and items that, on second thought, you don't want.

    b.   Check the abstractions so that you will know which items you will have to put on separate pages for further analysis.

4.   Write a complete statement for each performance, describing the nature, quality, or amount you will consider acceptable.

5.   Test the statements with the question: "If someone achieved or demonstrated each of these performances, would I be willing to say he has achieved the goal?"

The following are examples of appropriate and inappropriate goal statements as suggested by Mager's "goal analysis" procedure.

Poor	Better
1. Meet the needs of the consumer.	1. Provide an adequate quality and quantity of services to the consumer.
2. Understand the special vulnerability of the human service consumer.	2. Protect the rights of the human service consumer.

OBJECTIVES.   After specifying goal statements or performance areas for the program, the manager must expand them into more specific *objectives* that (1) describe a particular performance; (2) identify the key conditions under which the performance is expected to occur; and (3) indicate the level of performance considered acceptable. This expansion is similar to Mager's (1972) goal analysis procedure.

The pinpointing of performance is particularly important here since it provides the actual target for the planning, implementation, and evaluation that will follow. It is therefore important to use operational definitions of performance, that is, definitions that objectively specify the number of tasks to be performed, the length of time in which a given task is to be performed, the time and location of performance, and so on. This degree of specificity is essential if the target performance is to be reliably identified, observed, trained, and measured. Consider the following examples.

Poor	Better
1. Be able to meet needs of clients referred to program.	1. In response to a telephone survey, 90 percent of the clients served in the program will report satisfaction that their needs have been met; written report will be submitted to supervisor by ___(date)___.
2. Be knowledgeable about program policies and procedures.	2. In response to a written multiple-choice test given at six-month intervals, each staff member will score a minimum of 90 percent correct; written report will be submitted to supervisor by ___(date)___.

Performance-based goals and objectives must be developed for each area of program operation. This is a task that can be delegated to upper- and middle-management staff after they receive the necessary orientation and training in goal analysis. The following goals and objectives were developed by the director of outpatient counseling for a community mental health center providing services for children to thirteen years of age and their families.

Performance area	Objective
1. Community needs assessment	Written assessment of community mental health needs for report to Executive Director. Social validation via opinion survey to ensure that mental health services are based on the needs of individuals in the program's catchment area.
2. Staff knowledge	Staff members will demonstrate their knowledge of agency policies and procedures, progressive treatment strategies, and case record standards through monthly conferences with supervisor and by obtaining a minimum score of 80 percent correct on mastery test given at six month intervals.
3. Development of service programs a. Parent training b. Follow-up services	Parent protocol materials distributed as part of counseling service programs. Parent education program developed and implemented as part of community out-reach services. Eighty-five percent of counseling cases reviewed have appropriate follow-up services.
4. Provision of services	_____clients served in individual and group counseling programs. _____counseling hours submitted to business office for billing.
5. Client satisfaction	Ninety percent of clients contacted report satisfaction with agency services provided them.
6. Quality control	Ninety percent of cases reviewed include (a) treatment plan based upon specific needs of client, (b) evidence that least restrictive service is provided, (c) assessment of progress toward stated goals for treatment, (d) regular review of progress with client, and (e) follow-up.
7. Protection of clients' rights	Less than 1 percent of agency clients have their rights violated in the

	course of their involvement with the agency counseling service program.
8. Evaluation of program effectiveness	Eighty percent of cases reviewed include a method (graphical or tabular presentations, narrative summaries, check-lists, or rating forms) for evaluating effectiveness of treatment. Ninety percent of cases reviewed indicate overall effectiveness of the treatment program utilized. With only____exceptions per month, information provided to the program evaluator by counseling services staff according to the time schedule specified.
9. Documentation of services delivered	Ninety percent of case notes dictated within 48 hours of counseling session. Detailed intake summary present in 90 percent of the cases reviewed. Termination summary present in 90 percent of the cases terminated. Title XX documentation on each client submitted to Business Office on twenty-fifth day of each month for that month's service delivery, with only____exceptions per month.
10. Public relations	Positive image of agency and counseling service programs in the local community; 90 percent of individuals surveyed make positive statements about program. Placement of university practicum students in counseling service programs; two students placed by _(target date)_. Presentations given as requested by other local agencies and organizations, schools, parent-teacher associations, etcetera, as measured by follow-up contacts and 90 percent satisfaction ratings. Cooperation by counseling personnel with agency guidelines and interagency referrals, as measured by written performance evaluations at six-month intervals.
11. Research output	One conference presentation and one publishable manuscript written in area of service-related research each year.
12. Fee collection	Cost per service unit of____reached by ___(date)___. Clients notified of status with regard to agency fees as per requests by business office.

As this example illustrates, specific, performance-based objectives provide a great deal of structure for the manager and greatly facilitate his or her program evaluation efforts. Throughout this book, we will be providing the reader with other examples of performance-based objectives.

Identifying Contingencies

A contingency defines the relationship between a performance and its environmental antecedents and consequences. Positive contingencies strengthen, increase, maintain, or extend performance and may involve presenting some kind of reward to the individual (for example, a pay increase) or removing some kind of punisher or obstacle (for example, an employee may be taken off probationary employment status). Negative contingencies weaken, decrease, eliminate, or restrict performance and may involve operations opposite to those involved in positive contingencies. They may present some kind of negative consequence or punisher to the individual (for example, a decrease in pay) or remove him or her from some kind of positive situation (for example, an employee may be placed on temporary unpaid suspension from work for disciplinary reasons).

Figure 2–3 lists some of the antecedents, performances or behaviors, and consequences involved in personnel management contingencies.

The key questions for the manager to answer at this stage of the planning sequence are these: "What types of contingencies are appropriate to employ in my work setting?" "What antecedents and consequences appear to be presently contingent upon the performance or problem that I want to change?" Once the manager has found answers for these questions, he or she is ready to proceed to the selection of the actual procedural strategies to be employed in applying the contingencies.

FIGURE 2–3   Personnel Management Contingencies in Human Services

ANTECEDENTS	BEHAVIORS	CONSEQUENCES
Organizational structure	Adherence to legal and ethical guidelines	Type of work
Personnel policies and procedures	Compliance with program policy, procedure, and philosophy of service	Job security
		Pay
Work performance standards	Communication and feedback	Co-workers
Orientation and training	High quality and quantity of service to consumers	Supervision
Physical environment	Positive staff morale	Benefits
		Hours
Financial and material resources	Positive public image	Working conditions
	Staff longevity	

IMPLEMENTATION

Selecting Procedural Strategies

The manager now begins the task of "converting objectives into doing" (Drucker, 1974). This involves three steps: deciding what management strategies are to be implemented; providing a favorable environment for their implementation; and implementing them.

The manager generally looks to experience and/or to the literature to determine the specific strategies to be employed in meeting the program's goals and objectives. However, as we have previously discussed, the management literature does not always help and may even hinder the manager in the search for effective strategies.

EFFECTIVENESS. A variety of factors must be considered in selecting management strategies. For example, the strategy should be effective: it should help the manager achieve his or her objective. The manager is encouraged, therefore, to choose strategies that have a documented history of effectiveness in similar situations, although few of the strategies described in the management literature meet this criterion.

However, there is a growing body of literature in *behavioral management* and *organizational behavior management* that provides the manager with a variety of well-tested, performance-based strategies from which to choose. This literature includes studies on the effects of performance feedback and goal-setting on productivity and satisfaction; the use of positive reinforcement procedures to encourage the improvement of management performance; and the use of feedback and social reinforcement to increase the completion of graphs by staff members in a human service setting.

Strategies of documented effectiveness are also available for dealing with problems in the areas of staff productivity; tardiness and absenteeism; waste reduction; safety; attendance at staff meetings; staff management; staff orientation and training; client attendance at counseling sessions; staff feedback to management; fee collection; and Board of Trustee performance.

FLEXIBILITY. The manager should select procedural strategies that are easily adapted to the changing demands of the human service setting. For example, the manager's organizational design should provide the necessary flexibility for program staff to work in teams on special projects such as fund raising, program development, program evaluation, and/or public relations activities. The strategy must also be adaptable to changing goals, objectives, and needs of the manager. For example, it should provide for change in staff orientation and training procedures when testing indicates that staff members are not being equipped with adequate knowledge and skills.

However, while strategies must be capable of being problem-oriented, they must not be too problem-specific. Strategies must be generalizable; they must be replicable across a variety of problems, individuals, and situations. It is therefore important for the manager to have data at his or her disposal indicating a procedure's utilization history—when, where, how, and why the procedural strategy has been utilized.

Work performance contracting provides an example of a flexible management strategy with an impressive utilization history. The procedural steps of performance contracting are fairly standard. Goals and objectives for performance are defined; the individual's task or role is specified; consequences contingent upon completion of the contract are identified; the supervisor's role is identified; and the individual and his or her supervisor sign the contract. Consequences are then provided for individual and supervisor performance as per the terms of the contract.

Performance contracting has been used by the managers to improve staff performance and by Boards of Trustees to improve manager performance. Contracts have also been used to improve the consumer's participation in and cooperation with service delivery, and to define the nature of the relationship between public agencies and human service organizations.

FEASIBILITY.   The management strategy selected must be practical and feasible relative to (1) the manager's knowledge and expertise; (2) the resources available for its implementation; (3) the manager's ability to provide and maintain support for the utilization of the strategy; and (4) the properties of the strategy itself. The manager must understand the rationale for the strategy, that is, the conditions under which it is recommended and under which it can be expected to be effective. In addition, the manager must understand the steps to follow in the proper application of the strategy and how to determine whether it is producing the desired result.

We have already described the importance of knowing one's resources—what resources are required for the application of a particular management strategy and what resources are presently available. However, the effective manager also programs for the maintenance of the strategy once it has been applied. For example, the manager who utilizes a performance contract with an employee provides ongoing prompting, encouragement, corrective feedback, and so on, to ensure that the employee keeps to the terms of the contract. The manager also makes sure that no conflicting task assignment makes it impossible or unfeasible for the employee to continue with the contract.

The manager must also be careful to select procedural strategies with properties conducive to effective utilization in human service settings. For example, while on-the-job training may be an effective method of training for human service staff, it must not be the only method. The trial-and-error characteristic of on-the-job training makes it, in and of itself, an unreasonable risk in human service settings. Errors may result in violations of the client's rights as well as in harm to the client. Similarly, restrictive treatment procedures such as seclusion and restraint, while often effective in controlling disruptive client behavior, are not consistent with current legal and regulatory guidelines for human services. [1]

ACCOUNTABILITY.   Finally, management strategies must be accountable: they must involve manager and staff performance that can be measured and evaluated. An accountable strategy promotes quality assurance by resulting in performances and products that can be evaluated relative to program goals and objectives, as well as to the legal, ethical, and regulatory guidelines for human services. Accountable strategies, therefore, provide the manager with a way to identify problems in program operation so that they can be corrected.

Consider the process of federal, state, and local regulation of human services. The basic requirement of regulatory agencies is documentation. It must be documented that the program's consumers are receiving an appropriate quantity and quality of service, based on their needs, and within their rights as consumers and individuals. Documentation of a client's progress requires evidence that the client has benefited since his or her involvement in the service program.

This requires that each strategy utilized by the manager be data-based, that is, that the decision to utilize the procedural strategy be based on data and the decision to continue or discontinue it be based on data. For example, the manager of a residential treatment center for children notes that staff are interacting with clients only 40 percent of the time observed. He or she institutes a performance feedback procedure. When staff members are not interacting with clients, a middle manager provides immediate corrective feedback—for example, describing the importance of ongoing interaction with the client, or modeling a therapeutic interaction. When staff members are interacting with clients, the middle manager provides positive feedback.

After utilizing the feedback procedure for two weeks, the manager notes that staff are now interacting with clients 90 percent of the time observed. Since the procedure requires a large amount of middle-manager time, the manager decides to fade from continuous observation and immediate feedback to an intermittent schedule, observing and providing feedback several times each week. After six weeks on this intermittent schedule, the manager notes that therapeutic interaction with clients continues to occur 90 percent of the time observed.

In this case, an accountable strategy was employed. The manager was able to measure not only its effect on staff-to-client interaction (the increase from 40 percent to 90 percent), but the degree to which it was utilized (the change from a continuous to an intermittent schedule of observation and feedback, the amount of manager time required, and so on).

In subsequent chapters, we will describe procedural strategies that we have found to be effective, flexible, feasible, and accountable when applied in human service settings. Management strategies and organizational models will be presented in the areas of administrative organization, personnel management, budget management, and program evaluation.

Preparing the Environment

Before actually implementing a particular management strategy, the manager must provide a favorable environment for its implementation. Sometimes one's environment is simply not in the condition to provide adequate support for a particular procedural strategy. Environmental obstacles, constraints or deficiencies must be identified. They must be overcome, removed or remedied in an effort to increase the likelihood that a particular procedure will be effectively implemented and maintained.

A major component of this task has already been described—ensuring adequate resources, such as consumers, funding, space, staffing, and materials and equipment (see page 18). However, there remains the task of winning the support of the program's staff, Board of Trustees, supervising state officials, advisory board members, and others. In the case of a new management strategy that requires in any degree a break with tradition, there may be resistance from one or more of these groups.

Reasons for resistance may involve territorial disputes, fear of loss of autonomy, competition for limited funds, or the operation of special interest groups. However, the main reasons for resistance are probably, first, a lack of understanding as to the rationale for the new strategy, what it involves, and what it's probable results will be; and second, an impatience or naïveté on the part of the manager that results in the implementation of a strategy without sufficient planning and groundwork. The literature in organizational development generally indicates that employees need time and support to readjust, readapt, establish new perceptions and habits, and extinguish old habits or attitudes of mistrust. In the authors' experience, the same is true for board members and supervising state officials.

In short, a new management strategy such as work performance contracting cannot be forced. Staff and board members alike must be afforded a period of what has been referred to as "unfreezing"—unlearning and reducing the potency of old attitudes and behaviors. During this period, the manager must engage in a great deal of communication, information-sharing, and lobbying. For example, the manager might obtain support for the proposed procedures from professional consultants and from the available research literature. Staff training and orientation concerning the goals, objectives and operations of a new strategy are also recommended.

Raia (1974) has provided an excellent example of how a new strategy such as "management by objective" can be gradually introduced to management and direct service personnel with minimal resistance. His unfreezing process has the following goals (Raia, 1974, pp. 123–124):

1. Acceptance that present conditions are unsatisfactory.
2. Acceptance that something new is needed to move the organization ahead.
3. Time involvement of the top team in a program of change.

4. A clear idea of the ideal future state.
5. A large number of managers involved.
6. A comprehensive well-planned program to facilitate the change.
7. Early success experiences in moving from the prior state to the new.

Implementing Procedures

As should be obvious from the previous discussion, the implementation of management strategies demands much planning and preparation. The actual application of a specific strategy is no less systematic. It involves a series of operations designed to ensure that a particular system or strategy is properly implemented and that it produces the desired results.

There are two levels of implementation. One involves applications of what might be termed *organizational systems,* systems designed to improve the overall operation of the program. Organizational systems include (1) administrative organization; (2) personnel management; (3) financial management; (4) program evaluation; (5) public relations; and (6) quality assurance—adherence to legal, ethical, and regulatory guidelines. Recommended procedural strategies in each of these areas are provided in subsequent chapters of this book.

Another level of implementation involves working concurrently with ongoing organizational systems to solve specific problems. *Problem-specific strategies* supplement organizational systems and may include procedures designed to improve an individual employee's performance, to improve staff attendance at in-service training sessions, to provide increased funding for a special project, and so on.

The manager is thereby able to design and implement both an overall organizational system or model (such as work performance contracting for personnel management) and also a supplemental procedure specifically designed to motivate the employee who does not respond to the overall strategy. Each level of implementation involves the following operations:

1. Determining how the procedure will be evaluated. What data will be collected and analyzed to determine the effectiveness of the procedure? What measures of performance (dependent variables) will be used to determine the effects of the procedure being implemented (independent variable)? What observation and recording procedures will be used in data collection? (See p. 29, for a discussion of observation and recording strategies. Evaluation procedures are discussed in Chapter 7.)
2. Determining the level of performance, the status of program operation, the severity of the problem, and so on, that exist prior to implementation of the procedure. As previously discussed, this provides the manager with a baseline against which to assess the effects of implementing the procedure.
3. Applying the procedure. Various procedures for implementation in human service settings are discussed in Chapters 3 through 7.
4. Programming maintenance and generalization. How can the environment be structured to ensure that the effects of a particular procedure are maintained and extended to other situations?

MEASUREMENT

Evaluating Effectiveness

If the effectiveness, flexibility, feasibility, and accountability of an organizational system or specific strategy are to be adequately evaluated, there must be a continuous monitoring of their effects. Monitoring must include (1) systematically observing and recording the effects (dependent variables) that are produced by the system and/or specific procedure (independent variable); and (2) graphing the resulting data so that they can be visually inspected and more easily analyzed.

OBSERVING AND RECORDING. Hall (1975) has described three methods that are commonly used to measure and record performance: "Automatic recording, direct measurement of permanent products and observational recording." *Automatic recording* involves the activation of some sort of mechanical or electrical device (for example, a time-clock) to record performance (for example, work hours). However, automatic recording devices are typically expensive and afford the manager little flexibility. *Direct measurement of permanent products* involves the observation and measurement of the tangible products of performance (for example, written reports, data sheets, number of typing errors per page, units of product produced, and so on).

Observational recording involves an observer looking at performance and recording what he or she sees as it occurs. *Continuous recording* provides an anecdotal record of performance since the observer simply records everything he or she observes, compiling, for example, a daily diary of an employee's time-utilization. *Event recording* is more feasible than continuous recording since it involves the recording of discrete events or performances when they occur during the observation period (for example, the number of occasions that an employee was absent from work during a thirty-day period). *Duration recording* involves measuring how long a performance lasts (for example, the longevity of an individual's employment). *Latency recording* also involves a time-measure. Latency records indicate how much time elapses before a performance is initiated (for example, how soon after a phone prompt does a client pay his or her bill). *Interval recording* indicates whether or not a performance occurs during a specific interval of time. While interval recording demands the constant full attention of the observer, it does provide an indication of both the relative frequency (across intervals) and the duration of the performance observed.

A particularly useful recording strategy in human service settings is *time-sampling*. In time-sampling—an example of which is a spot check of staff performance—only that performance that occurs (or is occurring) at the end of a time-interval is recorded. One form of time-sampling, Planned Activity check or "Placheck" (Doke & Risley, 1972), deserves special attention since it can be used to evaluate the performance of groups of human service staff and clients. The

Placheck procedure consists of the following steps: (1) defining the behavior or target performance to be observed; (2) recording, at given intervals, the total number of individuals engaging in the target performance; (3) recording the total number of individuals present in the area of the activity; and (4) computing a percentage by dividing the number of individuals engaged in the target performance by the total number of individuals in the environment.

For example, a manager wishes to assess the amount of time his or her nursing staff spend on-task, attending to patients, assisting physicians, maintaining records, and so forth. Every hour or so, the manager enters the nurses' work area and unobtrusively observes the number of nurses on-task, and the total number of nurses present in the environment. One day, the manager finds four nurses on-task out of the ten nurses on duty—a Placheck rating of 40 percent (4/10 × 100%). After giving the nursing supervisor feedback concerning this problem, the manager is pleased to see Placheck ratings increase to 80 percent and 90 percent on subsequent observations.

Regardless of the type of measurement and recording procedure employed, it is important that observations be accurate or reliable. *Reliability* refers to the degree to which independent observers agree on what they have observed. Reliability can be determined using the following formula:

$$\text{Inter-observer agreement} = \frac{\text{Number of observations for which there was agreement}}{\text{Total number of observations}} \times 100\%$$

For example, two middle managers observed an employee's performance and recorded the number of times he took a coffee break each hour for eight hours. When the managers compared their recordings of coffee breaks per hour, they found that they were in agreement for six of the eight interval records. The reliability of their recording was therefore 75 percent (6/8 × 100%).

Accurate measurement is generally defined as inter-observer reliability above 80 percent. Inter-observer agreement can be improved by increasing the specificity of the performance definition and by providing training and practice for observers.

GRAPHING AND ANALYZING RESULTS. Graphing results greatly facilitates their analysis. Graphing provides a visual record of what is happening to performance during the implementation of a procedure. It therefore provides the manager with important feedback concerning necessary adjustments in his or her procedure, that is, what changes must be made when objectives are not being met. This kind of accountability is particularly important in the area of service delivery since consumer rights legislation requires that if a patient shows no improvement, his or her plan of treatment must be changed.

As illustrated in Figure 2–4, a graph consists of a vertical axis or ordinate

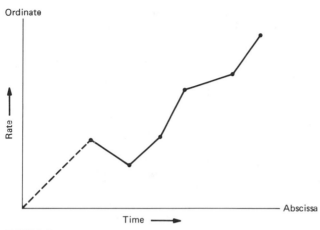

FIGURE 2-4

which is used to indicate the level or rate of performance, and a horizontal axis or abscissa that indicates the passage of time.

The following figures present sample data that might have resulted from the Placheck procedure described on page 30. Remember that the dependent variable (performance) in this case is on-task behavior by nurses and the independent variable (procedure being implemented) is manager feedback. The method of evaluation is Placheck recording. "Contingent feedback" consists of the manager's giving feedback to the shift supervisor at the time Placheck is conducted (for example, "Only 50 percent of the nurses on your shift are on-task at this moment. You can improve this rating by prompting them to get on-task").

In Figure 2-5, the manager can confidently conclude that the contingent feedback procedure had an effect on nurses' on-task behavior. Not only is it possible to see change by visual inspection of the data, but a return to the baseline (no feedback) condition in Phase III resulted in a decrease in on-task behavior. Furthermore, a return to the contingent feedback procedure in Phase IV resulted in another increase in on-task behavior. In short, a *functional relationship* between on-task behavior and contingent feedback has been demonstrated, as has the effectiveness of contingent manager feedback.

In a second case (Figure 2-6), a functional relationship between contingent feedback and on-task behaviors has again been demonstrated. Here, however, the effect of the contingent feedback was to *decrease* rather than increase task-related behavior. These data should prompt the manager to examine carefully the style and content of his or her feedback to nursing supervisors and to determine whether or not nursing supervisors are following through on their responsibilities in the feedback process.

Of course, it is not always possible for the manager to conduct reliability checks and/or to include a return-to-baseline phase in the implementation of procedures. However, the utility of the data will be greatly enhanced to the extent that

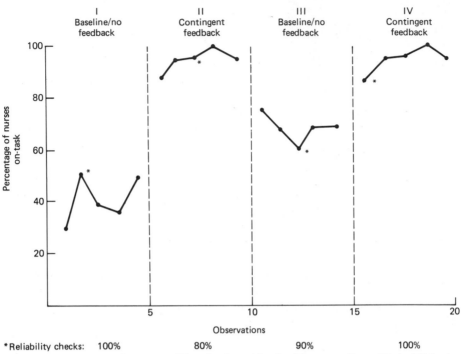

FIGURE 2-5   Example 1: The Desired Effect: Contingent Feedback Increases Nurses' On-task Behavior

the manager is able to include these operations. (For more information on graphing and analyzing results, the reader is referred to Hall, 1975).

Communicating Results

After results have been graphed, analyzed, and their reliability determined, they should be documented and communicated in the pertinent form to the appropriate parties. Results may be documented in the form of case notes in a patient's record, or as performance evaluations in an employee's personnel file (such as in the cases of the nurses, above). They may be communicated in training sessions and meetings of program staff, and in progress reports for the program's Board of Trustees, supervising state officials, and so on (See Chapters 7 and 9 of this book). When possible, results should also be shared with other professionals via conference presentations, publications, or newsletters. Care must be taken, however, in communicating information about patients, clients, and personnel, lest the confidentiality and/or privacy rights of these individuals be violated. (See Chapter 7 for a discussion of the rights of privacy and confidentiality and how they can be protected in human service programming.)

For such reports to be understandable and useful to patients, staff, board members and professionals, they should include the following information:

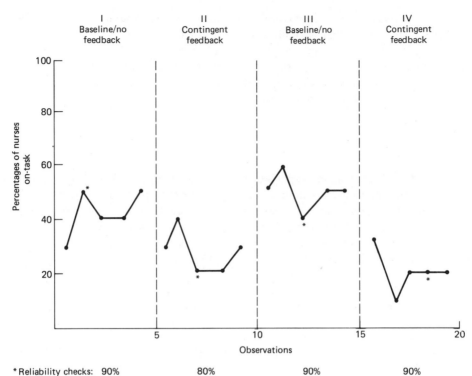

FIGURE 2-6   Example 2: An Undesirable Effect: Contingent Feedback Decreases Nurses' On-task Behavior

1. The *objective of the procedure* (what problem needed to be solved, what performance improved, etcetera).
2. An operational *definition of the problem* or performance (descriptions of the individual involved, of the performance in question, etcetera).
3. *Description of the setting* where the procedure was implemented.
4. An operational *definition of the procedure* that was implemented, the contingency involved, etcetera.
5. *Description of results* (effective, efficient, etcetera).
6. Brief *interpretation of the results* (their significance, implications for future programming, etcetera).

Incorporating Results

In this final step of the sequence, the manager must take the necessary steps to incorporate results of a particular procedure into his or her policies and strategies for the future. Here the manager seeks to profit from experience. For example, if the manager finds the Placheck/contingent feedback procedure to be effective in improving staff performance, he or she is likely to use that procedure more frequently in the future.

In this way, the manager is ensured of using procedures that have been adequately tested—those that actually work in his or her situation. In addition, the manager is constantly improving his or her management methods, thereby resisting the static, inflexible operational strategies characteristic of so many human service settings. Obviously, careful analysis and documentation of results is essential to any replication of a procedure.

SUMMARY

The AIM of effective management is to perform effectively the tasks of analysis, implementation, and measurement. *Analysis* includes the operations of defining or reviewing the program's mission; assessing needs and resources; specifying goals and objectives; and identifying contingencies. *Implementation* involves selecting procedural strategies; preparing the environment; and implementing procedures (determining baseline level of performance, determining how the procedure will be evaluated, applying the procedure, and programming maintenance and generalization). *Measurement* includes evaluating effectiveness (observing and recording, graphing and analyzing results); communicating results; and incorporating results.

3

Structuring the Human Service Organization

To this point, our prescription for effective human service management has included the tasks of forecasting and planning. A third essential task for the effective manager is that of *structuring* the human service organization. This involves efforts to *communicate* program goals and objectives and how they are to be achieved, and to *coordinate* staff performance in the pursuit of program goals and objectives.

While it is not the purpose of this chapter to review the literature on organizational theory and design, a working knowledge of organization is important. The manager must understand the basic requirements of functional organization before attempting his or her own organizational structuring.

An organization is basically a social system, consisting of both individuals and groups, created to achieve certain goals and objectives, and existing for that purpose. Groups within an organization may be formally established by managerial design or informally established by the interaction of group members. Both types of group membership have been shown to influence significantly the behavior of the individual employee.

Organizations are further characterized by rational planning, control, and coordination of members and activities. These characteristics stem from the mechanisms of authority, roles, norms, self-control, and implicit contract. Specifically, an organization features a *hierarchy of authority* that exercises the power of reward and punishment over subordinate members of the organization. Each member of the organization has a *role* or position with specified behaviors that are expected and considered appropriate by other members. This makes it possible for an organization to experience 100 percent member turnover, since new members can assume intact organizational roles.

Organizations are also characterized by *norms* or rules of conduct for members. Behavior discrepant with the norm typically results in pressure for conformance being exerted by other members. In addition, members tend to exhibit *self-control* relative to roles and norms; they have been socialized to accept and abide by the rules of groups and organizations. Finally, by his or her membership in an organization, an individual *implicitly agrees* to its rules and regulations in exchange for membership and its contingent rewards.

While all organizations have the characteristics described above, they differ in their design. The fact of organization is constant, but its form and function can be shaped by the manager to meet the special problems and needs of human service delivery as well as the special requirements of his or her program.[1]

ORGANIZATIONAL PROBLEMS

As described in Chapter 1, a particular organizational structure may not function to a program's advantage. Drucker has maintained, "There is no perfect organization. At its best, an organizational structure will not cause trouble" (1974, p. 546). When an organizational structure does cause trouble, it can prevent the manager from meeting program goals and objectives and may threaten the very existence of the program.

Every manager is familiar with the signs of organizational malfunction: overstaffing characterized by a proliferation of management levels, "coordinators" and "assistants"; recurring organizational problems; increased meetings with decreased attendance; greater concern for staff feelings and attitudes than for staff performance; poor communication at all levels of the organization; departmental isolation; poor service to consumers; violations of consumers' rights, and so on.

Structuring the human service organization is particularly problematic due to the complexity of the human service system. As previously described, human service delivery involves components (programs, providers, and consumers) that are rarely in harmony. Further, as Kouzes and Mico (1979) note, there are three distinct levels or domains of organization characteristic of human services. At the "policy" level (board members), the structure is representative and participative. At the "management" level (top and middle managers), the structure is bureaucratic. At the "service" level (service staff), the structure is informal and collegial. Kouzes and Mico describe how these various levels of organization may contribute to discordance, disjunction, and conflict.

Perhaps the major cause of organizational problems is the existence of a poor match between a manager's choice of organizational structure and the actual needs and special requirements of the program. The successful application of packaged solutions or popular organizational principles requires careful planning: *analysis, implementation,* and *measurement.*

Another general source of organizational problems is that, while the manager's organizational design may be potentially functional, he or she does not actually *utilize* the design to structure the day to day operation of the program. For example, an organizational chart may feature the most appropriate alignment of supervisory and service personnel, but it is useless unless it is adequately communicated to and followed by those personnel. Implementation of an organizational design, therefore, requires ongoing evaluation to ensure that the design is being applied and that it is functional.

A third cause of organizational malfunction concerns the tendency of management to focus more on organizational *procedure* rather than on organizational *performance.* For example, a manager may schedule meetings designed to improve performance only to find that meetings increase in number and there is no appreciable improvement in performance. Increased staffing may have the same result since this may create work without improving performance. Again we can see the importance of evaluation to ensure that organizational structure has the desired effect on performance.

SELECTING AN ORGANIZATIONAL STRATEGY

Criteria

According to Drucker (1974), any organizational structure must satisfy certain minimum requirements. *Clarity* refers to the requirement that "each managerial component and each individual within the organization, especially each manager, needs to know where he(she) belongs, where he(she) stands, where he(she) has to go for whatever is needed, whether information, cooperation, or decision, and how to get there" (p. 553). *Economy* refers to the fact that minimum effort should be required to control, to supervise, and to motivate individuals to perform—that is, the organization should permit self-control and encourage self-motivation. *Focus* refers to the requirement that the organization focus the attention of individuals and management units on performance rather that effort—that is, the organization should emphasize results and be goal-oriented.

The fourth requirement, *task-identity*, refers to the role of the organization in enabling the individual employee to understand his or her specific task as well as the task (mission) of the entire organization. This means that *communication* is one of the most important functions of an organizational structure. The organization must also *facilitate the decision-making process*—that is, facilitate the process by which decisions are met with organizational commitment and individual performance.

In addition, the organizational structure must provide *stability* without hindering the organization's *adaptability* and *flexibility* to respond to needs as they

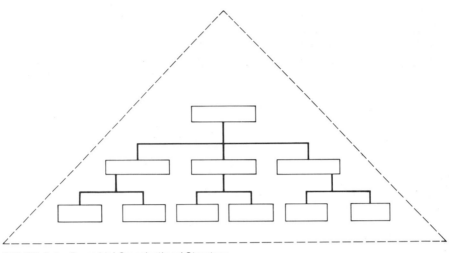

FIGURE 3-1   Pyramidal Organizational Structure

arise. Finally, the organizational structure must facilitate the organization's *survival, growth,* and *improvement.*

Categories

There are two general categories of organizational design most appropriate for use in human service management. The first is *pyramidal* and features a centralization of authority. Decision-making power is vested primarily with top management. Pyramidal structure may consist of several layers of managers and supervisors, or a broad base of personnel directly responsible to one or more of the supervisory layers. But, in both cases, power is ultimately exercised by a chief executive at the top of the hierarchical structure.

Criticism of pyramidal organizational structure has mainly been focused on its apparent rigidity and inflexibility. Wedel (1976) has noted that "in contemporary society, organizations are expected to respond constructively to constant and sometimes turbulent change" and that pyramidal organizational structures "impede effective responses to change and must give way to newer, more . . .temporary organizations." (p. 36)

In addition, pyramidal organization of the human service program may result in conflict between hierarchical and specialists' roles. Drucker (1980) has described such organizations as "'double headed monsters' which depend for their performance on professionals who are dedicated to their discipline rather than to the institution, who are the more productive the more dedicated they are, and, who at the same time, have to work toward the accomplishment of the goals of the whole" (pp. 130–131). He maintains that the transformation of organizations to include both business management and professional groups will require managers to develop new organizational strategies.

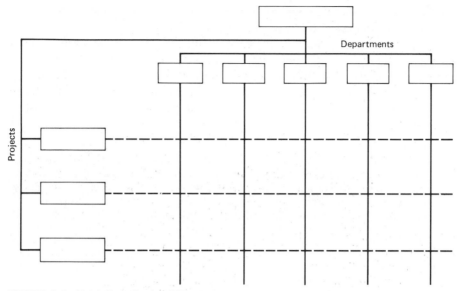

FIGURE 3-2   Matrix Organizational Structure

A second category of organizational structure applicable to human service programming is *matrix organization* or *project team management.* The matrix design first developed in the aerospace industry, structures the organization according to specific work projects rather than along departmental lines. It is composed of horizontal relationships formally superimposed upon the more traditional vertical, hierarchical organizational structure. These horizontal relationships are coordinated through project managers who direct a team of subordinates in the completion of an organizational task or project (fund raising, program evaluation, public relations, and so on).

The application of the matrix design to human service organizations is a relatively recent development. Wedel (1976) and Gray (1974) have provided descriptions of the matrix organization of social service agencies. Beckhard's (1974) comprehensive health care matrix included departmentalized professional services such as psychiatry, internal medicine, and social work as well as project-oriented teams collaborating on specific tasks. In Neuhauser's (1972) hospital unit system, patient care teams constantly form, dissolve, and are formed again.

The major advantage of the matrix organization, relative to the traditional pyramidal design, is that more attention is focused on the completion of specific work projects. However, not all activities are suitable for the project format. Moreover, project specification is only one aspect of matrix organization, since projects must be effectively managed once they are specified. Wedel (1976) has suggested that the most suitable activities are those that are temporary, must be completed by a specific date, and fit within a special budget category. In addition, not enough is known about the applicability of matrix organization in human services to provide the manager with adequate criteria for its selection.

Finally, matrix organizations are not immune to problems, for example, conflict between departmental and project managers. In fact, Wedel (1976) has observed that "problem areas cited in the literature for the matrix organization are about as numerous as those for any other organizational design" (p. 41). Butler (1973) has described some of the adverse effects of the matrix design on established patterns of human interaction within an organization:

> The institution of project management in functional organizations tends to violate established managerial practice with respect to: hierarchical authority and responsibility; procedural arrangements and accommodations; departmentation specificity; incentive systems; unity of command and direction; span of control; resource-allocation patterns; and establishment of relative priorities. Performance goals tend to be assigned in terms of interfunctional work flows and system requirements. Established work groups are disrupted and staffing patterns tend to involve duplication. FEs (functional or departmental employees) are forced into interaction in an environment which places a premium on interdepartmental consensus, they are required to participate in the forward planning of activities which previously may have been accomplished unilaterally, and the increased participation of others in this latter area tends to engender fears of invasion or absorption. [2]

Adaptive Organizational Structure

The ultimate test of any organizational structure is the degree to which it facilitates the manager's task of meeting program goals and objectives. Therefore, a functional organizational strategy is one that is need-oriented and flexible enough to be modified as needs change. In our experience, the most functional organizational structure is one that adapts relevant elements of both the pyramidal and the matrix designs to meet the special requirements of human service management. The need for such an *adaptive organizational structure* has been described by Drucker (1980, p. 133):

> There is a need for "top management" and there is a need for ultimate "command" —just as there is need for a skeleton in the animal body. There is need for a clear locus of decisions, for a clear voice and for unity of command in the event of common danger and emergencies. But there is also need for accepting that within given fields, the professionals should set standards and determine what their contribution should be.
>
> The hospital administrator, whether he has a medical degree or not, may decide to add fifteen beds in clinical neurology. But what then constitutes good clinical neurology is not within the administrator's purview. He can only demand that the neurologists think through what their objectives are, what their standards are, and how they propose to make effective their individual and collective accountability for the practice of clinical neurology within his hospital. But it is the administrator who has to make sure that the professional people do indeed take accountability, develop standards, set goals, and rigorously judge their performance against these standards and goals.

Adaptive organizational structure incorporates the following aspects of pyramidal design:

(1) *Centralization of authority* with decision-making power vested primarily with top management.

(2) *Formal rules and regulations for program operation.* These rules and regulations will be largely determined by (a) the requirements of regulatory agencies (for example, Joint Commission for the Accreditation of Hospitals); (b) legal policy (local, state, and federal statutes concerning the rights of individuals, clients, and patients); and/or (c) the mission and goals of the program.

(3) *Specific work performance standards* with the duties and responsibilities of each employee clearly defined. This is important in helping to ensure a high quality of service to the consumer by training employees and evaluating their performance relative to established criteria. (Work performance contracting is discussed in Chapter 4.)

(4) *Functional departmentalization* for organizational activities. For example, administrative support services may include organizational activities such as accounting, maintenance, and clerical services. Functional departmentalization requires that activities making the same kind of contribution (here, administrative support) be joined together in one component and under one management regardless of their technical specification.

(5) *A small span of control* in which each manager is responsible for as few subordinates as possible. However, a small span of control should not be established at the expense of greatly increasing the number of management levels. The ideal organizational structure will feature the finest possible management levels and the shortest possible chain of command. This is particularly important in human service delivery where poor communication and/or inadequate supervision of service staff may greatly increase the risk to the consumer. Every additional management level makes it more difficult to ensure programmatic consistency and increases the potential for poor communication.

Therefore, we prescribe a centralized, hierarchical structure for the human service organization. However, we have found that functional, adaptive organizational design must also allow for the temporary assignment of employees to teams for the purpose of completing special projects. This type of flexibility is best accomplished via work performance contracting rather than by some formal modification of the organizational structure, as in the case of the matrix design.

As previously noted, organizational activities best suited to a project format are those that are temporary, must be completed by a specific date, and fit within a specific budget category. Each project team should have a manager responsible for coordinating, supervising, and evaluating the performance of each team member and providing feedback to the member's departmental supervisor. In addition, feedback concerning the team leader's performance should be provided to his or her supervisor by the chief executive of the organization, who monitors the performance of the team leaders, receives reports from them, and so on. Project results also become an important source of data for program evaluation. Thus, *project management exists as the need arises and is established within the more formal, pyramidal structure of the organization.*

The adaptive organizational structure prescribed here differs from the traditional pyramidal structure in that the lines of authority are somewhat complicated by project management, and project managers represent a proliferation of management levels. It differs from the traditional matrix structure in that project management is an informal, albeit important, feature of the hierarchical structure. In short, the concept of *project orientation* has been incorporated in the hierarchical organization via work performance standards and policy/procedure. A horizontal organization has not been formally superimposed.

In our experience, the benefits of adaptive orgranizational structure have far outweighed its risks, which include the conflict that may develop between departmental supervisors and project managers, and the possibility that employees may become confused by, and respond inefficiently as a result of, dual supervision. However, these risks can be minimized through performance contracting, in which each employee (management as well as service personnel) has work performance standards that include a section describing the possibility of the employee's being assigned to work on special projects. Before a special project is initiated, the project manager, employees assigned as members of the project team, departmental supervisors whose employees are to be involved in the project, and the chief executive of the program all sign a performance agreement which delineates the nature of their involvement with the project.

For example, the project manager would agree to hold regular feedback sessions with departmental supervisors to ensure that conflict is minimized and communications to employees are consistent. Team members would agree to request a meeting with their project manager and departmental supervisor when there is evidence of conflicting communication. In addition, all employees to be involved in the project would be informed about and would agree to (1) the need for the project; (2) its goals and objectives; (3) the time for its completion; (4) the resources and procedural strategies that will be utilized; (5) its evaluation procedures; and (6) the criteria for its successful completion. The most important aspect of this approach is that everyone's role is carefully delineated and agreed to in advance of a project's being initiated.

The major benefit of adaptive organizational structure is that it provides the manager with flexibility without a significant loss of control. It enables the manager to maintain the advantage of functional specialization and centralized control while taking advantage of need orientation and task coordination. For example, when definite time-limitations are placed on an organizational activity (for example, the submission of a special report), output-oriented projects can often be specified and coordinated with greater precision than can departmentalized activities. A project team approach is also useful when there is a need for an interdepartmental approach to a particular problem (for example, the need for an interdepartmental team to review case records and provide feedback concerning needed improvements, violations of patients' rights, and so on). Finally, working on special projects may serve to enrich an employee's job and to increase his or her participation in and involvement with the organization.

IMPLEMENTING ORGANIZATIONAL STRUCTURE

As in the case of any management strategy, the test of organizational structure is in the performance it produces. Therefore, after the manager has selected an organizational strategy, he or she must go about the tasks of *implementing* the strategy in the day to day operation of the program, and *evaluating* its effects on staff performance and on the program's performance relative to its mission, goals, and objectives. The task of implementation comprises a number of mechanisms: (1) organizational charts; (2) policy and procedure manuals; (3) employee work performance standards; (4) orientation and training; (5) committees and project teams; (6) staff meetings; (7) written communications; (8) consultants and peer review; and (9) performance evaluation and feedback.

Organizational charts

An organizational chart is nothing more than a communication device. It represents an oversimplification of a program's organizational structure that attempts to assist the interested individual in understanding his or her *place* (department, supervisor, subordinates) and *function* (specialization relative to other employees) in the organization. Therefore, the basic criteria for a useful organizational chart are that it accurately and clearly represent the program's organizational structure, be understood by each employee, and be conveniently available for inspection by each employee.

DESIGN. The development of an organizational chart should be undertaken systematically. First, list the key functions or activities of the organization. These will become the functional components or "building blocks" of the organizational structure. To reiterate, the rule here is that activities making the same kind of contribution be joined together in one component and under one management regardless of their technical specification.

The simplest structure for the human service organization would include the following three components: top management, direct services, and support services. However, the size and degree of specialization charcteristic of most human service organizations require greater functional differentiation and a more sophisticated component structure.

The degree of functional differentiation is determined by examining the number of employees in each of the three major components, the specific function of each employee, and each employee's degree of technical specialization. However, as previously discussed, it is also important to consider the issues of clarity, simplicity, span of control, and chain of command.

For example, a private residential special education program for developmentally disabled children might require the following degree of differentiation:

Second, for each component, designate the position titles for the manager and his or her subordinates, indicating the hierarchical line of authority *within* the component. (Examples of position titles and lines of authority for various types of human service programs are provided in the sample organizational charts in the next section of this chapter.) Third, indicate how the various organizational components relate to one another and how they are integrated, that is, the lines of interaction *between* components. It is here that the hierarchical design of the structure becomes apparent. Solid lines may be used to indicate the line of authority. Broken lines may be used to indicate mechanisms independent of the lines of authority. Consider Figure 3–3. In this figure, the Human Rights Committee and the Professional Advisory Board have monitoring and advisory functions rather than control functions.

Figure 3–4 is an organizational chart for a private institution with a mission to provide twelve-month residential, special education, and basic health care services to its patients so that they can be moved to a less restrictive human service program (for example, outpatient care). The program is administered by a Board of

FIGURE 3–3

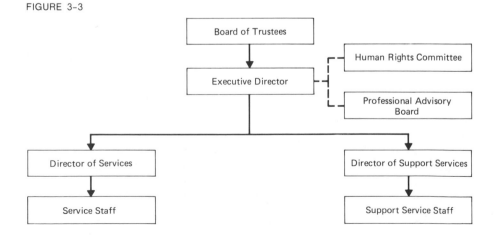

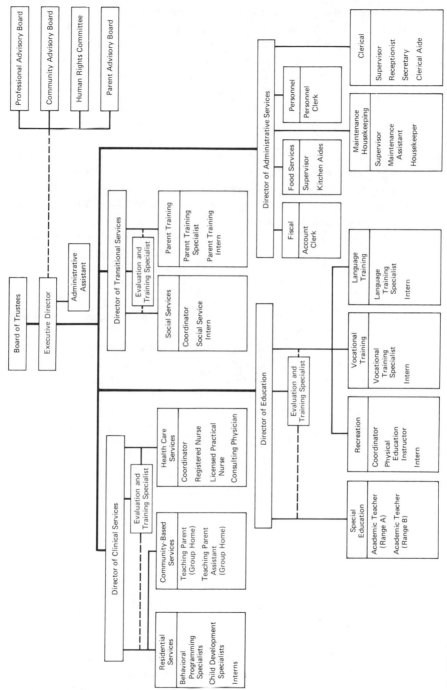

FIGURE 3-4

Trustees and has a staff of 125. The chart features the formal organizational structure that we have prescribed for the human service program, that is, functional departmentalization with centralized, hierarchical control. It must be remembered that the project team orientation that has been recommended is not a formal structural component of the organization but is accomplished via work performance contracting and program policy and procedure.

It is typically the case that employees are aware that an organizational chart exists for their program but do not know where to locate it. In preparing this chapter, one of the authors contacted a small community social service agency, a large acute-care hospital in a metropolitan area, an acute-care hospital in a small town, and a small outpatient medical center, in each case asking several employees how one could obtain a copy of the program's organizational chart. No employee knew where to obtain a copy of the program's organizational chart and more than half of those contacted had not even seen such a chart.

After an organizational chart has been developed, it should be posted in all areas of the work environment so that it is available for inspection by all employees, patients, and visitors to the program. A good rule of thumb is to post an organizational chart wherever a fire escape route is displayed. In addition, a copy of the organizational chart should be included in the program's policy and procedure manual along with additional information to ensure that the employee understands what the chart represents.

A final step involves the actual "field-testing" of the organizational chart, that is, determining if it does what it is supposed to do. Before posting the chart, the manager could obtain feedback from employees indicating their knowledge of the structure of the organization and how information about organizational structure can be obtained. After organizational charts are posted in the work environment and staff receive orientation and training in their use, the manager should obtain follow-up feedback from staff. The effectiveness of the organizational chart can be determined by comparing initial and follow-up feedback. (Did the posting of the organizational chart increase employee understanding of organizational structure? Are organizational charts adequately available to staff for inspection?) Based on this type of feedback, the manager can make the necessary changes in the method of posting the chart or in the chart itself (for example, indicating chains of command with bold lines; including information to make the chart more easily understood).

Policy and Procedure Manuals

Another potentially useful vehicle for organizational structuring is the program's policy and procedure manual, although such manuals are often neither appropriately developed nor effectively utilized. Typically, the policies and procedures of an organization represent an accumulation of management and employee efforts over a period of time. Policies and procedures which are determined by precedent are likely to be out of touch with an organization's current needs, goals, objectives, and/or structure. They may also not be consistent with current legal policy, regulatory guidelines, and/or state-of-the-art methods for human service delivery and human service management.

In addition, policy and procedure manuals are frequently dismissed by employees as just another form of "red tape" and are therefore either not taken seriously or are given little more than lip service. Moreover, manuals of policy and procedure are often put together to satisfy a Board of Trustees or a regulatory agency and may be forgotten once the immediate need is satisfied.

The purpose of the policy and procedure manual is to ensure that employees understand the goals and objectives of an organization and the methods that will be employed in their pursuit. Together with the organizational chart, the policy and procedure manual serves to integrate the various components of the organizational structure to ensure that the organization can be managed as a functional unit. There is probably nothing that contributes more to organizational malfunction and risk to the consumer than the inadequate development of, or ineffective adherence to, prescribed policies and procedures for program operation.

SOURCES.   The sources of policy effecting the human service program have already been described. They include the law (local, state, and federal); regulatory guidelines (for example, requirements of the Joint Commission for the Accreditation of Hospitals); standards imposed by third party payers (for example, Titles XIX and XX of the Social Security Act); professional codes of ethics; research in human service delivery and management (evidence of state-of-the-art methodology); and the individual program's mission, goals, and objectives. Therefore, the first step in the development of a policy and procedure manual is to review these sources carefully and to determine what policies and procedures are *required* of the program.

CRITERIA.   Like the organizational chart, the policy and procedure manual must be available for inspection and be capable of being understood by each employee. It should include information that is consistent with the program's organizational structure and with the standards and guidelines provided by the sources described above. In addition, policy and procedure should be written with the intent of providing criteria for evaluating the performance of individual employees, departments within the organization, and the organization itself. Therefore, policy and procedure must be operationally specific so that they are clearly understood both by the employee and by the person supervising and evaluating his or her performance.

While it is important that the manual be simple and not too detailed, it must also be sufficiently comprehensive to address all areas of program operation. Minimally, the manual should include such information as the program's goals, objectives, and treatment philosophy; a thorough description of the physical plant, so that work stations can be identified and located; personnel practices; policies concerning specific treatment procedures; health and safety regulations; policy and procedure concerning patient admission and discharge; standards for case record documentation; patients' rights and procedures designed to protect them; policies concerning the use of facilities; and staff orientation, training, supervision, and evaluation.

FORMAT.   The format of the manual contributes to its usefulness. It should begin with a table of contents which provides a ready reference to topic areas. The topics themselves should be logically organized, to the extent possible, so that the manual can be used for the orientation of new staff as well as serve as a reference for all personnel. While each program's policy and procedure manual must be geared to its specific needs, goals, and objectives, there are a number of topics that should be addressed by any human service program.

Sample Format for Human Service
Program's Policy and Procedure Manual

A.   *Table of Contents*
B.   *Program Description*
    1.   History.
    2.   Location.
        a.   Map showing geographic location of program.
        b.   Map indicating location and function of each building, wing, floor, ward, etcetera.
        c.   Brief description of local community.
    3.   Patients served.
        a.   Age.
        b.   Presenting problem.
        c.   Other criteria.
    4.   Personnel.
        a.   Board of Trustees or supervising state officials.
        b.   Administrative staff (position, academic degree or specialty area).
        c.   Service staff (position, academic degree or specialty area).
    5.   Administrative organization.
        a.   Organizational chart.
        b.   Brief narrative description of organizational structure.
    6.   Services.
        Brief description of the goals and objectives of each service program.
    7.   Philosophy of treatment.
        a.   Brief description.
        b.   Suggested readings for additional information (which should be available for inspection).
    8.   Licensing and certification.
    9.   Sources of funding.
    10.   Research, evaluation, and training.

11.   University and/or other affiliations.
12.   Public relations.
C.   *Use of the Manual*
  1.   Purpose of Policy and Procedure Manual
       The manual should include a statement such as the following:

> This manual represents a compilation and written statement of the policies and operational procedures of (program). In some cases, these policies and procedural guidelines have been mandated by local, state, and/or federal law; in others, they have been required by agencies that regulate and license the program. Policy and procedure are also determined by the existing literature concerning state-of-the-art human service delivery as well as the specific mission, goals, and objectives of (program).
> All staff should, therefore, be thoroughly familiar with the contents of this manual, particularly the sections which pertain to their specific responsibilities. This is necessary so that all staff know and understand policy and procedure before they interact with patients and perform their assigned tasks. Therefore, it is important that you contact your supervisor for clarification of any policy and/or procedure that you do not understand.

  2.   How Policy and Procedure is Interpreted
       The manual should include a statement such as the following:

> The policies and procedures included in this manual have been developed and approved by the administration of (program). Final decisions concerning the interpretation of any policy or procedure are made by *(the program's Executive Director and Board of Trustees, supervising state officials, etcetera, as applicable).*

  3.   How the Manual Is Revised
D.   *Personnel Practices*
  1.   Equal Opportunity/Affirmative Action guidelines.
  2.   Recruitment/hiring.
  3.   Employee classification (for example, salaried versus hourly wage, etcetera).
  4.   Job descriptions.
       Copies of work performance standards for each position (management and subordinate personnel) (See Chapter 4).
  5.   Probation.
  6.   Evaluation (forms and procedures) (See Chapter 7).
  7.   Disciplinary actions.
  8.   Grievance.
  9.   Resignation.
  10. Termination.
  11. Appearance/clothing (dress code, if applicable).

E. *Financial Information*
1. Pay day and pay periods.
2. Payroll deductions.
3. Wage garnishments.
4. Salary ranges.
5. Salary review.
6. Purchasing procedure.

F. *Leave Accrual and Use*
Description of each type of leave, how and when to apply for it, how and when it is approved, copies of pertinent forms.
1. Annual leave.
2. Sick leave.
3. Compensatory time.
4. Holiday leave.
5. Administrative leave.
6. Leave without pay.
7. Maternity leave.
8. Paternity leave.
9. Jury leave.
10. Military leave.

G. *Time and Attendance*
1. Work hours.
2. Attendance verification (duty log, time-card, etcetera).
3. Tardiness.
4. Absence.
5. Staff meetings.
6. Overtime.
7. Compensatory time.
8. Shift change.
9. Breaks (frequency, duration).

H. *Pay and Benefits*
1. Pay schedules (position, salary range).
2. Insurance benefit.
3. Social Security.
4. Pension plan.
5. Unemployment insurance.
6. Additional benefits.

I. *Health and Safety*
1. General safety.
    This section should describe each employee's responsibility to ensure the welfare and safety of patients, visitors, and other members of the program staff and the employee's duty to report any potential safety hazard to his or her supervisor.

2. Fire safety.
   a. Procedures.
   b. Escape routes for each work area.
   c. Fire drills.
   d. Equipment use (fire extinguisher, fire alarm, etcetera).
   e. Smoking.
3. Accidents.
   a. Reporting procedure.
   b. Workmen's compensation.
4. Infection control.
5. Cardiac pulmonary resuscitation procedures.

J. *Admission Policy*
   1. Criteria.
   2. Admission screening.
      a. Forms.
      b. Procedures.
   3. Intake.
      a. Forms.
      b. Procedures.
   4. Discharge/termination.
      a. Forms.
      b. Procedures.
   5. Follow-up.

K. *Service Delivery*
   1. Models or systems.
      In this section, models utilized by the program in service delivery should be described. For example, case manager function (See Chapter 4), the establishment and function of project teams (as previously discussed in this chapter), and work performance contracting (as described in Chapter 4) are appropriate.
   2. Procedures.
      Procedures described in this section are those that require the special attention of program staff. For example, this section might include policies and procedures concerning the prescription and distribution of medication, the use of restrictive procedures such as physical restraint and isolation, emergency medical care, and so on. This section can also include policy and procedures concerning (1) incident reports; (2) patients' trips off institutional grounds or out of the hospital; (3) religious services, etcetera.
   3. Ethical standards.
      The purpose of this section is to make it clear that, as a matter of policy, each employee should be aware of, and should conduct himself or herself in accordance with, pertinent codes of professional ethics.

L. *Patients' Rights*

This section should identify the rights of the human service consumer (especially those of informed consent, confidentiality, right to treatment, and right to refuse treatment) and describe procedures for ensuring that the consumer's rights are protected (see Chapter 8).

M. *Case Records* (see Chapter 7)

1. Location.

2   Organization.

3. Security and access.

4. Confidentiality.

5. Standards for case record documentation.

6. Record review procedures.

N. *Staff Orientation and Training* (see Chapter 4)

1. Importance of staff training and orientation.

2. Orientation (outline, time schedule, etcetera).

3. In-service training (outline, time schedule, etcetera).

O. *Feedback and Communication* (see Chapter 5)

In this section, policies and procedures concerning communications within and between departments of the organization are described. It is useful to include the following information:[3]

Policies:

1. All staff are encouraged to deal directly with each other, to support and encourage helpful activities, and to correct or solve problems that arise. The attached instructions for giving and receiving feedback and examples of how these instructions result in improved communication are intended to guide each staff member to a comfortable position with respect to giving and receiving feedback.

2. If a problem cannot be resolved by directly dealing with the person, or if you are not sure how to approach it, go to your supervisor for help. Your supervisor needs to know how you are getting along with other staff, and is there to help you get your job done. This requires open communication between you and your supervisor.

3. Behind-the-scenes grumbling can be very destructive to a program's functioning. Because we are developing ways to assure that communications can be open, any discussion of problems with persons other than your supervisor, or the individual involved, is not encouraged. There are always appropriate channels for expressing your concerns. The sequence of channels to use is: (1) the person involved, (2) your supervisor, (3) your supervisor's supervisor, (4) the Executive Director, (5) the Board of Trustees (or responsible state officials). If you find that you are being used as an audience for complaints, it is your responsibility to ask if that person has taken his or her concern to the appropriate parties, and if not, to remind the person to do so.

Procedures:

1. To assure that there is regular two-way job-performance feedback between program staff and their supervisors, forms have been

developed for regular use each month in meetings between these persons. It is the employee's responsibility to schedule and remind his or her supervisor to conduct these sessions. After scheduling a regular time, such as the last supervisory meeting in each month, both persons should come to the meeting with their portions of the review completed. The feedback can be discussed, and problems resolved at that time. Possible uses of this information, and the advantages that might accrue from using this feedback procedure are presented in the attached materials.

2. The cooperative functioning of all departments depends also on regular feedback between them. Again, each employee is encouraged to give direct and immediate feedback to the relevant persons to solve any problems that arise, but also, especially, to thank others for cooperative and helpful activities. Rather than rely on these informal understandings always working, all department directors should meet with their staff, prepare the interdepartmental feedback forms and then meet with the directors of the other departments to exchange feedback on a monthly basis. These meetings should be scheduled on the agency calendar, and checked off when they have taken place. In this way, the program's Executive Director will know that these lines of communicaiton are kept open and used.

3. Open communications must also involve the program's patients and provide the opportunities for their anonymous input. Thus, a feedback box will be available to concerned patients. The box will be opened once a week and all concerns raised will be responded to within forty-eight hours and publicly posted. This feedback will also be routed to the individual responsible for that department of the program for a reply.

In this section of the manual, it is also important to describe the various mechanisms that serve to integrate departments within the organization. Specific integrating functions can be described so that employees understand how departments communicate and interact while remaining functionally distinct. For example, while it may be a function of the Director of Nursing to hire, supervise, and fire nursing personnel, he or she may use the Personnel Department to advertise for and screen applicants for nursing positions. Similarly, the Business Department may be responsible for managing the program's payables and receivables, while relying on the Department of Nursing to change services and/or staffing in response to income and expense data.

P. *Use of Facilities*
   1. Telephone.
   2. Kitchen.
   3. Parking.
   4. Library.
   5. Vehicles.
   6. Grounds.

      7.   Equipment and supplies (for example, how to requisition).

      8.   Repairs and maintenance (for example, how to request).

Q. *Miscellaneous*

      1.   Cafeteria (if applicable).

      2.   Lost and found.

      3.   Gifts and tips (given to employees by consumers).

      4.   Mail (staff, patient).

      5.   Security for valuables.

In addition to the policy and procedure manual for overall program operation, it is often advisable for each department to develop a manual which focuses more specifically on policy and procedure of particular importance to its employees. Of course, a departmental manual must include only information that is supplemental to and consistent with the organization's policy and procedure manual and must be developed and utilized in accordance with the same criteria. For example, nursing staff might be provided with a manual which describes a hospital's policy and procedure concerning problem-oriented medical records, patient monitoring procedures, intensive care procedures, and so on. Similarly, a special education classroom in an institutional setting would be expected to have lesson plans for each student, and its staff would be expected to perform consistent with pertinent laws and regulations regarding special education (for example, Public Law 94–142 concerning the education of the handicapped) —policies and procedures that are not relevant to staff in other departments of the institution.

As in the case of the organizational chart, the policy and procedure manual should be made available to all members of the program staff. All new employees should be required to read and understand the manual as soon after beginning their employment as possible. Specifically, during orientation employees should be given a copy of the policy and procedure manual to read and return within ten work days. Employees should also be required to sign a brief statement indicating that they have read, understand, and agree to abide by the program's policies and procedures as a condition of their employment.

To ensure that new employees indeed understand the contents of the policy and procedure manual, they could be given a brief written or oral quiz on the manual's key topic areas. A brief test of this kind helps to emphasize the importance of each employee's understanding of program policy and procedure and makes it possible for the manager to evaluate the manual's effectiveness.

In-service training for all staff on program policy and procedure is also essential, especially when revisions are made in the manual. Copies of the manual should also be placed in each work area and should be available for checkout by employees. Employee feedback about the manual should be regularly solicited and should result in revisions when appropriate. In addition, once the manual has been made available to staff, it can be "field-tested" using procedures similar to those employed in testing the effectiveness of the organizational chart.

Work Performance Contracting

Work performance contracting is another useful mechanism for organizational structuring. In a work performance agreement, the employee (1) acknowledges the existence of organizational structure (that is, the chain of command with respect to his or her position), program policy and procedure, and the specific task that he or she is to perform; and (2) agrees to a certain standard of performance (quantity of work, time-lines for completion, etcetera).

Work performance contracting is the subject of Chapter 4. Briefly, work performance standards consistent with the program's goals, objectives, policies, and procedures, and with the employee's role in the organization, should be developed for each staff position. Performance standards are objective behavioral descriptions of an employee's work assignments, minimally consisting of the specific behavior required for completion of the assignment (for example, submission of a written report to one's supervisor), and the time-lines for its completion.

Work performance standards should be drawn up by the employee's supervisor and reviewed with the employee who should be encouraged to seek to negotiate changes in work assignment, time-lines, and so on, as he or she feels necessary. When both parties are in agreement, the standards are signed with the understanding that they will be used as criteria for the supervisor's periodic written evaluation of the employee's work performance and that they can be modified only with the agreement of both supervisor and employee. The employee is then given a copy of his or her work performance standards and encouraged to regularly review it.

Additional Mechanisms

Additional mechanisms for establishing organizational structure include (1) orientation and training; (2) committees and project teams; (3) staff meetings; (4) written communications; (5) consultants and peer review; and (6) performance evaluation and feedback. Each provides the manager with an opportunity to reinforce his or her organizational structure. For example, *orientation and training* for management and subordinate personnel should always be consistent with the structure of the organization. For this reason, it is advisable for department managers to take part personally in the orientation and training of their staff, thereby reinforcing the chain of command and establishing themselves as future sources of information for their employees.

The establishment of *committees and teams* to work on special projects serves to provide employees with examples of how a project team orientation can function within the formal pyramidal structure of the organization. *Staff meetings* provide opportunities for managers to exercise the communication, feedback, and integration mechanisms characteristic of the organizational structure. In addition, staff meetings provide opportunities for employees to further develop their departmental identity and to understand the line of authority within their department.

Organizational structure can also be established and maintained through *written communications.* Memoranda can be used to reinforce lines of authority (for example, correspondence between the program's top executive and department managers), integrate components of the organizational structure (for example, correspondence within and between departments), and facilitate the function of project teams (for example, correspondence across departments). Written communications also provide permanent product data for use in evaluating the quantity and quality of communication and feedback within the organization.

Feedback from sources external to the program can also be used in organizational structuring. Reports from *professional consultants and peer reviewers* can be used to provide an important source of validation for the program's organizational structure, thereby increasing the likelihood of its acceptance by program staff. Consultation and peer review also provide important sources of data for evaluating organizational structure and for prompting needed revisions in organizational design, program policy and procedure, and so on.

Finally, organizational structure can be used as a criterion for evaluating staff performance. Since organizational structure and program policy and procedure are reflected in each employee's work performance standards, *performance evaluation and feedback* is an important mechanism for ensuring that each employee's behavior is consistent with, and serves to promote, organizational structure. Staff performance is also the major source of data for evaluating whether the organizational structure is appropriate to the needs of the program and effective in helping the program meet its goals and objectives.

EVALUATING THE EFFECTIVENESS
OF ORGANIZATIONAL STRUCTURE

Throughout this chapter, we have stressed the importance of evaluating one's organizational structuring efforts to ensure that they are (1) responsive to program needs, and (2) effective in helping the program meet its mission, goals, and objectives. There are a number of evaluation systems that can be employed by the manager to ensure that his or her organizational structure, policy, and procedure meet these criteria. For example, evaluative feedback concerning organizational structure and program policy and procedure can be obtained from program staff. At regular intervals, staff members can be asked to provide feedback concerning what they consider to be the strengths and/or weaknesses of the administrative organization, communication and feedback mechanisms, and program policy and procedure, as well as to suggest ways in which each area might be improved. A suggestion box could be used if there is a need to ensure that feedback from staff is anonymous.

Program staff can also be evaluated concerning their understanding of organizational structure. Data of this type can be obtained via pre- and post-training written or oral quizzes as well as by actual observation of staff performance (for example, whether or not an employee follows the chain of command).

The degree to which communication and feedback mechanisms serve to integrate the various components of the organization should also be evaluated. Forms and procedures for generating this kind of data (for example, the interdepartmental peer review form) as well as for improving the quantity and quality of interdepartmental communication are presented in Chapter 7.

The adaptability and flexibility of the program's organizational structure should also be evaluated. For example, data concerning the goals, objectives, and accomplishments of project teams can be compiled and analyzed to determine if project management is a functional (and necessary) feature of the organizational structure. Feedback should also be obtained from project managers and project staff concerning team operation and how it can be improved.

The manager can also obtain evaluative feedback from sources external to the program. For example, evaluation of a program's organizational structure and administrative policies and procedures can be conducted by consultants with expertise in human service management or organization design. Similarly, peer review of the program can be conducted by a team of consultants representing various areas of expertise. Outside evaluation and consultation can also be obtained from consumers of services—patients, funding agencies, and the general public. (More information concerning evaluation strategies is provided in Chapter 7).

SUMMARY

The purpose of organizational structure is to *communicate* program goals and objectives and how they are to be achieved, and to *coordinate* staff performance in the pursuit of program goals and objectives. *Adaptive organizational structure* seems best suited to the special needs of the human service program. It is characterized by centralization of authority; formal rules and regulations for program operation; specific work performance standards for program staff; functional departmentalization; small span of control; and the flexibility for program staff to work in teams on special projects. Organizational structure can be *implemented* through development and utilization of mechanisms such as organizational charts; policy and procedure manuals; work performance contracting; orientation and training; committees and project teams; staff meetings; written communications; consultants and peer review; and performance evaluation and feedback. Evaluation of organizational structure is important to ensure that it is responsive to program need and effective in meeting program goals and objectives. Organizational structure can be evaluated via feedback from program staff, consultants, consumers, and the general public; testing, observation, and performance evaluation of program staff; evaluation of interdepartmental communications; and analysis of project team results and feedback concerning project team function.

4

Getting Staff On-Task

The best indicator of a manager's effectiveness is the level of achievement or productivity of those working in his or her program. The most effective planning and organization are of little consequence if the program's work force is non-productive. The effective manager, therefore, is successful in his or her efforts to get staff on-task and to ensure that tasks are completed so that program goals and objectives are realized.

   The first of these efforts, getting staff on-task, is best accomplished by staff orientation and training procedures that are systematically developed, implemented, and evaluated. *Orientation* procedures should inform each employee of the *task* that he or she is to perform and the *environment* in which it is to be performed. *Training* procedures should equip each employee with the knowledge and skills necessary to perform the task and to maintain a satisfactory level of performance in the future.

ORIENTATION

Work Assignment

   Orienting an employee to the task that he or she is to perform is best accomplished by developing explicit standards for task performance and contracting with the employee for a standard or above-standard level of performance. Each position in the organization should therefore have specific performance standards, including an objective behavioral description of the work assigned to the position. This should minimally consist of the specific product required for satisfactory completion of the assignment (for example, a written report to one's supervisor) as well as the time-lines for completion of the assignment.

Work assignments must be carefully worded so that they are *output*—rather than input-oriented. In addition, they must be measurable in dimensions such as time, quantity, quality, and cost. Finally work assignments must be *relevant* to the goals and objectives of the organization and to the employee's role in the organization as well as *feasible* with respect to program resources and the employee's skills and abilities.

The task of developing work performance standards can be simplified if the manager remembers to proceed according to an organizational framework such as that described in the previous chapter. Specifically, performance standards for the chief executive of the organization can be used as a model for developing performance standards for supervisory personnel. Supervisory personnel then use their performance standards to develop standards for their subordinate personnel. This strategy helps to ensure that each employee's performance standards are drawn up by his or her supervisor, thereby further reinforcing the line of authority characteristic of the organizational structure.

Each work performance agreement should be written so that it indicates the employee's position in the organization, line of supervision, work assignment, and timetable for performance evaluation. We have found the following format useful in a wide variety of human service settings.

Work Performance Standards

Position title: _____

Step, Grade: _____

Salary range: _____

Benefits: _____

Qualifications: _____

Employee: _____

Supervisor: _____

Date of employment: _____
    (in present position)

Date of performance standards: ___ _____

Description of assignment:

(Work assignments, products, and time-lines)

Evaluation:

Written evaluation of the employee's work performance relative to the assignments specified above will be made in six months ____(date)____ and at the employee's anniversary date. These work performance standards, jointly agreed upon by ___(employee)___ and ___(supervisor)___ will be used as criteria for evaluating performance when applicable. It is further understood that these may be modified with concurrence of the employee and the immediate supervisor. Proposed changes must be submitted to the program's manager (chief executive) for final approval.

Employee Signature _____ date _____

Supervisor Signature _____ date _____

Executive Director Signature _____ date _____

Following the rationale outlined above, the most detailed work performance agreement is that between the program manager and his or her supervising authority (for example, Board of Trustees, supervising state official). The manager's performance standards should specify goals, objectives, target behaviors, and time-lines for every area of program operation; call for performance consistent with legal and ethical guidelines as well as with the available research literature pertinent to human service programming; and describe the specific mechanisms that will be employed by the program in ensuring that legal and ethical criteria for service delivery are met. In short, since programming quality assurance while meeting the program's goals and objectives is the ultimate task for the manager, his or her performance standards should reflect this responsibility.

SAMPLE PERFORMANCE STANDARDS FOR THE HUMAN SERVICE MANAGER.   The following is a model work performance standards agreement for the human service manager, which has been adapted from our earlier work (Christian, 1981). This model is based on a human service organization such as that represented in Figure 3–4 on page 45 but can easily be adapted to meet the special needs of managers in other human service settings.

Position Title: Human Service Manager

Description of Assignment
I.   *Administrative Organization and Personnel Management.* Management of administrative structure and staff sufficient to support a progressive, comprehensive program of human services for the target population. Direction of administrative, direct service, clinical support, and support service staff with education, training, and certification (if applicable) sufficient to meet or exceed the requirements of pertinent state and federal licensing and funding agencies concerning personnel and the quality and quantity of services provided.

A. Recruitment, orientation, direct supervision and evaluation of administrative staff (for example, director of clinical services, director of education, director of administrative support services, director of transitional services). Assist administrative staff in recruitment, orientation, supervision and evaluation of direct service staff (teachers, teacher aides, and residential staff) and support service staff (for example, clerical, food service, maintenance personnel).

   1. Orientation of new personnel completed within first week of their employment.

   2. Training of new personnel completed within first month of their employment.

   3. Written work performance standards for each employee appropriate to the needs of the program, the skills of the employee, and pertinent regulatory and licensing requirements of supervisory agencies signed by the employee, his or her direct supervisor, and the program manager within the first six weeks of an individual's employment. Employee's work performance standards reviewed or revised when necessary and at the anniversary date of an individual's employment; written agreement of employee, direct supervisor, and program manager required for revision of standards.

   4. Written evaluation of each employee's performance relative to the standards specified for his or her position, completed and approved in writing by the employee, his or her supervisor, and the program manager at six-month intervals from date of employment.

   5. Weekly individual meeting conducted with each member of administrative staff and bimonthly meetings with the general staff to provide clinical consultation, ongoing communication, in-service training, and/or clarification of program policy and procedures.

   6. Staff performance monitored daily in visits to residential, classroom, and other areas of the physical plant.

B. Comprehensive manual of personnel policy and procedures describing all aspects of program operation submitted to the Board of Trustees/state officials for approval.

C. Current and complete personnel files for each employee maintained as per regulatory agency requirements and in-house standards.

D. Salary range for each position specified as per regulatory agency requirements; competitive salaries and benefits provided for all staff within the limits of the program budget.

E. Current profile of the program staff included in the biannual report to the Board of Trustees and/or department of state administration with supervisory authority over program. Profile to include: (1) positions; (2) name(s) of employee(s) at each position; (3) salary range for each position; and (4) employee's highest academic degree and certification (if applicable).

F. Equal Opportunity/Affirmative Action and regulatory agency guidelines concerning all aspects of personnel management followed.

II. *Service Programming.* Comprehensive, least restrictive human services geared to the special needs of the patients served in the program provided consistent with (a) the needs of the individual patient; (b) current research literature on the education and treatment of the patient population; (c) recommendations from the program's Professional Advisory Board (see Section XI); (d) supervisory agency regulations concerning quality and quantity of clinical, educational, transitional, and administrative services; (e) requests from parents and referral agencies; (f) the patient's approved individual educational plan (if applicable); and (g) accepted legal/ethical guidelines concerning the provision of human services.

A. Initial assessment of each new admission completed within first six weeks; assessment to include appropriate standardized instruments as well as observation of each patient in home (when possible), residential, classroom, and community settings. Follow-up assessment using the same instruments and procedures made at six-month intervals and/or when service is terminated.

B. Treatment plan for each patient completed within first month of admission specifying (a) target behaviors (based on behavioral and/or medical assessment) in areas of health maintenance and communication, social, motor, academic, and self-care skills; (b) treatment procedures to be employed; (c) alternative procedures attempted (in the case of a restrictive procedure to be employed); (d) goals and objectives for treatment; (e) criteria for success; (f) method of evaluating progress; (g) reasonable risks and benefits of the procedure; and (h) authorization from parent/legal guardian (if applicable).

C. Treatment procedures of demonstrated effectiveness used as per the specifications of the least restrictive procedure.

D. Each patient's progress reviewed at three-month intervals, with review addressing target behaviors on treatment plan and progress toward objectives specified. Written report of each patient's progress provided parents/legal guardians and/or referral agencies at three-month intervals from date of admission.

E. Treatment plan revised as indicated by review of progress to ensure that each patient is receiving *effective* treatment based upon his or her needs.

F. Written summary of behavioral assessment and quarterly progress notes entered in each patient's case record (see Section IV).

G. Existing service programs improved and new ones developed to ensure progressive service programming; community-based group homes, specialized foster parent programs, community-based consultation and training services for parents and helping professionals, and so on developed (see Section XIV).

III. *Budget/Accounting Operations.* Preparation, implementation, and monitoring of budget and accounting operations (in association with the program's director of administrative services) as per specifications and requirements of the Treasurer of the Board or state auditor/comptroller's office; monitoring of bookkeeping, billing, and payment mechanisms to ensure balanced budget in accordance with the regulations of the state comptroller's office and/or the state rate-setting commission.

A. Monthly report made to the Board of Trustees/state officials, including the following information for the previous month:*

*Each state has its own forms and procedures for budgetary reporting.

1. Budget control form.
2. Statement of fixed assets.
3. Record of working capital, including current balances of program's savings and checking accounts.
4. Statement of accounts payable and accounts receivable.

B. Reports prepared for the state rate-setting commission and as required for rate negotiations with other states; financial reports, tax statements, and so on prepared as required by other state agencies.

C. Regular communication with Treasurer of the Board/state officials maintained concerning current financial condition, financial problems anticipated, working capital, and so on.

IV. *Case Records and Patients' Rights.* Development of policy and procedures for the maintenance of a case record for each patient documenting (a) pre-admission status and presenting problems; (b) necessary authorizations for service and evidence of informed consent for treatment; (c) identification of pertinent patients' rights issues and their understanding by the patient and/or his or her legal guardian; (d) medical information (physical condition, allergies, special diets, etcetera); (e) treatment plan and appropriate data from intervention initiated through the program; (f) regular progress notes from program staff; (g) quarterly reviews of progress for each patient; (h) necessary identifying information for patient; (i) correspondence, test results, and so on pertaining to the treatment of each patient; (j) discharge information and follow-up status; and (k) other information as per regulatory agency requirements.

A. Manual of forms and standards for case records developed to ensure documentation and management consistent with patients' rights legislation, regulatory agency requirements, and program policy and procedure concerning case record documentation.

B. Program staff trained in record-keeping policy/procedures and the standards for case records.

C. Quarterly review and evaluation made of each active case record relative to manual of standards, with particular attention given possible violations of patients' rights. Rights of particular importance include: (a) confidentiality; (b) refusal of treatment; (c) individualized treatment based on client's special needs; (d) goals of treatment objectively stated with regular reviews of progress and revision of treatment plans as necessary to meet goals; (e) least restrictive treatment; and (f) informed consent to treatment, including information concerning treatment procedures to be utilized and what each entails. Patients and/or their legal guardians must be informed concerning the history and effectiveness of the treatment procedures with similar presenting problems, reasonable risks and benefits associated with each treatment procedure, and possible alternative treatments.

D. Notification of Board of Trustees/pertinent state officials made when a possible violation of patients' rights has been identified; notification of patient and appropriate state agencies made when a patient's right has been violated—this notification to contain a description of the extenuating circumstances (if any), and of the action taken to minimize the possibility of a similar violation in the future.

E. Security of patient records maintained (on-site) to ensure confidentiality of information concerning all aspects of the patient's treatment.

F.   Within the limits of the program's resources, no more than 1% of its patients to have their legal or personal rights infringed upon in receiving services.

V.   *Program Evaluation.*   Ongoing program evaluation, accountability, and quality control—utilizing accepted evaluation practices, reliability checks, and validation procedures—effective in monitoring the following: (a) demographic and treatment status data for patients served (age, length of stay, etcetera); (b) graphical presentation indicating the efficacy of services provided to each patient (the efficacy of the specific procedure employed to treat a specific target behavior); (c) the restrictiveness of the procedures employed; (d) patient status at follow-up; (e) the program's success in meeting its goals and objectives as specified by the Board of Trustees/pertinent state officials; (f) cost effectiveness and budgeting/accounting practices; (g) social validity and consumer satisfaction; (h) record-keeping procedures; (i) staff training and employee work performance; (j) program's impact on human services in general; (k) outcome of applied research projects; (l) protection of patient rights; (m) outcome of grant projects as per requirements of funding agency; (n) success of fund raising and public relations efforts; (o) success of parent involvement and parent training efforts (if applicable); and (p) compliance with guidelines of state and federal regulatory agencies.
A.   Procedural description and results of ongoing in-home evaluation and peer review on each of the areas listed above included in biannual reports to the Board of Trustees/responsible state officials (see Section XIII).
B.   Periodic outside evaluation conducted by recognized experts in the fields of health and human services; written report submitted to the Board of Trustees/state officials summarizing findings and recommendations of each outside evaluator (see Section XI).
C.   Ongoing revision of program's services, policy and procedures made as per the results of program evaluation efforts (for example, going to a new treatment procedure when evaluation indicates present procedure ineffective in meeting treatment plan objectives).

VI.   *Parent Involvement.*   Ongoing communication with parents/legal guardians to ensure (a) their understanding of the program's services and approach to treatment; (b) their participation in their child's treatment program; and (c) their notification concerning progress being made by their child as a patient. Ongoing outreach and on-site parent training and observation/consultation with the goal of helping each patient's parents and home environment to become as therapeutic as possible, so that skills trained by program staff will be maintained and refined in the home environment. Activities to promote parent involvement consistent with requirements of state regulatory agencies and with current literature on parent training.
A.   Quarterly written progress reports to parents/legal guardians describing the patient's progress toward each of the long- and short-term objectives identified in his or her treatment plan.
B.   Outreach parent training and in-home observation performed for as many parents as possible. Information concerning progress of parent training efforts included in biannual reports to the Board/responsible state officials.

C. Personal communication and consultation with parents by administrative staff concerning all aspects of program operation.

D. Development of a "Parent Interest Group" which meets a minimum of once each quarter and reports to the program manager concerning questions, parent recommendations, and so on.

VII. *Maintenance and Security of Buildings, .Grounds, Equipment and Supplies.*   Maintenance of physical plant to ensure compliance with state regulations and local codes and to provide for the health and well-being of patients.

A. Physical plant repaired and renovated within the limits of program budget and the guidelines concerning use of operating capital for repair/renovation (for example, limits imposed by state rate-setting commission).

B. Annual inventory of program equipment and supplies reported annually to the Board/state officials. The location and condition of equipment and supplies monitored via a requisition system.

C. Buildings monitored daily to ensure that they are clean and in a safe condition.

D. Grounds maintained to promote positive image of the program.

E. Ongoing communication maintained with Board of Trustees/responsible state officials concerning needed repairs and construction/renovation projects.

VIII. *Public Relations.*   Coordination of efforts to promote a positive image of the program—that of a progressive human service program effective in meeting the needs of its patients.

A. Brochure and other promotional literature developed for mailing to members of the local community, influential individuals in the state and across the country (for example, social service agency officials, legislators, officers of national organizations), colleges and universities, funding agencies, other human service programs, and so on.

B. A standard package of materials developed for mailing in response to inquiries concerning application for the program's services.

C. An audiovisual program describing the program and its services produced for use in admission interviews, public presentations, tours by the general public, conference presentations.

D. Professional activities of staff effective in promoting a positive image of the program. Report of professional activities of program staff included in each biannual report to the Board/responsible state officials.

1. At least _____ proposals submitted for presentation at a national professional conference each year.

2. At least _____ manuscripts submitted for publication as articles in professional journals or as books for parents and/or helping professionals each year.

E. Studies of social validation and consumer satisfaction included in ongoing program evaluation efforts and documented in biannual reports to the Board/state officials.

1. Social validity obtained to the extent possible on all applied research and program development.

2. Rating of at least 90 percent obtained on annual consumer satisfaction surveys; surveys to be sent to parents/legal guardians, school districts, social service agencies who have referred

individuals to the program and/or are responsible for purchase of services, etcetera. Results of surveys included in biannual reports to the Board/state officials.

F. A Community Advisory Board developed to assist the program in local public relations efforts.

G. Press releases concerning the program prepared for local and regional newspapers and periodicals.

IX. *Fund Raising.* Coordination of program's fund raising efforts.

A. At least _____ grant proposals prepared and submitted each year with an annual goal of $ _____ received in grant funding.

B. Proposals prepared for adjustment of the program's approved tuition/daily rate (for private, non-profit programs) or for increases in the program's state approved budget (for state-administered programs).

C. Local and other contributions secured with an annual goal of $ _____ .

D. Ongoing communication maintained with Board of Trustees/responsible state officials concerning fund raising efforts via biannual reports.

X. *Applied Research.* Direction of applied research designed to (a) improve the effectiveness of program services; (b) determine more effective individual and group training procedures for use with the program's patient population; (c) investigate new administrative and staff training/orientation systems effective in making human services more progressive; and (d) facilitate the return of the patient to his/her family and home community.

A. A Human Rights Committee consisting of members of the local community and helping professionals developed for the purpose of considering the reasonable risks and benefits to patients who are to be involved as subjects in applied research conducted by program staff. A description of the current membership and the function of the committee submitted to the Board of Trustees/state officials as a part of each biannual report (see Section XIII).

B. The program's applied research to be conducted according to guidelines established by the American Psychological Association, American Psychiatric Association, American Medical Association, etcetera, and those included in the following publications:

1. Protection of human subjects: Policies and procedures. *Federal Register,* November 16, 1973, *38,* No. 221.

2. Protection of human subjects: Research involving children. *Federal Register,* July 21, 1978, *43,* No. 141.

C. At least _____ major research projects completed each year, using experimental control rigorous enough to ensure the reliability and replicability of results. Reports on the progress of ongoing applied research included in biannual reports to the Board of Trustees/responsible state officials.

D. At least _____ grant proposal(s) for the support of applied research submitted each year.

XI. *Program Consultants.* Effective utilization of consultants with recognized expertise in the treatment and education of the program's patient population and in the areas of special education, medicine, residential treatment, psychiatry, nutrition, psychology, rehabilitation, and so on.

A. A Professional Advisory Board to provide consultation for program staff and outside evaluation of the program's services developed and coordinated. Current list of Professional Advisory Board members in-

cluded in biannual reports to the Board of Trustees/state officials.
   B. Biannual report provided to Board/state officials concerning scheduled visits by consultants and including written evaluative reports submitted by consultants.
   C. Periodic newsletters/progress reports sent to members of the Professional Advisory Board to keep them informed of program developments.
XII. *University Affiliation.* Development of productive affiliations with universities which prepare graduate and undergraduate students for effective education and management of the program's patient population.
   A. University practicum students and/or interns placed with the program.
   B. Ongoing research projects conducted in collaboration with colleges and universities.
   C. University affiliations sought that would enable the program's direct service staff to earn academic credit contingent upon their work performance.
XIII. *Communication with Board of Trustees/Responsible State Officials.* Frequent communication with members of the program's Board of Trustees/state officials to ensure their ongoing interest and participation in the program. Cooperation with recommendations made by members of Board/state officials.
   A. Biannual reports submitted to the Board/state officials in _____ and _____ of each year describing any change in status relative to the previous six-month reporting period (new programs, data concerning patient progress, fund raising, staff changes, etcetera) for each of the previous twelve assignment areas.
   B. Additional correspondence during each reporting period to be entered upon as needed to keep Board/state officials current concerning all aspects of program operation.

SAMPLE WORK PERFORMANCE STANDARDS FOR ADMINISTRATIVE STAFF.   As previously described, work performance standards for the program manager provide an overall framework for specifying work assignments and performance standards for program staff. For example, the personnel management tasks in Section I(A) of the standards listed the above and the budget/accounting tasks in Section III provide the nucleus of the performance standards for the Director of Administrative Services (following organizational structure represented in Figure 3-4, page 45). Similarly, Section II (Service Programming) is translated into performance standards for the Director of Clinical Services and the Director of Educational Services. Sections IV (Case Records and Patients' Rights) and VI (Parent Involvement) are delegated via work performance standards to the Director of Transitional Services. Sample work performance standards for these key administrative positions are presented in Appendix A.

These examples serve to illustrate how work performance standards actually accomplish much more than work assignment. They *reinforce* the organization's lines of authority and *integrate* the various components of the organizational structure. As previously described, in such a work performance agreement the employee (1) *acknowledges* the existence of organizational structure, program policy and procedure, and the specific work assignments associated with his or her position; and (2) *agrees* to a certain standard of performance.

In integrating the various departments within the organization, work performance standards also help to coordinate employee efforts and to allow each employee the flexibility to realize personal as well as program goals and objectives. For example, each of the sample work performance agreements listed above prompts administrative personnel to meet regularly with each other and with their supervisors to promote open communication among departments as well as to ensure their frequent interaction with the program manager. In addition, the sample agreements have been designed to encourage cooperation by providing (1) opportunities for an employee to work on special projects that involve employees from other departments of the organization (the *project team* characteristic of the *adaptive organizational structure* discussed in Chapter 3); and (2) tasks that employees can work together to complete (such as applied research assignments).

Another integrating function is an employee's involvement in a regular work assignment (as opposed to a special project) that crosses departmental boundaries without disrupting lines of authority. For example, the sample agreement for the Director of Administrative Services (see Appendix, pages 219–20) includes the following assignment: "Recruitment, interviewing, hiring, and time-scheduling of non-administrative personnel subject to guidelines and requirements (for example, qualifications, special needs of a particular department) specified by the supervisor and the Directors of Clinical Services, Educational Services, and/or Transitional Services." Thus, while the Director of Administrative Services does not exercise supervisory authority over all non-administrative personnel, he or she works closely with other administrative staff in the recruitment and scheduling of these personnel.

It is also important to note how work performance standards can serve to promote program accountability and quality control. Specifically, in each of the sample performance agreements, the employee is required to collect certain types of data and conduct regular reviews of progress—progress of patients, staff in training, parents in parent training, maintenance staff in keeping facilities clean, the program's budget via reports of payables and receivables, and so on. In addition, the sample agreements presented in this chapter stress timely documentation in the form of entries in the patient's case record, reports to the program manager and to the program's ultimate supervisory authority (Board of Trustees, state officials).

SAMPLE WORK PERFORMANCE STANDARDS FOR NON-ADMINISTRATIVE STAFF.   As we have seen, work performance standards for administrative staff can be an important step toward ensuring that organizational structure, goal orientation, and quality control become truly pervasive. What remains, then, is to continue this trend in the delegation of work assignments to the subordinate personnel in each department of the organization. Appendix B contains sample work performance standards for non-administrative personnel.

Each of the samples in Appendix B follows the format illustrated on page 59 of this chapter. The samples were chosen to illustrate how each administrative staff member delegates his or her work assignments to employees in his or her department. Therefore, the performance agreement for one position from each department (clinical, educational, transitional, and administrative services) is presented.

It is important to note that the integrating function of the sample work performance agreements for administrative staff (see Appendix A) is also characteristic of the sample agreements for non-administrative personnel. Specifically, (1) work assignments prompt an employee to interact with, and seek assistance from, personnel in his or her own department as well as from personnel in other departments; and (2) employees have opportunities to work on special projects that may involve employees from other departments.

The samples also indicate that work assignments for non-administrative personnel should be output- or product-oriented. This is important since staff directly involved in the delivery of human services must be accountable, that is, their performance must result in their patients receiving services that are effective in meeting their needs and are appropriate relative to pertinent legal, ethical, and regulatory guidelines.

THE CASE MANAGER SYSTEM.   One work assignment strategy that we have found to be very effective in human service settings is the *case manager system*. In this system, each direct service staff member is assigned (via work performance standards) the task of case manager for a particular patient. In this role, the employee is responsible (in consultation with other program staff) for (1) assessing the patient's needs; (2) setting goals and objectives for treatment; (3) planning, conducting and evaluating the success of human service projects (see below), (4) documenting change in the patient's case record (providing graphical representations, progress notes, etcetera); (5) assisting in transitional planning for the patient (for example, discharge and follow-up); and (6) generally monitoring the patient's program of services to ensure that his or her needs are being met and rights are being protected.

The *human service project* is the product or output of the case manager system. Indeed, it can be viewed as the basic unit of accountability for the human service program. The human service project features:

(1) *Baseline assessment* of the patient's behavior to indicate his or her treatment needs as well as to serve as a basis for evaluating the change (or lack of change) in the patient's behavior in response to treatment.

(2) *Determination of a goal for treatment* with an explicit *criterion for success.*

(3) The use of an *evaluation procedure* that will enable program staff reliably to determine if the treatment administered or service delivered has actually had some effect on the patient's behavior, *and* if a change seen in the patient's behavior or baseline condition is actually a result of the treatment administered or service delivered, as opposed to some other factor or factors (for example, age, treatment administered by someone other than a member of the program staff, and so on).

(4) Implementation of a treatment procedure or delivery of a service using *procedures that have been demonstrated to be effective* when used with individuals having a condition and presenting problem similar to the patient's.

(5) *Measurement, analysis and documentation* of the results of treatment or service delivery with ongoing peer review provided by other members of the program staff (administrative, non-administrative, and consultants).

(6) *Maintenance and generalization* of treatment results by continuing to monitor the patient's progress and by enlisting the support of other program staff.

Thus, in conducting a human service project, a staff member follows the same essential steps that we have prescribed for the manager in his or her implementation of a procedural strategy or an organizational system: assessment, implementation, evaluation, maintenance, and generalization (see page 15). This kind of operational specificity and consistency contributes to program accountability and quality control. In addition, since the manager is most familiar with this operational framework, he or she is able effectively to train, supervise, and evaluate staff performance within a similar framework. In short, it is possible for employees in all areas of the human service program to become more product-oriented in their jobs and to utilize a more systematic, problem-solving approach to their work assignments.

Other advantages of the case manager/human service project approach to work assignment include its emphasis on patient advocacy and the likelihood that it will result in job enrichment for human service staff. The case manager is in a unique position to advocate for the patient, having expert knowledge concerning the patient's needs and how the patient's present plan of treatment is meeting those needs. In addition, our experience has been that the case manager does have a definite degree of control over a particular patient's course of treatment. The human service project also increases task-identity for the employee and adds a degree of challenge to the task, since the employee must follow well-specified procedures. Finally, with its emphasis on output and accountability, it facilitates the supervisor's task of providing frequent, appropriate feedback to the employee. Autonomy, task-identity, challenge, and feedback have been identified as factors characteristic of highly enriched jobs (Hackman & Lawler, 1971).

In summary, when developing work performance standards, the manager should be sure to meet the following criteria:

(1) All goals and objectives of the organization should be translated into work assignments for the program manager, who delegates assignments to other program staff via work performance standards.

(2) Work assignments should be clearly specified and should call for some product or output from the employee within explicit time-lines. They must lend themselves to measurement and evaluation.

(3) The number of employee positions within the organization and the number of work assignments per position should be minimized as far as possible without jeopardizing the personnel and task-specificity necessary to ensure that program goals and objectives are met or exceeded. Work assignment overlap across positions should be minimized as far as possible.

(4) Work performance standards should call for performance consistent with legal and ethical guidelines for human services; the best interest of the program's consumers; and the program's mission, goals, objectives, and available resources.

(5) Work performance standards should serve to integrate the various components (departments) of the organizational structure as well as to reinforce the organization's line of authority and its operational policies and procedures.

NEGOTIATION.   After work performance standards have been developed for a particular position, there remains the task of *communicating* them to the employee and *contracting* with the employee for performance consistent with the standards. The employee probably has some general knowledge of work assignments for his or her position as a result of the recruitment process. However, in accepting the position, the employee is not always asked to agree to specific products and time-lines for the work assignments. (While it is possible to negotiate work performance at the time the employee formally accepts the position, this is not recommended unless the negotiation is between supervisor and employee rather than between, for example, personnel officer and employee. Most programs, especially large ones, will probably find it inefficient or impossible to have the employee's supervisor involved to this extent in the recruitment and hiring process.)

Therefore, as soon after his or her employment as possible, the employee should be asked to meet individually with his or her supervisor to discuss the following: the employee's work assignments; the employee's work assignments relative to other employees in his or her department; the supervisor's personnel management methods; department policy and procedure and how it interfaces with organizational policy and procedure; the line of authority within the department and within the organization, and so on. (We have found it most efficient to make this meeting part of the employee's overall orientation program, which will be described in the next section of this chapter.)

Discussion of work assignments and performance standards should consist of the supervisor's reading through the performance standards, calling particular attention to products and time-lines, and answering any questions raised by the employee. If the supervisor feels that the employee does not adequately understand a particular work assignment, he or she should employ restatement, that is, he should explain a work assignment to the employee and ask the employee to restate the work assignment as he or she understands it. Obviously, work performance standards are of little utility if they are not understood.

While this meeting should be conducted as far as possible in the spirit of negotiation, the supervisor should identify the limits for negotiation—the tasks that *must* be performed, the products that *must* result, the time-lines that *must* be met for the position to be "filled." However, areas should also be identified where the employee can have input and negotiate change. These areas will typically be limited to time-lines, the form of a particular product (for example, oral versus written reports), and the nature of special projects to which the employee is being assigned. The supervisor can therefore plan for a certain degree of flexibility in negotiation by specifying adjustable time-lines, identifying areas where products different than those specified might be acceptable, and by making tentative special project assignments.

In our experience, special project assignment is the best way to allow for employee input in work performance contracting. The supervisor should have a list of special projects (with products and time-lines specified for each) from which the employee may choose. Even this limited input means that the employee has had some involvement in determining the job which he or she is to perform.

One last point about the negotiation conference. Work performance contracting may be a totally new experience for the employee. Seeing work assignments and their time-lines for completion specified in writing can be disconcerting. Therefore, it is important that the supervisor adequately communicate the main purpose of the procedure, which is to equip the individual with *information* so that he or she will know the tasks and level of performance expected of him or her and will thus be better able to be effective in (and positive about) his or her employment. If properly conducted, therefore, the employee should leave the negotiation meeting with a positive attitude toward his or her supervisor, understanding of the job that he or she is to perform, and enthusiasm about his or her future with the organization. If the supervisor feels that this is not the case, he or she should schedule a subsequent meeting so that the employee can spend more time looking over the performance agreement, formulating questions for his or her supervisor, and so on.

AGREEMENT.   The agreement stage of work assignment consists of the employee and his or her supervisor signing the work performance agreement and forwarding it to the program manager for approval. When all parties have signed the agreement, the employee is given a copy and encouraged to review it regularly. A copy of the agreement is also placed in the employee's personnel file and another forwarded to the employee's supervisor. (Copies of the work performance standards for each position in the organization should also be included in the program's policy and procedure manual, as described on page 49.)

EVALUATION.   The final section of the work performance agreement indicates the way in which performance standards will be used by the supervisor to evaluate employee performance. To reiterate, this section should include a statement such as the following:

> Written evaluation of the employee's work performance relative to the assignments specified above will be made in six months (date) and at the employee's anniversary date. These performance standards, jointly agreed upon by (employee) and (supervisor) will be used as criteria for evaluating performance when applicable.

Forms and procedures for use in evaluating employee performance will be presented in Chapter 7.

REVISION.   The work performance agreement is not meant to be a static, inflexible procedure. As the needs, goals, and objectives of the program change, work assignments may need to be modified. Thus, work performance contracting, as in the case of organizational structure, must be *adaptive* if it is to be feasible and effective. Therefore, each performance agreement should include the following statement:

> **It is further understood that these performance standards may be modified with the concurrence of the employee and the immediate supervisor. Proposed changes must be submitted to the program manager (chief executive) for final approval.**

When revision is necessary, the supervisor should make sure to proceed through the steps of *negotiation* and *agreement* for the revised document. A copy of the revised agreement, with a revised evaluation schedule, should then replace the existing agreement in the employee's personnel file.

Another way that work performance contracting can be revised and adapted to meet the special needs of the human service manager is the use of the procedure with Boards of Trustees, Human Rights Committees, Professional Advisory Boards, volunteers, practicum students, and so on. For example, with the President of the Board assuming the role of supervisor and a board member assuming the role of employee, the procedural steps of developing standards, negotiation, agreement, and evaluation can be adapted to ensure the active involvement of a Board of Trustees. We have found these procedures of particular value in contracting with outside consultants. More about this use of performance contracting is included in Chapter 7.

Work Environment

Work assignment is actually just one of the topics that should be addressed when orienting the employee to his or her new job. As soon as possible after hiring, the new employee should be equipped with information sufficient to enable him or her to survive in the work environment. This should include information concerning (1) location and function of program facilities; (2) administrative structure; (3) program policy and procedures (with particular emphasis on personnel practices); (4) codes of conduct for employees; (5) the needs and characteristic behaviors of the patients served by the program (with particular attention given to behaviors of patients with whom the new employee will be working most closely); (6) program staff (in particular, those staff working in the employee's immediate environment as well as those individuals with authority over the employee and/or those over whom the employee has authority); and (7) legal and regulatory guidelines concerning the services delivered and patients served by the program.

Orientation for human service personnel may be accomplished in various ways. Many programs conduct orientation and training conferences for groups of new employees. Others leave orientation up to the individual employee, assuming that on-the-job experience, or exposure to printed material such as the program's policy and procedure manual, will provide sufficient information about and introduction to the work environment. However, we have found that these procedures have several disadvantages and limitations. For example, *group orientation* is not always responsive to the needs of the individual employee. In addition, group orientation is often conducted by a personnel officer or training specialist and, therefore, does not bring each employee in contact with key members of the program staff. Reliance on group orientation may also mean that, if there is only one employee in need of orientation, he or she may be asked to wait until the next group session or be given a scaled-down version of the group procedure. The major advantage of group orientation is that it is convenient and time-saving for administrative staff.

On-the-job orientation offers the advantages of providing the new employee with a role model and of better gearing orientation to the special needs of the individual employee. However, this approach assumes, first, that the role model exhibits a high standard of performance consistent with program policy and procedures, his or her work performance agreement, and so on; and, second, that the new employee's errors during this orientation period will be negligible. Since these assumptions are not always true, on-the-job orientation may result in inappropriate or inadequate performance by the new employee, thereby placing the consumer at risk. In addition, on-the-job orientation requires that the program's most experienced, competent service personnel take time away from their work with patients to assist a new employee. While a certain amount of on-the-job orientation and training is important for any new employee, problems such as those described above suggest the use of other procedures as a program's main method of orienting new staff.

THE ORIENTATION CHECKLIST.   An alternative to these more traditional orientation procedures is the orientation checklist. This procedure involves the use of a written schedule which routes each new employee to key personnel whose responsibility it is to provide the employee with information about their specific areas of programmatic responsibility. In our experience, this procedure has been more effective and efficient, more preferred by staff, and more advantageous than either the group or on-the-job methods of orientation.

The first step is the development of the checklist which begins with a determination of the types of information that the procedure is intended to provide the new employee. Sources of this information include (1) the program's policy and procedure manual; (2) the employee's work performance standards; (3) input from the program's administrative staff concerning what they would like each new employee to know; and (4) input from existing staff (in positions similar to the new employee's) concerning what it is important to learn during orientation (or what it would have been nice to have learned when they went through orientation). When a list of this information has been generated, each item should be matched to a responsible administrative staff member. The best rule to follow is, "If I had a problem in this area, who would I go to?" since this is precisely the lesson that one wishes to teach the new employee.

The following is an example of an orientation checklist which might be used by a human service program such as that represented in Figure 3–4 (page 45).

Orientation Checklist

Employee name_____

Date of employment_____

Target date for checklist completion____(within ten work days)_____

Instructions: (if applicable)

Recruitment

_____   I . *Position offered to applicant* - Director of Administrative Services
             (for non-administrative positions) or Executive Director (for ad-
             ministrative positions).
             A.   General description of assignment.
             B.   Review of salary and benefits.
             C.   Time schedule.
             D.   General description of program and patients to be served.
_____ II. *Letter of Agreement* - Director of Administrative Services or Ex-
             ecutive Director.

Orientation

_____ III. *Personnel Practices* - Director of Administrative Services
             A.   Tax forms.
             B.   Leave and accrual information.
             C.   Blue Cross/Blue Shield.
             D.   Life insurance.
             E.   Sign-in procedure.
             F.   Use of facilities (keys, autos, maintenance).
             G.   Emergency routine (incident reports, accident forms, fire
                  escape information, etcetera).
             H.   Personnel practices and policies.
_____ IV. *Administrative Services* - Director of Administrative Services.
             All staff:
             A.   Goals and future plans for department.
             B.   Department's organizational structure and key staff.
             C.   Special projects (planned and in progress).
             Administrative services staff:
             D.   Review of position and patients served.
             E.   Review of work assignments and evaluation procedures;
                  negotiate and sign work performance agreement; copy of
                  agreement retained by employee after approval by Executive
                  Director.
             F.   Staff meetings.
             G.   Training.
_____   V. *Clinical Services* - Director of Clinical Services.
             All staff:
             A.   Goals and future plans for department.
             B.   Department's organizational structure and key staff.
             C.   Special projects (planned and in progress).
             Clinical services staff:
             D.   Review of position and patients served.

E. Review of work assignments and evaluation procedures; negotiate and sign work performance agreement; copy of agreement retained by employee after approval by Executive Director.
F. Case manager system and human service projects.
G. Staff meetings.
H. Training.

_____ VI.   *Educational Services* - Director of Education.
All staff:
A. Goals and future plans for department.
B. Department's organizational structure and key staff.
C. Special projects (planned and in progress).
Educational staff:
D. Review of position and patients served.
E. Review of work assignments and evaluation procedures; negotiate and sign work performance agreement; copy of agreement retained by employee after approval by Executive Director.
F. Case manager system and human services projects.
G. Staff meetings.
H. Training.

_____ VII. *Transitional Services* - Director of Transitional Services.
All staff:
A. Goals and future plans for department.
B. Department's organizational structure and key staff.
C. Special projects (planned and in progress).
Transitional services staff:
D. Review of position and patients served.
E. Review of work assignments and evaluation procedures; negotiate and sign work performance agreement; copy of agreement retained by employee after approval by Executive Director.
F. Staff meetings.
G. Training.

_____VIII. *Medical Conference* - Coordinator of Health Care Services.
A. Medication routine and policies.
B. Confirmation of TB test within past twelve months (appointment to be made within one week of starting work).

_____ IX.   *Conference with Executive Director.*
A. Role of the Executive Director.
B. Organizational structure.
C. Board of Trustees/state administration.
D. Professional Advisory Board (consultants).

_____ X.   Submit completed policy and procedure manual form and orientation checklist to supervisor.

_____ XI.   Filed in individual's personnel file.

Each employee should also be required to sign a form indicating that he or she has read, understands, and agrees to comply with the program's policy and procedure manual. A sample format is as follows:

I have read and understand the contents of the ____(program)____ policy and procedures manual. I agree to comply and work in accordance with these policies and procedures during the course of my employment at (program) .

Employee: _____

(date)

This form should be signed and submitted to your supervisor.

The supervisor acknowledges receipt of this form by initialing Item X on the orientation checklist.

After the checklist has been developed, it should be shared with the program's administrative staff and modified in response to their feedback. Care should be taken to ensure that each staff member listed on the checklist understands his or her responsibilities in the orientation procedure, that is, what information is to be conveyed, how to ensure that the information is understood by the employee (for example, use of restatement), and how to advise the employee so that his or her completion of orientation is facilitated. We have found it desirable to have a few practice trials with individuals acting out the roles of the new employee and the staff member to ensure that this meeting is conducted as effectively and efficiently as possible.

There are several methods for *implementing the checklist.* The *manager-controlled* method makes it the responsibility of program staff to route the checklist, thereby controlling the orientation procedure. According to this method, a staff member listed on the checklist contacts the new employee, schedules a conference for his or her area of the checklist, initials his or her area when the conference is completed, and forwards the checklist to the next staff member on the checklist. The last staff member on the checklist to have a conference with the employee forwards the completed checklist to the employee's supervisor who enters the checklist in the employee's personnel file and notifies the employee that he or she has successfully completed orientation. Thus, using the manager-controlled method, the employee has little control over the course of his or her orientation.

The *employee-controlled* method makes the new employee responsible for scheduling conferences with program staff, completing the checklist, and submitting the completed checklist to his or her supervisor. When this method is employed, the following instruction should be added to the checklist.

This checklist becomes the permanent record of your orientation and, when completed, will be entered in your personnel file. It is your responsibility to proceed through work areas III - X listed below by obtaining the signature of the staff member responsible for each work area in the space provided to the left of the area. The attached map of the facility indicates the location (building, floor, office number) and phone number for each of these individuals. This form should be completed and returned to your supervisor by the target date indicated above. Any questions about this procedure should be addressed to your supervisor.

The manager's choice between these two methods will be determined by factors such as the skill level of the employee; convenience; preference (by administrative staff and by staff members who have actually been exposed to the orientation procedures); and effectiveness. We have attempted to evaluate the use of the orientation checklist procedure in a human service setting (Christian, Troy, Lipsker, Czyzewski, & Luce, 1981). We have been particularly interested in the extent to which this procedure is more effective and more preferred by staff as compared to a more traditional approach to orientation, such as on-the-job experience. It is useful to review this research briefly, since it not only provides evidence concerning the applicability of the orientation checklist, but also gives an example of how one can go about *evaluating the effectiveness of orientation training.*

Forty-five employees of a human service program were randomly assigned to groups according to the type of orientation training that they were to receive. Employees in Group A were exposed to the *employee-controlled* orientation checklist procedure; those in Group B were exposed to the *manager-controlled* orientation checklist procedure. Employees in Group C, who were not exposed to either of the orientation checklist procedures, had at least one month of on-the-job experience as their orientation training. A pre-test was administered to all employees prior to the initiation of orientation procedures. The test was designed to assess general knowledge of program policy and procedure, that is, the type of information that a thorough orientation program would be likely to address.

When the checklist procedure had been completed for the members of Groups A and B, a post-test was administered to all forty-five employees. A satisfaction questionnaire was also completed by each employee as well as by each of the administrative personnel involved in orientation. The questionnaire asked each individual to indicate which of the orientation procedures he or she preferred and which he or she felt was most efficient. Employees and administrative staff were also given an opportunity to provide additional feedback and comments about the various orientation procedures.

This research revealed that either of the checklist procedures was more effective in communicating information to new employees and was more preferred by both new employees and administrative staff, compared to on-the-job orientation without a checklist. An interesting finding was that while the employee-controlled checklist procedure resulted in the greatest pre/post test score increase and was preferred by administrative staff, the new employees involved in the study preferred the manager-controlled procedure and felt that it was the most efficient. Apparently, both new employees and administrative staff preferred the course of least effort with respect to their involvement.

TRAINING

While orientation is concerned with exposing the employee to organizational policies and practices, training is concerned with developing job-related skills and task-related knowledge. The goal of every training effort is *positive transfer*, that is, the successful transfer or generalization of skills learned in the training session to the staff member's interactions with patients and with other employees in the work environment.

Developing a Training Program

There has been a considerable amount of research conducted in the area of staff training and it has provided a number of important guidelines for the program manager who is interested in developing or improving a training program for employees. For example, we know that positive transfer is more likely to occur when the training and job situations are similar; when trainees are provided with a wide variety of and experience with job-related stimuli (situations that actually occur in the work environment); and when trainees understand the general principles underlying the rationale of the training sessions (Bass & Vaughn, 1966; Ellis, 1965).

In addition, we know that trainees must be motivated to learn if training is to be effective. While this motivation should be intrinsic (that is, training should be seen by the trainee as a worthwhile experience in and of itself), extrinsic motivation, which may involve reward, punishment, and/or coercion by the organization, has also been shown to be effective. Indeed, numerous research investigations have demonstrated the importance of contingent reinforcement (written and verbal feedback for staff performance on the job as well as during training) for motivation and learning. The active practice and repetition of skills during training, rather than simply passive listening, is also recommended.

Many methods for training staff have been described in the literature. We know that training in human service settings is typically delivered in workshops and consists of lectures, audiovisual aids, case presentations and *in vivo* demonstrations, discussion groups, handbooks and texts, specially prepared instructional materials, and questionnaires allowing trainees to evaluate the workshop. However, we know little about the relative effectiveness of these procedures in improving staff performance. This is because much of the available literature on staff training, while it describes training programs conducted by specific human service organizations, does not view training as a performance measure. In fact, there is ample evidence from the research literature to suggest that staff training does not always result in improved staff performance and that demonstrations of effectiveness should be required of any staff training procedure before large amounts of time and money are invested in it.

In short, while it is generally assumed by program managers that staff training leads to improved staff performance, such is not always the case. Quilitch (1975) has described research in which contingent cash bonuses to staff for leading training sessions greatly increased the number of such training sessions, but had no significant effect on the performance of students in the sessions. In addition, managers should never assume that improved staff behavior will necessarily result in improved patient behavior.

CRITERIA.   In developing a training program, the human service manager should attempt to meet the following criteria:

(1) Utilize training procedures with *demonstrated effectiveness* in improving the performance of similar staff in similar settings.

(2) Program for *similarity* in training and work environments.

(3) Ensure that trainees have a sufficient *understanding of the basic principles* underlying the procedures that they are being trained to employ.

(4) Provide *feedback* for appropriate staff performance in training sessions as well as in the work environment.

(5) Provide opportunities for trainees to *practice* new skills.

(6) Promote *maintenance* and *generalization* of new skills through ongoing training and contingent feedback.

JOB ANALYSIS.   After identifying the criteria for an effective training program, the manager must determine the skills, knowledge, attitudes, and standards for effective staff performance. The first step in this job analysis, the specification of explicit performance standards for each job, has already been described. The second step is to list the skills and knowledge required for an employee to perform consistent with the performance standards for his or her job. It is this list that becomes the objective of the training program.

For example, consider the task of case manager described earlier in this chapter.

Job analysis: Case manager

Performance standards	Knowledge/skills
1. Assessment of patient's needs	a. Ability to administer, score, and interpret results of standardized behavioral assessment instruments.
	b. Ability to unobtrusively and reliably observe and record patient behavior in a human service setting.
	c. Knowledge of normal, age-appropriate human development and behavior.
2. Specification of goals, objectives, and procedures for treatment	a. Ability to describe human behavior in objective, operational terms.
	b. Skills in goal analysis (Mager, 1972).
	c. Knowledge of state-of-the-art treatment procedures with tested effectiveness in meeting needs similar to the patient's.
	d. Understanding of legal and ethical issues regarding the delivery of human services to the patient population.
	e. Knowledge of appropriate forms and procedures for use in the development of a treatment plan.

f. Ability to develop a treatment plan based on a patient's special needs.

g. Knowledge of basic principles of research design; ability to plan treatment so that the effect of the treatment procedure can be isolated.

3. Implementation of treatment procedure

Ability to implement a procedure as per recommended guidelines.

4. Evaluation of treatment effectiveness

a. Ability to administer, score, and interpret behavioral assessment instruments.

b. Ability to reliably observe and record human behavior.

c. Ability to determine the reliability of results.

d. Ability to graph data.

e. Ability to analyze data using basic statistical methods.

f. Ability to write an evaluation summary for the patient's case record as per the program's case record standards.

PLANNING.   Once skill areas have been identified, the manager must develop an operational plan which specifies the *objectives* of the training program, the *methods* it will employ, and the specific *instructional techniques* that will be utilized. We have found the following training plan effective in structuring individual and group training programs for human service staff.

Training plan

Objective	Method	Instructional technique
1. Preparation	1. Put trainees at ease. 2. Tell them the title of the job.	1–2. Lecture; discussion or conference training.
	3. Explain the purpose of the job.	3. Lecture; audiovisual training.
	4. Explain why they have been selected for training. 5. Help them relate past experience to the job.	4–5. Lecture; discussion or conference training.
	6. Assess pre-training skill levels.	6. Role playing and situational testing; audiovisual recording.
2. Instruction	1. Introduce trainees to tools, materials, equipment, and important terms.	1. Lecture; programmed instruction; audiovisual training.

2. Demonstrate the job, explaining each step slowly and clearly.	2. Role playing; audiovisual training; modeling; on-the-job training.
3. Review with them what they should know up to this point: title of job, purpose of job, and procedural steps.	3. Conference or discussion training; lecture; audiovisual training.

3. Practice

1. Supervise each trainee's performance of the job.	1. Role playing; modeling; on-the-job training.
2. Question them on weak and key points.	2. Lecture; conference or discussion training.
3. Have them repeat until each trainee has developed the skills necessary to meet the performance standards for the job.	3. Role playing; modeling; on-the-job training.

4. Evaluation

1. Have them do the job alone.	1. Role playing; on-the-job training.
3. Inspect job against standards of performance and pre-training skill levels.	2. Lecture; audiovisual recording.
3. Discuss with each trainee his or her readiness for the job or need for further training.	3. Lecture.

Promoting Trainee Attendance and Participation

The manager's training plan should also incorporate procedures designed to promote interest, attendance, and participation on the part of the trainee. In our experience, a manager must program for trainee involvement if he or she expects to get it. Therefore, we recommend including the following in every training program:

1. *Training contract.* A brief training agreement should be developed, specifying the roles of trainer and trainee; the criteria for successful completion of training; how trainee attendance, participation, and performance will be evaluated; and the consequences for successful and unsuccessful completion of training. (This can also be accomplished by adding a brief consent section to the training syllabus.)

2. *Syllabus.* A written syllabus or agenda for a training program should include a list of the training modules and a time-schedule for the initiation and completion of each module. In addition, the following information should be listed for each module: (a) workshop title; (b) topic; (c) rationale; (d) reading assignments; (e) study questions; (f)

in-session assignment; (g) independent assignment; and (h) review questions for quiz. Study questions might be designed to structure note taking for trainees, as discussed later in this chapter. Notice that the trainee is required to participate actively in the completion of each module.

3. *Resource packet.* A collection of assigned readings should be provided or made available to each trainee to increase the likelihood that readings and other assignments are completed. A small reference library is therefore an important supplemental resource for staff orientation and training programs.

4. *Rehearsal.* The training program should be carefully rehearsed. A professional consultant might be asked to critique the trainer's presentation skills, use of audiovisual aids, and so on, so that skills can be refined and the program improved.

5. *Access to trainer.* Each trainee should be provided with information concerning how to contact the trainer outside of the training session. This provides encouragement for those individuals in need of special guidance or assistance.

Conducting the Training Program

The format typically used in training human service staff is the *workshop* or training session. A group of employees with similar work assignments and varying pre-training skill levels complete training *modules* based on the specific skill areas identified through job analysis. Each training module (for example, Observing and Recording Patient Behavior) reflects the overall structure of the training program in that it systematically works through the objectives of *preparation, instruction, practice,* and *evaluation.* This format can be used in training supervisory as well as service delivery skills and is appropriate for the initial training of new staff as well as for ongoing in-service training programs.

The major disadvantage of the workshop format is that it is not always sufficiently responsive to the skill levels and needs of the individual trainee. Workshop training must, of necessity, be pitched to the skill level thought to be characteristic of the ''average'' trainee in the group. The obvious result is that highly skilled trainees and very unskilled trainees are less likely to benefit from their training experience. Great variability in trainee skill level also complicates the task of the workshop leader.

When faced with this problem, the manager should consider the development of a more *personalized program of instruction* for those trainees who are apparently not benefitting from workshop training; the workshop format can continue to be used for other trainees. A personalized program of instruction is developed in much the same way as a workshop, that is, by the establishment of standards or criteria, job analysis, and the development of a training plan that calls for preparation, instruction, practice, and evaluation of each skill area. The difference between the two methods lies in the role of the trainee.

In a personalized program of instruction, the trainee is required to learn the material, all of it, and to set his or her own pace. For example, the trainee may be given a list of assignments (for example, to read a book) and required products (for example, a brief written report) with liberal time-lines. He or she individually learns each assignment and, contingent upon completion of the product for that assignment, receives immediate feedback. In the workshop format, the trainer sets the pace and assumes that the trainees are keeping up (even when there may be evidence to the contrary).

We have found many uses for personalized programs of instruction in human service settings. One reason for this is that the work performance contracting procedures that we have employed lend themselves so readily to the development of individualized training schedules—they prompt the manager to analyze a job and to specify the output required for its completion.

For example, consider the problem of the human service program that needs a computer but employs no one (and cannot afford to hire someone) with computer programming expertise. It is not practical for the program to conduct a workshop on the technical aspects of computer programming, since it is not important that more than one employee be equipped with such skills. In this situation, the manager (in consultation with a computer science professional) could develop a personalized program of instruction that would actually become a special project for the individual (as per his or her performance agreement). The plan for such a program might look like the following:

Personalized Training Plan

Goal: To prepare employee for position of computer programming specialist.

Unit I. Computer programming

assignments	Products
A. Attend two-day computer programming seminar.	A. Passing grade; proof of attendance; participation rating; oral or written quiz on seminar content.
B. Complete selected readings on topics including: 1. How computers work. 2. Tasks that computers can be programmed to perform. 3. How to design and run a computer program. 4. Computer hardware and software.	B. Oral or written report; quiz on seminar content.
C. Complete programmed instruction manual on computer programming.	C. Record of correct answers to questions in programmed text.
D. Complete night course on computer programming at local community college.	D. Passing course grade.
E. Competency examination on computer programming.	E. Mastery test—take as many times as necessary until score of 100 percent correct is attained.

Unit II. Computer programming for human service organizations

A. Attend training seminar on uses of computer technology in human services.

A. Passing grade: proof of attendance; participation rating; oral or written quiz on seminar content.

B. Visit ten human service organizations which make use of computers. Complete a brief written report of each site-visit including the following information:
  1. Name and location of organization.
  2. Mission of organization.
  3. Type of computer equipment being utilized.
  4. Computerized functions.
  5. Evaluative feedback from organization staff concerning the cost effectiveness, advantages/disadvantages, etcetera of computerization.

B. Evaluation of written reports; reliability check by contact with several of the organizations reportedly visited.

C. Complete list of selected readings on topics including:
  1. Basic concepts for designing a functional hospital information system.
  2. Computerization and hospital data processing.
  3. Uses of computers in medical diagnosis, processing of clinical laboratory data, administering screening tests and health examinations, patient monitoring, medical records and automated medical histories.
  4. Ensuring cost effectiveness of computerization in human service settings.
  5. Preparing human service data for computer processing.
  6. Hardware and software for human service application.
  7. How to utilize technical consultants.
  8. Time-sharing strategies for increasing the benefits

C. Oral or written report; quiz on content.

of computer use in human
services.

D. Competency examination on
the applications of computer
programming in human
services.

D. Mastery test—take as many
times as necessary until score
of 100 percent correct is
attained.

E. Develop a three-year plan for
submission to program
management describing the
introduction of computer
technology to trainee's
human service organization
specifying:
1. goals;
2. objectives;
3. time-schedule;
4. hardware and software
requirements;
5. operational procedures;
6. budget;
7. evaluation systems.

E. Evaluation of written proposal with aid of technical
consultant to determine appropriateness, feasibility,
probable cost effectiveness,
etcetera. Evaluation of results
following actual implementation of the proposal.

We have found the personalized instruction format particularly useful in training practicum students, interns and fellows, volunteers, and staff members who either were not able to attend or were not successful in completing workshop training. In general, we have found that the more skilled the employee and/or the higher his or her professional level, the more he or she is likely to prefer personalized instruction. In our experience, unskilled and/or nonprofessional staff tend to prefer workshop training and may have difficulty following through with a self-paced program.

INSTRUCTIONAL TECHNIQUES.   The techniques used in staff training can be grouped in two categories: *on-the-job* and *off-the-job* training techniques. *On-the-job* techniques include orientation training, job-instruction training, apprentice training, coaching, and job rotation. Coaching involves matching the trainee with an experienced peer or supervisor. Job rotation involves placing the trainee in a number of jobs so that he or she learns a number of skills, observes and participates in a variety of work situations, and is exposed to a variety of patients and service programs.

However, as previously described, on-the-job training for staff involved in service delivery may result in unnecessary risks to the consumer. In addition, experienced peers are often unskilled trainers and on-the-job training may be scattered and unfocused. Nevertheless, on-the-job techniques are effective in eliminating problems associated with transfer of training. They provide for active participation by, and ongoing feedback to, the trainee, and ensure the relevance of the training experience.

Off-the-job training techniques have the advantage of focusing on specific elements of a job and of allowing the trainer to present the type of supplemental information that may be essential for some trainees. Most importantly, however, off-the-job techniques are more conducive to trial-and-error learning and thereby minimize risk to the consumer during the training process. On the negative side, off-the-job training requires trainee time off the job and does not always result in high employee motivation and positive transfer to the work situation.

For example, lecturing is perhaps the most efficient and widely used off-the-job training technique. However, the use of lectures alone results in problems of one-way communication and passive listening, and is heavily dependent on the skill of the lecturer. Audiovisual techniques, although they have advantages and limitations similar to those described for the lecture, are particularly useful in the human service environment. Specifically, we have found audiovisual recordings of correct and incorrect staff-to-patient interactions an essential element of any training program for human service personnel. Audiovisual techniques are also useful in documenting the effectiveness of staff training, since a post-training audiovisual record of performance can readily be compared with one obtained prior to training.

Other off-the-job instructional techniques include discussion (conference) training, programmed instruction, role playing, and social skill/assertive training. In *discussion (conference) training*, the trainer acts as a resource person and provides non-directive feedback as trainees exchange information. *Programmed instruction* involves breaking down the content of training into a sequence of small elements. As the trainee individually learns each element, he or she answers questions, and receives immediate feedback.

Role playing is a frequently used procedure in which the trainee is asked to assume the role of someone else with a specific problem to resolve (for example, a staff member confronted by an aggressive patient, a manager who must fire an employee). The obvious limitation of such training is that positive transfer of role-played skills may not occur. *Social skill/assertive* training is designed to teach the trainee to develop and maintain mutually reinforcing interactions with other individuals in his or her environment. In this type of training, modeling, role playing, and audiovisual recording are used to (1) present the trainee with a hypothetical interpersonal situation; (2) assess the individual's level of social and assertive skills; (3) develop and improve social skills such as eye contact, positive voice tone, speech content and so on; and (4) evaluate the trainee's use of his or her newly learned social repertoire.

Evaluating the Effectiveness
of Staff Training

Evaluation of staff training requires advance planning. Since training is essentially a performance measure, the manager must plan to collect the kind of data that will enable him or her to evaluate *change in trainee performance*. Therefore, the manager must obtain data concerning the trainee's performance and job-related knowledge prior to training as well as after training has been completed. In addition, the manager must be sure that data obtained are valid and reliable indicators of trainee performance and job-related knowledge. Unfortunately, many managers rely on impressionistic or anecdotal data ("It was a beneficial experience; training helped me a lot") rather than on systematic assessments of behavior change.

We recommend several strategies for evaluating the effects of training on staff performance.

1. *Behavioral observation.* This involves pre- and post-training observations and recordings of the trainee's performance in the work situation. The manager should develop a checklist of work behaviors to be observed and a time-schedule (preferably variable) for observation. Observers should then be trained to ensure that their ratings are reliable. (Observation and recording procedures are described in greater detail on pages 29-30).

2. *Situational testing.* This procedure may be used as either an on-the-job or off-the-job assessment procedure. As an off-the-job procedure, the trainee might be asked to role play therapeutic interactions with a patient (role played by the trainer or another trainee), with a colleague in solving some hypothetical problem in the work environment, and/or with his or her supervisor (for example, receiving positive and negative feedback). As an on-the-job procedure, the trainee would be asked to model these interactions in the actual work environment, with patients, colleagues, or supervisory personnel. Ideally, an audiovisual record should be made of the pre- and post-training situational tests. These permanent products are then compared to determine how training has effected the trainee's performance.

3. *Written tests.* The trainee might also be asked to complete a written test before and after training which samples the content of the training program. Care must be taken, however, to ensure that the pre- and post-training tests are equivalent (covering the same content with a similar level of difficulty) so that variation in difficulty does not confound the effect of the training program. When training a large number of staff, the manager should consider the use of a training model or package that includes prepared reading materials and mastery tests.

4. *Assignments and special projects.* Another procedure for pre-/post-training assessment of staff knowledge, attitude, motivation, and performance involves the use of assigned readings and special projects. For example, a training module concerned with treatment planning might require that the trainee read several "how-to" articles on treatment plan development, give a brief written report of the articles read, and design a treatment plan for a hypothetical patient. If the trainee had been required to design a similar hypothetical treatment plan prior to training, the manager would have permanent product data for determining how training affected the individual's treatment planning performance.

Attendance and participation in staff training should be required of every employee and specified in his or her work performance agreement. It is important, therefore, that an attendance record be maintained for each trainee. Records should also be maintained of employees who attend optional in-service training sessions. These data are useful in documenting and providing reinforcing feedback for employee motivation.

Each trainee's participation should also be evaluated. One measure of trainee participation is the trainee's completion of work assignments and special projects,

Participation Evaluation

Participant: _____

Session number	Attendance Present —2 Tardy/left Early —1 Absent —0	Participation Maximum —3 Adequate —2 Minimal —1 Excessive —1	Assignments Return data —1 Complete quiz —1 Read assignments —1	Total points earned

Points earned — (y-axis, 0–10)
Training sessions — (x-axis, 1–10)

FIGURE 4-1

for example, number of assignments completed, adherence to established time lines, quality of completed assignments. Another measure is the *participation rating* recorded for each trainee by the trainer at the conclusion of each training session. We have found the following form useful in rating training session attendance and participation. The same form, incidentally, is useful in providing contingent feedback to staff and patients (e.g., in group therapy).

Another way to evaluate training participation is to represent the major issues to be addressed in a particular training session in the form of questions. Answers to each question are provided by the trainer during the course of the session. The trainee is provided with a list of these questions and instructed to listen carefully to the trainer, fill in the answer to each question as it is discussed, and submit the completed answer form to the trainer at the conclusion of the session. In this case, the trainer has *structured note taking* to promote and evaluate trainee attention and participation.

It is also important to obtain feedback from trainees concerning their satisfaction with the trainers, the materials used, the scheduling of training sessions, session content, and so on. This is best accomplished by developing an evaluation form that can be completed anonymously by each trainee. We have found the following form to be useful in assessing employee satisfaction with orientation and training programs.

Trainee Satisfaction Survey

Workshop _____   Instructor _____

Date _____

1. Were the prerequisite skills for the workshop clearly specified in the workshop description? (a) yes   (b) no.
2. If yes, how would you judge the usefulness and appropriateness of these skills to the workshop objectives? (a) very appropriate   (b) somewhat appropriate   (c) not appropriate.
3. Were the objectives of the workshop clearly stated during the presentation? (a) yes   (b) no   (c) somewhat.
4. If yes, were the activities of the workshop appropriate to the objectives of the workshop? (a) yes   (b) no   (c) somewhat
5. Were written materials distributed at the workshop? (a) yes   (b) no.
6. If yes, how would you rate the quality and appropriateness of these materials to the objectives of the workshop? (a) excellent   (b) acceptable   (c) not acceptable.
7. Please indicate the types of activities which were provided in the workshop. (a) mostly lectures   (b) lectures and practical experiences   (c) mostly practical experiences.
8. Were audiovisual presentations used in the workshop? (a) yes   (b) no.
9. If yes, how would you rate the quality of these presentations? (a) excellent   (b) good   (c) fair.
10. How well did the type of presentation assist you in meeting the learning objectives of the workshop? (a) very well   (b) somewhat   (c) not at all.
11. How would you describe your general activity level in this workshop? (a) mostly active   (b) active/passive   (c) mostly passive.
12. If you answered active, did you complete structured activities which required that you learn various concepts and principles as you progressed through the activity? (a) yes   (b) no   (c) sometimes.
13. If you answered passive, would you conclude that the structure and content of the presentation has advanced your knowledge in the field? (a) yes   (b) somewhat   (c) no.
14. Please comment on the style of the instructor's presentation. (a) exciting   (b) acceptable   (c) boring.

15. Please comment on the general overall quality of the workshop activities. (a) excellent   (b) average   (c) below-average.
16. Review the objectives of the workshop. How well do you consider that the workshop activity met those objectives? (a) very well   (b) acceptable (c) unacceptable
17. How well do you think you have mastered the material presented in this workshop? (a) very well   (b) some mastery   (c) very little.

Additional Comments:

Finally, it is important to document any *patient behavior change* apparently resulting from staff training. It is very difficult to ascertain with any degree of certainty whether a particular training program resulted in a particular patient's improvement—there are so many variables in the human service environment that can act or interact to influence the patient's behavior. Nevertheless, we have found it important for staff morale to document when a pre-/post-assessment indicates significant improvement (that is, a greater *rate* of improvement) in a patient's behavior following a staff training program. The *human service project* described earlier in this chapter (see page 69) is a particularly useful mechanism for relating patient behavior change to improved staff performance. We have found, also, that human service projects are conducted more effectively and more efficiently by staff who have been properly trained. Other strategies for evaluating patient behavior change will be described in Chapter 7.

Graphing and Communicating Results

As described in Chapter 2, the best way to indicate change in behavior is to represent it graphically. Graphing pre- and post-training data provides a visual record of how training has affected the trainee's performance and his or her job-related knowledge. It also provides a clear indication of the trainee's strengths and weaknesses, thereby facilitating decision-making concerning remedial training. Finally, graphing facilitates communication of training results to the trainee and provides a permanent record for inclusion in the trainee's personnel file. (How to graph and analyze data is described on page 30.)

When the trainee's pre- and post-training data have been graphed and analyzed, they should be communicated to the trainee in an individual meeting with the trainer. (Some supervisors may prefer to obtain this information from the trainer and personally pass it on to trainees under their supervision.) The trainer (or supervisor) should take advantage of this opportunity to provide positive feedback for the trainee's participation in training as well as for the trainee's improved performance. If the data indicate that the individual is in need of additional training, he or she might be advised to participate in the next training program or to begin a personalized training program designed to improve areas of weakness. In addition, all of this information should be summarized for entry in the individual's personnel file.

The manager should provide feedback for the individual responsible for conducting the training program. This feedback can be based on trainee attendance, participation and satisfaction data, as well as on data indicating the overall success of the training program (for example, number of trainees successfully completing the program, average scores for module quizzes). A memorandum including this type of feedback should be entered in the trainer's personnel file.

Promoting Maintenance and Generalization

The generalization of instructional gains from the training session to the work environment cannot be taken for granted. If generalization is the objective of the training program, training for generalization must be made an integral part of the program and should be implemented during training or after the trained employee has entered the work environment. We have already described some of the ways to promote generalization *during* training. These include: (1) ensuring similarity between training and job situations; (2) providing a wide variety of and experience with job-related stimuli; and (3) providing for the practice of new skills.

Promoting maintenance and generalization *after* the completion of training can be accomplished by procedures such as the following: (1) providing feedback contingent upon performance in the work environment; (2) fading the density of feedback from continuous feedback immediately contingent upon performance to intermittent feedback not as immediately contingent upon performance; (3) cueing or prompting the staff member to perform as he or she was trained to perform and (4) ongoing training to ensure that skills are maintained and further refined. Taken together, these procedures add up to *good supervision*, a subject that we will address in more detail in the next chapter.

SUMMARY

Getting staff on-task is best accomplished by *orientation* and *training* procedures that are systematically developed, implemented, and evaluated. *Orientation* procedures should inform each employee about the *work assignment* and the *environment* in which it is to be performed. Orienting an employee to the work that he or she is to perform is best accomplished by *developing work performance standards*, and by *negotiating* and *contracting* with the employee for an acceptable level of performance. The most detailed work performance standards are the program manager's since they serve as the framework within which performance standards for other program staff are developed. Orienting the employee to the work environment is best accomplished by the use of an *orientation checklist*, a procedure which routes each new employee to key program personnel who provide the employee with information about their specific areas of responsibility.

Training is concerned with developing job-related skills and task-related knowledge. Training procedures should be *effective*; program for *similarity* between training and work environments; provide *feedback* for trainee performance; encourage the *practice* of new skills; and promote *maintenance and generalization* of new skills. A *training plan* specifies objectives, methods and instructional procedures. *Job analysis* determines what skills are taught. Trainee attendance and participation can be promoted by the use of a training contract, syllabus, and resource packet, and by rehearsing training procedures and providing trainees with access to the trainer outside of the training session. Training may be conducted in *workshops* or via *personalized programs of instruction*. Both *on-the-job* (for example, coaching) and *off-the-job* (for example, role playing) *instructional techniques* are used in staff training, although on-the-job training may result in unnecessary risk to the patient. The effectiveness of training is evaluated by examining its effect on *trainee performance*. This can be accomplished by using strategies such as behavioral observation, situational testing, written tests, and assignments and special projects. It is also important to assess trainee attendance, participation, and satisfaction. Evaluation results should be *graphed and communicated* to the trainee. *Maintenance and generalization* of training effectiveness can be promoted by contingent feedback for staff performance, going from continuous to intermittent performance feedback, cueing or prompting desired performance, and providing ongoing supervision and training.

5

Ensuring Job Completion

We have characterized the effective manager as one who is successful in his or her efforts to get staff on-task and to ensure that tasks are completed so that program goals and objectives are realized. As we discussed in Chapter 4, the first of these efforts, getting staff on-task, is best accomplished by orientation and training procedures that are systematically developed, implemented, and evaluated.

To ensure job completion, the manager must effectively schedule, supervise, and evaluate staff performance. *Scheduling* procedures should result in an employee's being present in that part of the work environment—and for that period of time—in which his or her skills, expertise, and personal goals are most likely to be maximized. *Supervision* procedures should result in an employee's having the support and direction necessary to maintain effective performance and positive morale, and to improve ineffective performance and negative morale. *Evaluation* or *performance appraisal* should result in an employee's understanding his or her level of performance relative to the work performance standards for his or her position, and how that level of performance can be maintained or improved upon.

SCHEDULING

Scheduling is the procedure whereby the manager assigns personnel resources to areas of need. Effective scheduling is particularly critical to the operation of those human service programs that provide some form of residential treatment, for example, hospitals, nursing homes, and institutional programs which rely on shifts on employees to provide services on a twenty-four-hour basis. We have found a number of steps essential to effective personnel scheduling in these kinds of settings: identification of scheduling criteria; development and implementation of a personnel schedule consistent with those criteria; evaluation; and maintenance.

Criteria

Scheduling of staff must be consistent with the needs of the patients to be served. For example, the available literature indicates that patients with severe behavior problems typically require a more intensive staff-to-patient ratio than patients with less severe problems. Similarly, the staff-to-patient ratio sufficient at night (11:00 p.m. to 7:00 a.m.) may be less intensive than that required during the day, although this may not always be the case (for example, when working with patients for whom there is a risk of attempted suicide or for whom there is significant medical risk, as in the case of the intensive-care patient). However, to ensure consistency and quality of treatment, it is important that night-shift personnel be no less qualified than personnel working the day shift.

The quantity and quality of personnel needed in a particular place during a particular period of time are best determined by identifying the *specific tasks that must be performed and the skills needed to perform them.* In addition, it is important to examine daily records and progress reports and to solicit feedback from staff concerning the adequacy of a particular staffing pattern once it has been scheduled. Shift supervisors should be capable of providing the program manager with this kind of feedback on a regular basis. While the need for these procedures may be obvious to even the most inexperienced manager, it has been our experience that managers often fail to base their personnel-scheduling decisions on performance data of this kind.

The scheduling of human service personnel must also be consistent with *the patient's legal rights and the requirements of pertinent state and federal regulatory agencies.* A number of legal cases have established that a patient's right to treatment implies a quantity and quality of staffing adequate to meet his or her special needs. For example, in *Wyatt* v. *Stickney* (1972), the court stressed the importance of "qualified staff in numbers sufficient to administer adequate treatment." Similarly, the court in *Morales* v. *Turman* (1973) suggested that placing a patient's program of treatment in the hands of poorly trained staff violated constitutional requirements. The court specifically referred to risks posed to the patient by (a) insufficient staff; (b) poor screening that results in staff being hired who are psychologically unfit for the job they must perform; (c) staff members making decisions beyond their level of competence; and (d) staff with inadequate training and supervision.

Other criteria for personnel scheduling are provided by state and federal regulatory agencies. For example, Titles XVIII and XIX of the Social Security Act of 1964 specify minimum staff-to-patient ratios and staff qualifications for programs receiving Medicaid/Medicare reimbursement. In addition, most states specify minimum staffing standards for human service programs (for example, the ratio of certified teachers to special education students being served in a state mental health institution or private, non-profit residential treatment center).

Development and Implementation

After applicable standards or criteria have been indentified, the manager develops an adequate staffing schedule and sees that it is effectively implemented. This begins with the development of a *master staffing schedule* which lists the work hours and location for each employee and is followed by the scheduling of each employee consistent with the master plan. As described in the previous chapter, we have found it useful to negotiate time and location scheduling with each employee as part of his or her work performance standards. Accordingly, the work performance agreement would specify (1) time (hours per day, days per week) to be worked by the employee; (2) location (department, place in the facility) where the employee will be working; and (3) the employee's obligation to adhere to program policy and procedure regarding the documentation and reporting of hours worked, tardiness and absence, coffee breaks, obtaining a variance in the work schedule (for example, "switching" with another employee), resignation, and so on. While every effort should be made to accommodate the employee in time and location scheduling, the manager should minimize the amount of part-time scheduling as far as possible. A large number of part-time employees is an obstacle to effective personnel scheduling, supervision, and evaluation.

After time and location assignments for program personnel have been completed, the master staffing schedule should be disseminated by posting it in the work environment and including it in the program's policy and procedure manual. In large programs, it is most important that *department staffing schedules* be made available. When staffing schedules are kept current (by indicating vacancies or projected vacancies, new employees, and so on), they provide a way for management to (1) advertise positions that become available through staff turnover to potential in-house applicants; (2) facilitate "switching," finding substitute staff, and maintaining consistency of staff scheduling; and (3) promote the orientation of new and existing staff concerning the program's work force.

The task of developing and implementing the master staffing schedule is typically the responsibility of the program's personnel manager or director of administrative services. However, the program manager and department supervisors must be involved in orienting employees to the schedule and in working to ensure that they adhere to it.

Evaluation

It is of course important continuously to evaluate the adequacy, efficiency, and effectiveness of personnel scheduling relative to the criteria identified above. The most useful evaluation strategies are those that yield data concerning staff performance and morale. *Performance* data can be obtained by observing the work behavior of employees on each shift and by monitoring the quantity and quality of human service projects completed by staff (see page 69). Staff *morale* can be evaluated using satisfaction surveys and by monitoring staff behaviors that are typically associated with poor morale and dissatisfaction (absenteeism, turnover, complaints and grievances, alcoholism and drug abuse, mental and physical health problems, and low job involvement).

We have also found it useful to record the employee's initial attitude toward his or her work schedule (hours/location) so that it is possible to assess the effects of the staffing schedule—for example, change or lack of change in attitude after working in the schedule for a period of time. It is also a good idea for the personnel manager to have an ''exit interview'' with each outgoing employee to obtain feedback concerning the staffing schedule and recommendations concerning how it might be improved. Performance evaluation will be discussed in greater detail later in this chapter; program evaluation is the subject of Chapter 7.

Maintenance

Problems and breakdowns in scheduling can be costly and may result in risk to patients. We have found that an effective staffing schedule can be maintained and many scheduling problems can be prevented by (1) employing a staff scheduling specialist; (2) orienting and training staff members in schedule maintenance procedures; and (3) engaging in proactive recruitment/hiring practices.

The first of these strategies involves hiring a *personnel clerk* or personnel scheduling specialist, whose job it is to assist the personnel manager in making adjustments in the staffing schedule as they become necessary (for example, filling temporary vacancies in the schedule). This individual must be thoroughly familiar with the staffing schedule, and program policy and procedure. He or she must also know what substitute staff are available to the program; what tasks, shifts, and work stations they are qualified to assume; their current addresses and phone numbers; and each substitute's preferred tasks, shifts, and/or work station. When a staff member is unable to report to work, he or she contacts the personnel clerk who finds a suitable substitute employee and notifies the personnel manager of the schedule change. Since much of the personnel clerk's work is done by telephone and may be conducted in the evening or early morning hours, the job may be performed at home. We have found that the position of a personnel clerk provides an excellent employment opportunity for a disabled or handicapped individual.

Our experience has been that the employment of a personnel clerk is the most efficient way to manage personnel scheduling. We have been able to meet the needs of programs with up to 150 full-time staff with one part-time personnel clerk. In larger programs, it might be desirable to employ several individuals whose responsibilities are department-specific. In addition, care must be taken to ensure that each staff member knows how and under what conditions to contact the personnel clerk.

A second strategy is to orient and train program personnel in *schedule maintenance procedures*. As previously described, each employee should understand the role of the personnel clerk. Staff should also receive orientation and training in (1) the staff-to-patient ratio that must be maintained in their work area; (2) procedures for documenting hours worked (the forms and procedures for employee sign-in and sign-out); (3) procedures for ''switching'' work hours with another employee (the forms to be completed, prior approval by supervisor, and so on); (4) policy and procedure regarding resignation (especially with respect to giving at least thirty days' notice); and (5) procedures for reporting scheduling problems to management.

A third schedule maintenance strategy is to utilize a well-coordinated *staff recruitment and hiring program* so that qualified applicants are readily available to fill vacancies in the schedule as they occur. Unfortunately, many managers engage in *reactive* recruiting—that is, they wait until a staffing vacancy occurs before they begin efforts to fill it. While reactive recruiting is an efficient strategy for filling low-turnover positions, such as management and support staff, it is an inefficient way to maintain a staff which consists of a large number of high-turnover direct service positions (for example, nurses, nurses' aides, child care workers, and so on). Recruiting personnel for positions with a high rate of turnover should be *proactive*. Recruitment should go on continuously so as to maintain a pool of potential employees. In addition, it is important to recruit qualified individuals for work as substitutes continuously (and selectively).

Proactive recruitment is most effective when outgoing employees give management at least thirty days' notice prior to their resignation. In fact, we consider such early notification so critical to schedule maintenance that we recommend (1) making a two-week minimum advance notice of resignation part of each employee's work performance agreement, and (2) paying the employee a small bonus for giving a full thirty-day advance notice.

SUPERVISION

There are four characteristics of effective supervision: productivity, quality control, morale, and education. *Productivity* refers to the supervisor's monitoring and/or directing the activities of his or her staff to ensure a quantity of output consistent with the employees' work performance standards and the program's goals and objectives. *Quality control* refers to the supervisor's operating to ensure that staff performance results in a quality of service consistent with patient need, legal policy, regulatory guidelines, and program policy and procedure. *Morale* refers to the supervisor's functioning to promote the positive morale and job satisfaction of his or her staff. *Education* refers to the supervisor's working to improve his or her own job-related knowledge, skill level, and personal adjustment, as well as that of staff.

Given the complexity of the supervisor's task, it is not surprising that good supervision is rare. Unfortunately, this complexity has prompted many supervisors to rely on procedures based largely on tradition, with the result that many supervisory problems have remained unsolved and the technology of supervision in human services has not been significantly improved upon. It is important to reiterate, therefore, that we view supervision as a *performance measure,* that is, good supervision is what a good supervisor does. In the remainder of this section, we will identify criteria for good supervisory performance and describe specific supervisory strategies that we have found effective in human service settings.

Criteria

The characteristics of good supervision previously enumerated suggest a number of specific performance criteria for the effective supervisor.

1. The effective supervisor *specifies rules of conduct for the employee.* Every employee wants to know (and deserves to know) what his or her supervisor considers to be good behavior or conduct. Furthermore, it has been our experience that employees are more likely to accept and abide by rules of conduct if they have had a role in their development (for example, by serving on a committee responsible for drafting proposed rules of employee behavior). When rules of conduct have been specified, they should be entered in the program's policy and procedure manual, included in the agenda of each employee's orientation and training, and used as standards to evaluate employee behavior.

2. The effective supervisor *sets reasonable work performance objectives for the employee.* As described in Chapter 4, each employee should be provided with explicit standards for task performance which specify the *product* required for the satisfactory completion of a work assignment as well as the *time-lines* for completion. The effective supervisor further ensures that an employee's performance objectives are *relevant* to the goals and objectives of the organization and to the employee's role in the organization as well as *feasible* with regard to the program's resources and the employee's knowledge and abilities. It is often the case that, given the opportunity, employees set and maintain higher, more feasible, and more relevant performance standards for themselves then their supervisors would have or could have set for them. Unfortunately, many supervisors tend either to overestimate employees' knowledge or underestimate their intelligence in this regard.

3. The effective supervisor *creates a favorable work environment.* A supervisor committed to providing a favorable work atmosphere for employees must be concerned with physical, financial, social, and task-related factors. More specifically, the effective supervisor provides a work environment with *physical conditions and material resources* adequate to facilitate productivity and promote staff comfort and morale. He or she also provides *financial resources* (salary, benefits) appropriate to the quantity and quality of work performed by the employee and, as far as possible, consistent with salaries paid other employees with similar qualifications and productivity. The effective supervisor also works to develop a *positive interpersonal relationship* with the employee, as well as to promote friendly, trusting interpersonal relations between the employees themselves. Finally, the effective supervisor works to ensure that each employee views his or her job as challenging, interesting, and self-regulated.

    One of the most important features of the favorable work environment is the *open channel of communication* between supervisor and employee. This can be established by adhering to the general principle that every employee should have the opportunity to discuss a problem with a higher authority, provided that he or she follows established organizational structure (lines of supervision). Therefore, the effective supervisor (a) is accessible to the employee, being present in the employee's work environment and having office hours for employee consultation; (b) listens to employee grievances when they arise; (c) assists the employee in the self-management of problems as far as is possible; (d) acts to adjust a situation if an adjustment is called for and if the supervisor has situational control sufficient to effect the desired change; and (e) assists the employee with a formal grievance procedure if necessary.

    In short, the effective supervisor establishes a relationship with employees in which they feel free to offer suggestions for improvements in physical, financial, and/or work conditions and to report grievances when these arise. The effective supervisor understands that while the existence of grievances among employees is not necessarily a reflection of supervisory skills, not knowing that grievances exist does reflect on the supervisor.

4. The effective supervisor *models, prompts, and instructs employees in appropriate conduct and productive performance.* The effective supervisor realizes that he or she sets the pattern of acceptable conduct and performance for employees. In addition, he or she acknowledges the responsibility and develops the skills necessary to provide the orientation, training, monitoring, and contingent feedback necessary for employees to meet their work performance standards and to preserve their positive morale.

5. The effective supervisor *exercises fair, impartial control in his or her management of employee behavior.* The effective supervisor is consistent in efforts to encourage and strengthen appropriate employee behavior as well as to discourage and correct inappropriate behavior. He or she realizes that if infractions of established rules of conduct are not corrected, there is the danger that employees will come to regard such infractions as accepted practices. In addition, the effective supervisor is proactive as far as is possible in dealing with problematic employee behavior. Problems are not allowed to accumulate to the point that the first corrective action is an overreaction (for example, recommending some punishment inconsistent with the single infraction that occasioned it). However, the supervisor is aware of his or her capabilities and limitations and seeks the assistance of a higher authority when unable to exercise fairness and impartiality.

Strategies

We have found a number of procedural strategies essential to ensuring that there is effective supervision in a human service program. From recruiting the right individual for a supervisory position to evaluating that individual's supervisory performance, the manager will most likely be successful when making use of the following strategies.

RECRUITMENT OF COMPETENT SUPERVISORY PERSONNEL.   The most important qualifications to look for when recruiting a supervisor for human service staff include (a) interpersonal skills; (b) prior experience in human service supervision; (c) ability to observe, record, and evaluate change in human behavior; (d) academic training consistent with the type of service delivery/employees to be supervised; (e) writing skills; (f) ability to model appropriate behavior (conduct, performance, concern for patients, morale, compliance with program policy and procedure and work performance standards, appearance, professionalism, ethics, and personal integrity); (g) ability to train subordinate personnel in the skills consistent with their work performance standards; (h) ability to accept direction as well as to work well independently; and (i) ability to work well with existing administrative and supervisory personnel. (In this last instance, a similar degree of professional commitment, common research interests and a common philosophy of supervision are valuable.)

Interpersonal skills are particularly important. If the applicant is to function effectively as a supervisor, he or she must be able to initiate and maintain mutually rewarding social interactions with others and to be appropriately assertive—as opposed to passive or abrasive. Clearly, such skills are important since the very nature of supervision is interpersonal. Indicators of good interpersonal skills include (a) frequent eye contact; (b) appropriate use of gestures; (c) good posture; (d) appropriate facial expressions; (e) appropriate voice (loudness, tone, pace); (f) adequate duration of speech; (g) brief latency of speech; and (h) speech content appropriate to the situation.

Interpersonal skills can be assessed in the interview and by the use of situational testing. For example, the applicant might be asked to role play his or her most probable response to a hypothetical interpersonal situation (for example, one that demands giving negative feedback to an employee.) The applicant's response is then evaluated relative to the indicators listed previously. The use of audiovisual recording can be very useful in this regard, both in terms of presenting the hypothetical situation as well as providing a record of the applicant's baseline level of interpersonal skills for use in training in the event that the individual is hired.

As when recruiting and hiring any new employee, the manager should be familiar with pertinent laws and regulations. For example, Title VII of the Civil Rights Act of 1964 established the Equal Employment Opportunity Commission (EEOC), an agency responsible for eliminating discrimination based on age, sex, race, color, religion, and/or national origin. The manager must understand EEOC regulations and comply with them. Recruitment and hiring practices must also be consistent with program policies and procedures regarding affirmative action and employment of the handicapped, as well as with applicable union guidelines.

ORIENTATION AND TRAINING FOR SUPERVISORS. Orientation and training as described in Chapter 4 are no less important for supervisory personnel than they are for other program staff. In fact, it is the supervisor who must have a working knowledge of organizational structure, program policy and procedure, job-related skills, service programming, and legal and regulatory guidelines sufficient to serve as a model and resource person for subordinates and to plan, direct, and evaluate their efforts. Therefore, the manager must (a) develop work performance standards for supervisory personnel so as to provide an analysis of the job they are to perform and to structure the job-related training they are to receive; (b) negotiate a performance agreement with each supervisor calling for an acceptable level of performance; (c) provide appropriate orientation and training; (d) evaluate the supervisor's on-the-job performance; and (e) maintain an acceptable level of supervisory performance.

Perhaps the most important aspect of training for supervisory personnel is that which is concerned with how to evaluate employee behavior and to provide the employee with evaluative feedback. We have made extensive use of audiovisual recording in teaching and reinforcing these skills. Audiovisual records of the supervisor's behavior can be used to communicate areas of strength and weakness as well as areas in which improvement is being made (relative to pre-training assessment). Role playing and coaching can also be used to prepare the supervisor for the situations that he or she will be exposed to on the job. Finally, there are a number of useful protocols that the supervisor can learn to follow in evaluation and feedback situations. These include positive teaching interaction, disciplinary procedures, Placheck evaluation, and forms for evaluating employee performance, all of which are discussed in the last section of this chapter.

DEVELOPMENT OF A PROFESSIONAL WORK FORCE. We have found that when human service employees are oriented, trained, and supervised as professionals they are more likely to perform as professionals. In addition, the more professional the work force, the easier it is to supervise. Developing a professional work force begins with the *selection of job titles* that communicate management's expectation of the employees and provide them with task-identity and prestige. This may involve using titles such as "child development specialist" or "patient care specialist" in place of the more traditional "child care worker" or "attendant."

Another step is to provide each employee with as much *autonomy* and opportunity for *self-management* as possible. We have seen how this can be accomplished via work performance contracting which provides for individualized work performance standards for each employee, employee participation in goal selection, the case manager system, and work on special projects negotiated by the employee with his or her supervisor. Similarly, the supervisor should allow the employee to have input in decision-making that effects his or her job or the immediate work environment.

Ongoing *staff development* is also essential to the establishment and maintenance of a professional work force. Each human service program should attempt to target from one to five percent of its total personnel budget for the purposes of staff development. The supervisor can use these funds to provide the following types of staff development activities: (a) staff attendance at professional workshops and conference presentations both in and out of state; (b) development of an up-to-date library to assist staff in their work; (c) encouragement of research and program development by staff; (d) provision of bonus payments or other special rewards for work related to career development (see the incentive system described in Appendix E; (e) regular exposure of staff to external consultants with expertise relative to some aspect of staff work or career development; (f) development of affiliations with universities and other human service programs so that academic credit and practicum experience can be arranged for qualified staff; (g) job rotation so that each employee has maximum exposure to other tasks and individuals in the program environment and increased opportunities to develop new skills and varied career interests; (h) ongoing orientation and in-service training to ensure that staff are exposed to the most current human service technology, career opportunities, laws and regulations, and so on; (i) provision of all possible procedures and resources to assist staff in their work performance (for example, routines or checklists as described in the next section, supplies and materials, equipment such as a copying machine); (j) utilization of mechanisms to provide ongoing two-way communication between staff and management and to ensure that staff feedback is acted upon; and (k) two-way performance appraisal to ensure that both employee and supervisor learn how to work together more effectively and professionally.

UTILIZATION OF ROUTINES AND CHECKLISTS. We have found that developing routines and checklists for the tasks most frequently performed by human service staff greatly facilitates performance of the task as well as the supervision and evaluation of the performance. More specifically, a routine or checklist provides the supervisor with a means of structuring his or her monitoring of staff behavior and of giving staff immediate written feedback. The checklist includes a number of criteria that must be met for task completion and a space next to each criterion for the supervisor to indicate a "yes" or "no" rating. The completed checklist provides permanent product data for program evaluation and can be used by the manager and his or her external consultants to monitor supervisor behavior and to determine the reliability of a supervisor's observations and recordings. It can also be used to encourage staff self-management, as when a staff member completes the form as he performs the task and then submits the form to his supervisor. An example of a staff monitoring checklist is presented in Appendix C.

ESTABLISHMENT AND MAINTENANCE OF AN EFFECTIVE FEEDBACK LOOP. A "feedback loop" refers to the two-way communication between personnel and management that is essential to effective supervision. We have already described the methods used by management to communicate organizational structure, policy and procedure, and so on to staff through organizational charts, policy and procedure manuals, work performance standards, orientation and training, written memoranda, and meetings. It is important to note that each of these methods provides a mechanism for employees to give feedback to management; they should be encouraged by their supervisors to do so. For example, the dissemination of organizational charts, policy and procedure manuals, and written memoranda can be accompanied by requests for feedback from staff. Meetings, orientation and training activities, and work performance agreement negotiation also present opportunities for two-way communication. We have found, however, that such communication will not occur unless it is prompted. We have used a combination of the following strategies in prompting and maintaining two-way communication:

1. *Communication as Policy and Procedure.* As previously described, it is important to include a section in the policy and procedure manual describing how communication among staff and between staff and management should occur (see pages 52-53).

2. *Patient Status Report.* The patient status report is a written statement of the treatment and evaluation procedures currently in use with each patient. This type of communication helps to improve the consistency of treatment by prompting staff and management to behave in a particular way in the presence of a particular patient (for example, patient John S. has seizures and is presently receiving *(dosage)* of *(drug)*; in the event of a seizure, the following procedure should be followed: *(procedure)*). The patient status report should be updated weekly or monthly; we recommend holding treatment team meetings (discussed below) for this purpose. The tasks of preparing and updating the patient status report are greatly facilitated by the use of a memory typewriter or a word-processing unit.

3. *Shift Communication Checklist.* Consistency of human service programming is often difficult to achieve, especially in situations where employees work in shifts. Too often, shifts of employees tend to function so independently that those working the day shift seldom know what those on the night shift are doing, and vice versa. As a result, there is little communication and carry-over of procedures across shifts, often resulting in the patient's receiving a lower quantity and quality of service than that which he or she

requires. We developed the shift communication checklist to remedy this situation. A copy of this form is included in Appendix C.

Staff members are instructed to complete this form during the course, or at the conclusion, of their shift and to give the completed form to members of the incoming shift. If each shift completes the checklist, the supervisor is provided with permanent product data concerning staff performance and patient behavior during the previous twenty-four hour period. When the completed lists are checked to ensure that they are reliable, they provide an excellent ongoing record that can be used to evaluate the effects of changes in service programming, staffing, supervisory strategies, and so forth. With the use of such an instrument, staff are usually able to control the quality of shift communication with little supervisory support. For example, peer pressure will be directed toward the individual who fails to fill out the checklist or fills it out incorrectly.

4. *Effective Staff Meetings.* Perhaps, the most effective way to ensure two-way communication is for the supervisor to meet with his or her staff on a weekly basis. We recommend an interdisciplinary/interdepartmental treatment team meeting which is scheduled and conducted as follows:

Treatment Team Meeting

Attendees:	Service staff (direct and support service personnel) working with a particular group (unit, ward, therapy group) of patients.
	Supervisors of departments represented; team leaders.
	Other staff (for example, administrative personnel, consultants, staff from other treatment teams) by invitation.
Scheduling:	Weekly; written schedule posted monthly.
Duration:	One hour, unless special arrangements made.
Supervision:	Meeting run by team leader (if applicable) or by supervisors of departments represented.
Agenda:	Prearranged case presentations.
	Brief review of each patient's treatment and progress (for example, analysis of graphs).
	Revisions of treatment plan (if needed).
	Feedback from staff.
	Feedback from supervisor.
	Announcement of next scheduled meeting; assignment of case presentations.
Products:	Attendance register.
	Record of treatment plan and human service project changes.
	Participation ratings.
Additional features:	Manual including each patient's current treatment plan, human service projects, and graphs of pertinent data to facilitate discussion.
	Refreshments.
	Relaxed atmosphere.
	Peer and supervisory feedback contingent upon staff attendance and participation.

As evident from this description, the treatment team meeting fulfills a number of functions in addition to promoting frequent two-way communication. It facilitates evaluation of staff performance, in-service consultation and training, orientation of new staff, treatment planning, coordination of various professional disciplines, quality control, and review of ongoing programming and staff performance by the program manager. In addition, if it is conducted properly, staff typically come to view the treatment team meeting as a very positive aspect of their employment.

Given the potential value of treatment team meetings, it is important regularly to solicit feedback from program staff, administration, and outside consultants concerning ways in which meetings can be improved. We have found that the most important variables to monitor are: (a) attendance; (b) staff participation; (c) the tone of the meeting (negative/destructive versus positive/constructive); (d) any changes in the status of treatment procedures/programs discussed (reviewed, revised, changed, initiated, etc.); (e) the duration of the meeting; and (f) satisfaction ratings. We have learned that good meeting behavior, like any other type of performance, must be carefully planned, trained, and evaluated. Thus, it is advisable to (a) prepare agenda; (b) provide instruction and training in how to present topics at meetings, keep to the established time limits, and so on and (c) provide feedback following meetings regarding how well participants followed instructions and how closely behavior adhered to the meeting's agenda.

UTILIZATION OF PROFESSIONAL CONSULTATION AND PEER REVIEW. The supervision of human service personnel is too difficult and risky a task to attempt alone. As we have seen, patients' presenting problems, patients' rights legislation, and regulatory guidelines leave only a slight margin for error. As we have also noted, managers and supervisors tend to wait until a problem occurs before taking action (or *reaction*) to solve it. For these reasons, we have learned constantly to seek the advice of colleagues and outside consultants regarding the extent to which our supervisory practices are consistent with legal and ethical guidelines and whether there are any developing problems of which we may not be aware.

We recommend, therefore, that the program manager take the following steps to ensure that his or her supervisory personnel are afforded adequate consultation and review: (a) include consultants with expertise in the supervision of human service personnel on the organizations' Professional Advisory Board (see Chapter 7); (b) encourage ongoing communication and consultation among supervisors; (c) conduct regular professional (external) peer review of the organization's policy and procedure for personnel management; (d) schedule regular meetings with each supervisor to discuss progress, problems, and recommendations; and (e) require regular written reports from each supervisor sufficient to evaluate the performance of his or her staff relative to the goals, objectives, policy, and procedure of his or her department as well as of the organization as a whole.

UTILIZATION OF ADDITIONAL SUPERVISORY PERSONNEL. The supervisor may also find it desirable to identify an additional level of supervision within his or her department. For example, a ''team leader'' might be assigned the responsibility of coordinating and monitoring the performance of staff working in a particular unit, ward, or wing. This approach may have the advantage of coordinating the efforts of individuals representing a number of different disciplines, but has the disadvantage of confusing lines of authority within the established organizational structure. It is important, therefore, that staff understand that the addition of a team leader is intended to *supplement* rather than supplant existing supervision.

In addition, the team leader must be carefully recruited and trained using criteria similar to those specified for the recruitment of supervisory personnel (see page 100). Typically, a senior staff member with demonstrated leadership ability will be selected for such a position.

Unfortunately, many human service managers and supervisors tend to believe that the addition of team supervision or the use of team-oriented organizational structure such as "unitization" is as far as they need to go in providing effective supervision for direct service personnel. They fail to understand that any such strategy will be inadequate without effective *performance evaluation and feedback*. As we will discuss in the next section of this chapter, performance evaluation and feedback must be the essential ingredient of any effort to ensure job completion.

We have conducted a study designed to investigate the effect of introducing team leaders in a human service setting.[1] The study was conducted in a residential treatment center for severely disturbed children. Staff members were college graduates with an average of nine months' experience (range of from one to eighteen months) in the setting. All staff members had been thoroughly trained in procedures for maintaining a high degree of therapeutic interaction with the patients in their care. The average staff-to-patient ratio during the study was 1:3. Team leaders were individuals with advanced academic training and/or experience in the treatment setting or similar settings. In addition, each received special training in team supervision and coordination.

The study utilized the Placheck method of observation described in Chapter 2. During the study, trained observers went to each of six residential units at different times each day and recorded the total number of patients *active* (that is, interacting with staff or engaging in an appropriate task) and the total number of patients present. The percentage of active patients was calculated by dividing the number of active patients by the total number of patients and multiplying by 100.

As indicated in Figure 5-1, the introduction of a team leader without provision for performance feedback resulted in only a slight improvement in the performance of staff (that is, their effectiveness in keeping patients actively involved in a task or social interaction) in Cottages 1-4. (No team leader was introduced in Cottage 5 during this period.) However, when the team leader was provided with written feedback immediately following each Placheck observation in Cottages 1-5, significant improvement was seen and high level of appropriate patient behavior was maintained over time. Feedback in this case consisted of the date, time, percentage of patients active, the activities of the patients, comments, and suggested ways to get more patients active. If the team leader had questions, they were discussed later that day, or within two days of the observation.

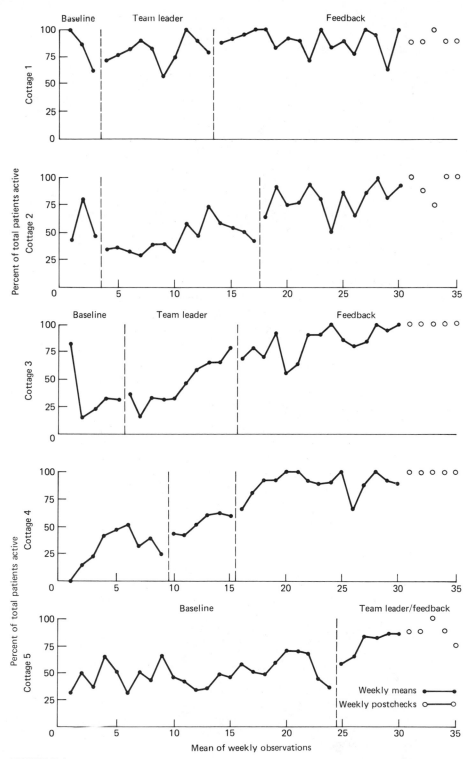

FIGURE 5-1

PERFORMANCE APPRAISAL

To ensure job completion, the manager must be able to *shape* the performance of his or her staff so that it approximates an acceptable level with respect to quantity and quality of effort and also to *maintain* that level of performance once it has been reached. This requires that each employee's performance be regularly *evaluated* and that the employee be *provided feedback and environmental consequences* sufficient to motivate and assist him or her to maintain or improve upon that level of performance. In short, systematic change in or maintenance of staff performance requires a systematic application of performance appraisal procedures in conjunction with the scheduling and supervision procedures that we have previously described.

Criteria

In general, performance appraisal should be conducted consistent with program policy and procedure and should involve procedures of proven relevance, feasibility, efficiency, and effectiveness when used in similar settings with similar staff. In addition, performance appraisal must be viewed as an *educational procedure.* It involves learning about staff performance through evaluation, informing staff about their performance, and teaching them how to maintain or improve it through feedback.

More specifically, evaluation procedures should meet the following criteria:

1. *Work Performance Standards* (work assignments, expected products, and required timelines) should be used as criteria to evaluate performance. In this way, evaluation is more likely to be objective than to be based on subjective feelings and impressions.

2. A *representative sample* of performance should be evaluated. An employee should be observed at different times, performing different tasks, and in different settings to ensure that an accurate indication of his or her overall level of performance is obtained. Observation and evaluation of work performance should be conducted as unobtrusively as possible and on a variable time schedule so that a representative, unbiased sample of behavior is obtained.

3. A *variety of evaluation procedures* should be employed to ensure that an adequate quantity and quality of information about the employee's performance is obtained. Procedures might include observation, reports from supervisors and co-workers, personal interviews, performance on special projects (for example, completion of a personalized sequence of instruction), situational testing, and paper and pencil assessment instruments (for example, a test designed to assess knowledge of program policy and procedure).

4. Evaluation procedures should possess an acceptable level of *validity* and *reliability.* Observers and raters should be well trained; observation and recording should be checked for reliability; tests and checklists employed should be valid and reliable and should be used consistent with the standardization sample specified for each instrument.

    Unfortunately, these criteria are frequently not met. Individuals with the task of observing and rating performance are often poorly motivated to complete rating scales and checklists accurately and conscientiously. Typically, this is due to their not having been included in the development of the checklists, or to their not having been consulted as to the importance of accurate performance ratings.

In addition, when observers and raters are not sufficiently trained, their responses are more likely to be biased. For example, an employee (or patient) may be rated highly in a particular area because he or she is viewed favorably in another area (the "halo effect"); an employee (or patient) may be rated in the "high" or "low" ranges with little attention given to the "middle" range (the "leniency effect"); employees may be rated in the middle range with little attention given to high or low ranges; or ratings may reflect the personal bias of the rater (for example, rating a female employee lower than her male counterpart because "a woman belongs at home"). However, research has shown that brief training sessions for raters can help to alleviate these problems.

5. Evaluation should be conducted at *regular intervals*. We recommend a verbal evaluation/feedback session with each employee at three-month intervals and written evaluation at six-month intervals from the employee's start date. Each evaluation (written and oral) should be documented in the employee's personnel file.

6. A *systematic design* should be utilized so that the results of each evaluation are analyzed relative to previous and subsequent evaluations. For example, an employee's six-month evaluation can be used as a baseline against which to assess the improvement, maintenance, or decline in his or her level of performance six months later.

7. Methods employed should be *adequately field-tested* in human service settings and should represent the state of the art as per the current research literature. Often the most useful evaluation strategies are those that a manager develops and field-tests to meet his or her special needs. To reiterate, when using any evaluation strategy, it is important that definitions for "target" performance are clearly understood by observers; that observers are given preliminary training sufficient for them to rate occurrences of the target performance reliably, that is, with a better than 80 percent agreement with a second rater; and that periodic checks of reliability be conducted as performance ratings are being recorded.

   Methods for behavioral observation, recording, and determining interobserver reliability were described in Chapter 2. To review, these observation and recording methods included (a) automatic recording, (b) direct measurement of permanent products, (c) event recording, (d) duration recording, (e) latency recording, (f) interval recording, and (g) time-sampling.

8. Results of performance evaluation should be treated as *confidential information*. Only after obtaining the employee's express written permission can they be shared with other personnel (the employee's supervisor and members of the program's administrative staff excepted) or with individuals outside the organization.

Procedures used to provide performance *feedback* and *environmental consequences* to employees must also meet a number of criteria:

1. Feedback (written and oral) should be *data-based* and *highly specific* so as to be clearly understood by the employee and to provide an objective criterion for the employee's future performance. In addition, feedback should be *fair* and *impartial* and should not be influenced by factors unrelated to the employee's performance.

2. The *methods* used to generate feedback (the procedures used to observe and record performance, the use of work performance standards as criteria, etcetera) should be carefully explained to the employee.

3. The supervisor should employ whatever forms, guidelines or procedures are necessary to ensure that (a) the employee is put at ease and is likely to be *receptive to feedback;* (b) the *feedback is understood* by the employee; (c) the *supervisor's expectations* for the employee's future performance are understood by the employee; and (d) the feedback session is a

mutually reinforcing event likely to promote positive morale on the part of employee and supervisor. In general, the tone of the feedback should be positive and educative.

4. The employee should be given an *opportunity to respond* to feedback. In addition, the employee should be able to request an in-house reveiw of his or her performance evaluation, to present relevant performance data on his or her behalf, and to file a grievance if he or she feels that performance feedback is inaccurate, unfair, and/or biased.

5. *Ongoing two-way performance feedback* should be provided—the employee and his or her supervisor should regularly provide *each other* with evaluative feedback. (Forms and procedures for two-way feedback are presented later in this chapter).

6. *Effective environmental consequences* should be made contingent upon staff performance in such a way as to ensure that productive performance is strengthened, increased, and/or maintained; and that nonproductive performance is weakened, decreased, and/or eliminated. In addition, it is important to provide *bonus* consequences for performance that far exceeds the employee's work performance standards. (See Appendix E)

7. *Follow-up* should be provided to ensure that the employee is performing consistent with the feedback he or she received and that the consequences contingent upon the performance were effective.

8. *Ongoing professional peer review* of evaluation and feedback procedures should be obtained. *In-service training* should be conducted for supervisors in how to evaluate performance and give feedback, and for employees on how to receive and respond to feedback.

In addition, the manager must be concerned with *employee perception* of the program's performance appraisal system. Appraisal systems are most likely to be accurate and effective in an atmosphere characterized by employee perception that (a) the appraisal system actually and fairly measures performance and not factors such as "favoritism"; (b) performance appraisal is linked to extrinsic, tangible rewards such as salary and bonuses; (c) the extrinsic reward system is relatively non-competitive, with sufficient valued rewards and incentives available for anyone who receives a highly positive performance evaluation; (d) they have some control over the appraisal system, and can criticize or modify it when necessary; (e) they will be informed of the results when their performance has been evaluated; and (f) they will be given help or training in improving deficient areas of performance (cf. Lawler, 1975; Porter, Lawler, & Hackman, 1975).

Strategies

Performance appraisal must therefore consist of a number of procedural steps: (1) *determining sources of data* for performance evaluation; (2) *sampling environmental consequences* to determine what strengthens, increases, or maintains performance and what weakens, decreases, or eliminates it; (3) *observing, recording,* and *evaluating change* in performance; (4) *informing the employee* of evaluation results; (5) *delivering effective consequences* in an attempt to change or maintain employee performance; and (6) *providing follow-up* evaluation and feedback.

SOURCES OF DATA. Evaluating staff performance requires that we measure what a staff member does *(activity)*, what he or she produces *(productivity)*, and what the staff member thinks and feels about what he or she is doing *(satisfaction)*. These data are then compared to the activity and productivity criteria for the employee's job assignment (work performance standards) to determine whether he or she should receive positive or negative feedback.

Productivity is easiest to measure, especially if one has followed the recommendations made in Chapter 4 and has required that each employee submit *permanent product data* (written reports, completed forms, etcetera) in meeting his or her work performance standards. Activity may be more difficult to measure unless managers and supervisors are committed to the regular monitoring and recording of staff performance as it occurs, and to taking the necessary steps to ensure that their recordings are representative and reliable. Data concerning staff satisfaction can be obtained using personal interviews and rating forms. The latter ("satisfaction surveys") are most appropriate since the most candid satisfaction ratings are those that are anonymously reported.

While managers and supervisors should never assume that desirable staff performance will lead to patient progress, patient activity, progress, and satisfaction data must be considered in evaluating staff performance. For example, research has suggested that patient activity can serve as an outcome or product measure of staff performance (Pomerleau, Bobrove, & Smith, 1973). We therefore recommend the ongoing monitoring and recording of patient progress as a useful variable in evaluating staff performance and, even more importantly, in evaluating the effectiveness of the overall program of services.

We have used the following sources of data for evaluating staff performance. The methods utilized to collect these data are described throughout this chapter.

A. Staff Behavior
   1. Activity
      a. Attendance records.
      b. Daily monitoring and recording of performance (Appendix C).
      c. Shift change checklist (Appendix C).
      d. Treatment team meetings.
   2. Productivity
      a. Routines and checklists (Appendix C).
      b. Patient progress reports.
      c. Human service project forms (Appendix C).
      d. Daily monitoring and recording (Appendix C).
      e. Assessment results.
      f. Written correspondence to and interviews with supervisor.
      g. Treatment team meetings.
      h. Bonus performance reports (Appendix E).
   3. Satisfaction

        a.   Staff satisfaction ratings.

        b.   Records of staff turnover and absenteeism.

B.   Patient Progress

    1.   Activity

        a.   Human service project forms (Appendix C).

        b.   Patient status reports.

        c.   Daily monitoring and recording of patient behavior (for example, Placheck ratings).

        d.   Shift change checklists (Appendix C).

        e.   Patient tracking system (see Chapter 8).

        f.   Treatment team meetings.

        g.   Problem behavior checklists (Appendix D).

    2.   Progress

        a.   Graphed data from extended periods of daily monitoring and recording.

        b.   Assessment results.

        c.   Progress reports.

        d.   Human service project forms (Appendix C).

        e.   Treatment team meetings.

    3.   Satisfaction

        a.   Patient satisfaction ratings.

        b.   Patient interview with patient advocate.

        c.   Satisfaction ratings and feedback from parents, concerned persons, referring agencies, etcetera.

CONSEQUENCES.   Research and our own experience have shown us that an employee's performance is difficult to change unless he or she is *motivated* to make that change. Motivation is not the same as job satisfaction. Motivation pertains to a person's inclination to exert effort; satisfaction refers to his or her overall attitude toward the job. Thus, it is possible for an individual to be generally satisfied with his or her job, while lacking the incentive to work hard and be productive. However, we strongly agree with researchers such as Porter and Lawler (1968) that *if* the employee perceives that there is a high probability that his or her performance will be rewarded, and *if* the rewards or incentives contingent upon performance are perceived as desirable and equitable (relative to amount of effort expended), *then* job satisfaction will occur. In short, motivation leads to performance which in turn leads to job satisfaction.

    Therefore, it is not only important that we provide "rewards" for good job performance but that those "rewards" or "incentives" be considered *equitable and desirable* by the employee. Many managers and supervisors assume that they know what will be rewarding to their employees (for example, money and benefits). However, when employees are actually asked to choose their rewards they tend to select things like change in type of work, increased job security, more time off, and varied work hours as being as rewarding as pay and/or benefits.

Recent research literature indicates that the American work force in general is increasingly characterized by (a) a concern with "quality of work life" rather than economic considerations alone; (b) a desire for a greater voice in decision-making; (c) an orientation toward long-term career growth; (d) a desire for greater control over the technology and work operations that are part of the job; (e) a desire for supportive, informational supervisors as opposed to directive, autocratic ones; and (f) a desire for greater flexibility and choice in pay, benefits, work hours, work schedules, tasks, and vacation and retirement options (Dunnette, 1973). Evidence of these trends has received support from Jurgensen's (1978) thirty-year study of job preferences, in which he pointed to "...the gradual increase in importance of type of work and the gradually decreasing importance of those factors that fall most clearly in the extrinsic group" (p. 275).

All of this has led us to the conclusion that the best way to determine what will serve as positive and negative consequences for a particular employee's performance is to *ask the employee.* This type of information can be obtained at the time of an individual's employment, maintained in the employee's personnel file, and updated at six-month intervals with each written performance evaluation. One might use a form such as the incentive survey presented in Appendix C to obtain this information.

After this information has been obtained from each employee, the results should be analyzed and the mean (average) rating by the group for each consequence should be determined. This process should be repeated at six-month intervals to be sure that information about employee preference is current. In addition, all employees should be informed of the results.

The next step is for managers and supervisors to make every effort to provide the incentives preferred by staff. This often requires special budgeting (for example, bonus payments, raises, funding for staff to attend conferences), flexibility of personnel scheduling (for example, providing more annual leave for a particular employee), and so on.

Each employee should also receive feedback indicating what incentives are available for standard to above-standard performance, what extra incentives are available for above-standard to outstanding performance (see Appendix E), and what consequences are contingent upon below-standard performance. It is important to note, therefore, that the incentive survey form included in Appendix C also yields information concerning what the employee feels is most negative (least preferred), and this may be useful in the event that some disciplinary action must be taken against the employee.

OBSERVING AND RECORDING PERFORMANCE.   The general methods for observing and recording staff performance have already been described. In addition, there are a number of other strategies that we have found useful in ensuring that representative samples of staff performance are regularly and reliably evaluated.

Routines and checklists.   As we noted earlier in this chapter (see page 102), checklists such as the staff monitoring checklist (Appendix C) provide a way to record the quantity and quality of staff performance on an ongoing basis. We therefore suggest that checklists or routines be developed for the tasks that staff members are required to perform most frequently and that supervisory personnel be trained in their use.

Daily monitoring of staff behavior.   In addition to employing checklists for specific tasks, staff performance in general should be monitored each day on a variable time-sampling schedule. Each day, the supervisor should briefly note whether or not employees are at their assigned work stations and are engaged in activities consistent with the personnel schedule and their respective work performance standards. This type of monitoring is most efficient when the supervisor develops categories of behavior that can be quickly marked with a "yes" or "no" or a " + " or a "–" dependent upon the staff behavior being observed. For example, Risley and Favell (1979) have described the use of the following categories in monitoring the behavior of staff in a large state institution for the developmentally disabled:

1. Social interaction with patients.
2. Non-social interaction with patients.
3. Environmental maintenance.
4. Clerical work.
5. "Other" activities.
6. "Unaccounted for" (for example, out of area).

One might also choose to include a number of other categories that are less concerned with patient interaction than with an employee's appearance and demeanor. These might include the following:

1. Appearance (dress, personal hygiene).
2. Morale (number of positive statements/negative statements made about work, patients, co-workers, etcetera).
3. Diplomacy in contacts with patients, patients' families, supervisors, peers, and the public.
4. Sociability (likeability).
5. Verbal expression.
6. Assertiveness.
7. Professionalism.

In addition to facilitating the monitoring and evaluation of performance, these procedures help to ensure that a supervisor keeps his or her attention and staff behavior focused on activities that are likely to result in the highest productivity, quality, and efficiency of effort. Of course, the program manager can use these same strategies (routines, checklists, and behavior ratings) to monitor the performance of supervisory personnel and to ensure that the information received from them about staff performance is reliable.

Daily monitoring of patient behavior.   As previously described, patient activity is an important dependent measure of staff performance. We have already described the use of the Placheck procedure to monitor the amount of patient activity (see page 106). However, it is also important to determine the *quality* of patient activity, that is, whether the patient's activity is task-oriented, consistent with his or her plan of treatment, and so on.

Several of our colleagues have conducted a study in which patient behavior was rated relative to a number of descriptors.[2] Each day, on a variable schedule, trained observers rated the behavior of eight severely handicapped children and adolescents in each of five residential units. Each patient was observed for ten minutes, during which the following categories were scored:

On-task behavior (check *each* that applies)
_____   Functional task.
_____   Functional, task-related materials.
_____   Age-appropriate task.
Off-task behavior (check if applicable)
_____   Engaged in treatment to reduce socially deviant behavior.
Nature of task (check *one* that applies)
_____   Community-related.
_____   Recreation/leisure.
_____   Domestic.
_____   Self-care.
_____   Vocational.

This simple rating scale yields a total possible score of four if the patient is *on-task* when observed (one point for each of the three "on-task" categories and one point for the "nature of task" category) and a total possible score of one if the patient is *off-task* but "engaged in treatment to reduce socially deviant behavior." If the patient is simply idle or out of the area at the time of the observation, no points are scored. When scores obtained for a particular group of patients are compared to their total possible scores, the supervisor has a basis for providing feedback to staff and for suggesting steps that can be taken to improve their performance and, it is hoped, their patients' behavior.

It is also useful to make note of certain problem behaviors that patients exhibit during the day or during a particular work shift. The shift change checklist (see Appendix C) can be used for this purpose, although we recommend designing an instrument that will be more specifically geared to the patient population and to the behavioral data that one wishes to obtain. A list of patient problem behaviors that can be adapted for use by most human service managers is included in Appendix D.

Other methods that can be used to monitor and record patient behavior include the patient status report (see page 103), the patient tracking system (see Chapter 7), and human service projects. Human service projects are particularly useful since they provide the manager with permanent product data (for example, completed project forms, graphed data) indicating that the patient's behavior is being changed and, it is hoped, that his or her needs are being met. In addition, human service projects function to get services (treatment plans, goals, and objectives) *from the paper to the patient.* The human service project form (Appendix C) can be used to document the initiation, progress, and completion of human service project.

Copies of each human service project form should be placed in the patient's case record and in the patient's treatment team manual, a collection of all current and recently completed human service project forms that is reviewed and updated each week at the treatment team meeting (see page 104). However, it is important to check the reliability of data generated by human service projects as well as the correlation between service project forms, the patient's treatment plan or individual educational plan and the patient status report. Human service project forms should also be regularly reviewed by the program's Human Rights Committee (see Chapter 7).

Knowledge of results.   After evaluating an employee's performance, it is important that he or she be informed of the results. Research has indicated that when employees receive evaluative feedback they are more likely to improve their performance and to be satisfied with their job. However, while most managers and supervisors agree on the necessity of regular performance feedback, they do not always provide it. This problem is typically due to competition with other job-related priorities and/or to a lack of skill and enthusiasm for the task of communicating evaluative information to another individual. Therefore, managers and supervisors should be *required* to give regular feedback to their employees, *trained* in how to do it effectively, and *monitored* to see that they follow through.

Evaluative feedback can be communicated through smiles, grimaces, gestures, verbal statements, and written correspondence. Whatever the form of the feedback, the basic content should be fairly standard. Specifically, four areas should be addressed: (a) *personal characteristics* such as cooperativeness and leadership; (b) *performance criteria* that have been specified in the employee's work performance standards; (c) *job results,* that is, the effectiveness and productivity of the employee's performance relative to his or her performance standards; and (d) *recommendations* for the future (for example, more attention to a particular task, participation in remedial training).

We recommend the use of the following guidelines to ensure that verbal and written feedback is communicated positively and educationally. [3]

Person Giving Feedback

1. *Express affection* by smiling, greeting.
2. Acknowledge what has been accomplished by giving *positive feedback* first.
3. *Describe behaviors* that need improvement, getting to the point but using "I-messages," for example, "I would like you to finish your work on time," instead of "You have a problem finishing your work on time."

4. *Describe improvement needed* and how it can be achieved, maybe offering to help.
5. Give *rationale* for the desired alternative.
6. Describe the *present consequences.*
7. Request *acknowledgement,* for example, "Do you understand what I want you to do?"
8. Prompt *practice* of improved performance.
9. *Give feedback* for improved performance.
10. *Deliver consequences.*

Person Accepting Feedback

1. Maintain *eye contact.*
2. *Acknowledge* by saying something.

The following is an example of a feedback session between the evaluator and the manager of a human service program that follows these guidelines. [4]

EVALUATOR: Hi, Jim. How's your day going?

PROGRAM DIRECTOR: Well, okay so far.

EVALUATOR: Have you got a few minutes?

PROGRAM DIRECTOR: Sure, now that you're settled into that chair.

EVALUATOR: I've just collected and summarized the forms from the anonymous review of the Program Director's performance that was recently completed by program staff. You'll be pleased to know that the ratings you received from staff were excellent on problem solving, concern for the clients' welfare, and leadership. However, on the item, "serves as buffer between my job and the state bureaucracy," the ratings were consistently in the dissatisfied range. I followed up to identify just what seemed to be the problem here. Two things seem to be relevant. First, the staff seem to think that you are in a position to allow them to ignore agency regulations, clearly a misunderstanding of your role as director. Second, staff are concerned that you hide in the bathroom every time Alex Wyatt, the division chief, comes to visit. It seems that he then corners one of them with a barrage of questions about what's going on at the center.

It's my opinion that you could clear this up with a memo to staff describing the importance of following agency guidelines and your role as "buffer" from outside influences that detract from accomplishing our service mission. The other you could probably handle by inviting Wyatt over for a personal tour, guided by you.

It is really important for staff morale to see that you are willing to endure the same hardships you ask them to submit to. And I really think that these simple actions would clean up your ratings so that they are all very favorable. Is this making sense to you?

PROGRAM DIRECTOR: Well, I guess so, but I need some time to think it over.

EVALUATOR: Fine, how about setting up an appointment for the day after tomorrow? I'd be happy to help you draft a memo or whatever you decide to do.

PROGRAM DIRECTOR: Thanks, I hope improving the ratings is as easy as you think it may be.

Two-Way Feedback. Regular two-way feedback between supervisor and employee can be initiated and maintained using the supervisor feedback form and the employee feedback form which have been included in Appendix C.[5] Each month, employees and their supervisors are required to fill out these forms and exchange them. (It is also advisable to conduct *entrance* interviews—what an employee expects of the job—and *exit* interviews—what the employee thought of the job, staff, and so on—for two-way feedback). After reading each other's feedback, each person initials the form he or she has received and retains a copy of the form in his or her file. This information should then be kept confidential except in the event of a personnel problem or grievance.

The effectiveness of this procedure will, of course, depend on situational variables and on the personal style of the individual employee and supervisor. However, we have found that two-way feedback has a number of advantages relative to more traditional one-way feedback: (a) employees can have an impact on the quantity and quality of supervision they receive; (b) feedback forms provide a record so that comparisons can be made between present and future performance, thereby prompting employees and supervisors to compliment each other for progress made on problems mentioned earlier; (c) problems are solved proactively, that is, before they become serious obstacles to effective supervision and performance; and (d) employees are protected from arbitrary actions of the supervisor by a written record of feedback which is always available for reference. We have also used similar procedures to encourage two-way performance appraisal between ''peers'', employees working at the same position within the organization.

Evaluation Forms. As previously described, each employee should receive a written performance evaluation from his or her supervisor at six-month intervals in addition to any other feedback that he or she may receive. We recommend two types of forms for this purpose: narratives and checklists. The *narrative* evaluation includes a written statement of the employee's present performance (relative to performance standards for his or her position) and recommendations for maintaining or improving performance. Checklists typically include a number of categories for use in rating the employee's performance. While employees report that the narratives are more personalized and are likely to include more detailed and explicit information than checklists, checklists are easier and more feasible when evaluating a large number of employees and are likely to address more performance areas than narratives.

For these reasons, we have devised a form that combines the advantages of both narrative and checklist. This form is based on work performance standards, provides a performance rating scale for each performance area, and includes brief narrative sections that can be used for clarification, recommendations, and so on. The use of this format is also feasible when evaluating a large number of personnel. Examples of both the narrative and checklist/narrative formats are included in Appendix C.

Delivering consequences. The next step is to "reward" or "punish" an employee contingent upon the quantity and quality of his or her performance. This should be done in a verbal feedback session and in writing on the performance evaluation or in a separate memorandum. If the employee's performance is standard or above-standard, he or she will be provided with a desirable consequence (for example, praise, increased pay). Sub-standard performance should be met with some undesirable consequence (for example, verbal or written reprimand, demotion), although it should be delivered as positively and educationally as possible. It is also important to identify and reward "bonus performance"—above-standard to outstanding performance. Whenever possible, rewards and punishers should be selected on the basis of preference ratings by the employee. (See incentive survey form in Appendix C.)

Rewards. As previously described, employees should be allowed to select rewards for their performance whenever possible. In addition, managers and supervisors must understand that whether or not a consequence is rewarding depends entirely upon *its effect on staff performance.* If performance becomes more frequent, or is maintained in the future, we say that it has been "rewarded." Examples of consequences in the human service environment that are *potentially rewarding* for staff performance include (*not* in any order of importance):

1. Increased pay.
2. Increased benefits.
3. Positive verbal and/or written feedback.
4. Job rotation.
5. Advancement in status (promotion).
6. Attendance at conference and workshops.
7. Involvement in special projects.
8. Letter of commendation.
9. Opportunity for greater voice in program policy and procedure (for example, committee membership).
10. Improved working conditions.

In addition, we have described the importance of knowing when employees far exceed their work performance standards and delivering bonus rewards when they do so. Such a system is described in Appendix E; it is a system in which human service employees *prompt their supervisors for bonus rewards.*

Disciplinary Procedures. In any organization, it is inevitable that a few employees will unwittingly or willfully violate established standards of conduct and job performance. Such instances, if uncorrected, can threaten the morale of other employees, disrupt their work efforts, or reflect unfavorably on supervisors and program managers. It is important, therefore, that supervisors and managers take prompt corrective action in such situations.

There are two levels of corrective action. When the immediate welfare of the program or its patients is not endangered, the supervisor may choose to conduct a *corrective interview* as an informal disciplinary procedure. In conducting the corrective interview, the supervisor should follow the general guidelines for providing feedback previously listed (see page 116). The supervisor should also specify a definite plan for improvement in employee conduct or performance and designate a time when formal corrective action will be taken unless improvement has been made.

In addition, the supervisor should use the corrective interview to establish a record upon which to build any further action should it be necessary. A written summary of the interview should be prepared and the employee should be provided with a copy. Taking notes during the course of the interview greatly facilitates preparation of the written summary.

When there is a need for more immediate action and/or when the corrective interview has had little effect on employee performance, the supervisor should take *formal corrective action*. It is important that the supervisor proceed thoughtfully when taking formal disciplinary action since the employee has a number of rights in this process that must be respected. We recommend the following steps:

1. *Know* the applicable standards of conduct and performance.
2. *Obtain* an accurate statement of the disciplinary problem and collect full information about the case (time, place, individual(s) involved or present, analysis of available permanent product data, frequency of occurrence, history of problem, etcetera).
3. *Select* the corrective action to be taken or recommended after considering the seriousness of the problem, the probable cause of the employee's behavior, and possible extenuating circumstances.
4. *Apply* the corrective action consistent with program policy and procedure, regulatory guidelines, Affirmative Action requirements, etcetera.
5. *Follow up* to see if the action taken has been effective or if a more serious step should be taken (for example, termination of the individual's employment).

As in the case of selecting rewards, selecting forms of corrective action can be based at least in part on feedback from the employee (for example, ratings on the incentive survey included in Appendix C). Types of corrective action in order of increasing severity include:

1. Verbal reprimand from supervisor (corrective interview).
2. Letter of formal reprimand from supervisor.
3. Suspension without pay.
4. Demotion to a lower class or level.
5. Reduction of pay within class.
6. Termination.

Every manager wants to avoid the necessity of formal corrective action. This can only be achieved if one manages and supervises *proactively* as characterized by (1) preventive planning including the development of explicit, realistic standards for employee conduct and performance; (2) effective communication including the systematic use of two-way performance appraisal procedures; (3) prompt delivery of rewards when they are earned; and (4) prompt, fair, and impartial corrective action when it is needed.

Follow-up.   The final step in any performance appraisal procedure is to monitor employee performance to assess the effect of feedback and the delivery of positive or negative consequences. For example, verbal feedback sessions at three-month intervals can be used to follow up six-month written performance evaluations. Procedures for monitoring and evaluating employee performance have already been described. It is also important to document the results of follow-up evaluations and to communicate follow-up results to the employee as per the guidelines described above.

SUMMARY

To ensure job completion, the manager must effectively schedule, supervise, and evaluate staff performance. *Scheduling* is the procedure whereby the manager assigns personnel resources to areas of need. Scheduling must be consistent with patient need, the tasks to be performed and the skills needed to perform them, the patient's legal rights, and the requirements of state and federal regulatory agencies. Recommended strategies for scheduling human service personnel include developing and disseminating a master staffing schedule; negotiating time and location of the employee's job as part of his or her work performance agreement; minimizing part-time scheduling; hiring a personnel clerk for schedule maintenance; orienting and training personnel in schedule maintenance; utilizing a well-coordinated recruitment and hiring program; and evaluating the effectiveness of staff scheduling.

Effective *supervision* of human service personnel involves specifying rules of conduct for the employee; setting reasonable work objectives; creating a favorable work environment; modeling, prompting, and instructing employees in appropriate conduct and productive performance; and exercising fair, impartial control in the management of employee behavior. Recommended strategies for supervising human service personnel include recruiting competent supervisory personnel; orienting and training supervisors; developing a professional work force; utilizing routines and checklists; establishing and maintaining an effective feedback loop; utilizing professional consultation and peer review; utilizing additional supervisory personnel; and conducting regular performance appraisal and providing feedback to staff.

Performance appraisal involves regularly evaluating employee performance, providing evaluative feedback, and delivering positive or negative consequences to change or maintain performance. *Evaluation* procedures should be based on the employee's work performance standards and a representative sample of his or her performance. A variety of evaluation procedures should be employed, each having been adequately field-tested and possessing an acceptable level of validity and reliability. Evaluation should be conducted at regular intervals. A systematic design should be used, in order to facilitate the analysis of results obtained. Results of performance evaluations should be considered confidential information. *Feedback* should be data-based, highly specific, fair, and impartial. It should be provided as positively and educationally as possible so as to ensure that it is viewed as mutually reinforcing for supervisor and employee. The employee should be given an opportunity to respond to the feedback he or she receives and should also have the opportunity to give performance feedback to his or her supervisor. Effective environmental consequences should be made contingent upon employee performance and follow-up should be provided to determine the effect of feedback and contingent consequences. Ongoing peer review of performance appraisal procedures should also be obtained and in-service training should be provided for supervisors in how to evaluate, and give feedback contingent upon, staff performance.

Recommended strategies for performance appraisal in human service settings include determining appropriate sources of data for evaluation; sampling environmental consequences to determine how each is likely to effect performance; observing, recording, and evaluating change in performance; informing the employee of evaluation results; delivering effective consequences contingent upon performance; and providing follow-up. Sources of data should include measures of employee activity, productivity, and satisfaction. Effective consequences can be best identified by asking each employee what is desirable and undesirable to him or her. Performance can best be evaluated using routines and checklists to monitor and record employee performance and patient behavior on a daily basis. Feedback to the employee should address personal characteristics, performance criteria, job results, and recommendations for the future. Feedback can be given in meetings between employee and supervisor and in written evaluation forms. Each program should specify policy and procedures for providing formal and informal corrective feedback for employees as well as for providing bonus rewards for outstanding performance.

6

Solving Budget
Management Problems

The development and implementation of a budget and the raising of funds are essential to the effective management of a human service organization. Every manager must be able to control and balance these two factors because an organization cannot fulfill its mission without funds to give it life and a budget to give it direction.

In recent years, human service organizations have had to maximize their use of limited resources without decreasing services. Some have described this situation as "having to do more with less." Given the economical forecast for the 1980s, managers will have to be more skilled in developing budgets and seeking funding. A reduction in funds does not necessarily mean fewer services. It does mean that managers must be assured that their organization is providing efficient and effective services and providing only services that its consumers need. As far as funding goes, managers must begin to cut their umbilical cord to governmental funding agencies. Today, the funding of human service programs is a state and local community problem. It will take a few years for state and community funding agencies to refocus their funding priorities, but even then state revenue cannot totally replace the loss of federal funds. Therefore, managers of the 1980s must develop new skills, procedures and systems for addressing the financing of their organizations.

This chapter describes *how to increase funding* independent of governmental support and introduces a *new budget model* for ensuring a balance-base budget.

INCREASING FUNDING

A revenue department plan should be an integral part of an organization's budgeting process because it ensures that the financial needs of the organization's programs are realistic. Such a plan consists of a list describing all the organization's potential sources of revenue, such as patient fees, individual and private corporation contributions, private foundations, community service groups, and government agencies. The revenue department plan is developed and monitored continuously by the manager and the Governing Board's Finance Committee made up of influential citizens representing both the financial and professional sectors of the community—bankers, large and small business leaders, elected public officials, and so on.

In this section, you will learn how to develop and implement five revenue-producing models: patient fee collection, philanthropy funding, soliciting contributions by mail, planning annual fund raising events, and soliciting community service group sponsorship. Keep in mind that you might need to modify the procedures slightly in order for them to be successful in your organization.

Patient Fee Collection System

A major problem in fee collection is that the procedures are not taken seriously and are not managed. Many of the staff of human service agencies have the attitude that a fee-collection system is not appropriate for an agency that receives government or philanthropic support. The Joint Commission on Mental Health and Mental Illness Report to Congress (1974) cited numerous agency problems including (1) long billing-time lags; (2) absence of an explicit billing and collection system; and (3) inadequate billing records. Mazade, Surles, and Akin (1976) have observed that poor eligibility determination, inadequate records, sloppy accounts, lack of procedures for billing patients, and inefficient follow-up of delinquent accounts often prevent collection of fees.

The present inadequacy of fee-collection procedures may create a problem for human service programs in receiving additional funds. The fees collected, in other words, purchase additional funds for the programs. Hence, poorly managed fee-collection procedures could inhibit potential funding resources. Also, a poorly managed fee-collection system might create a cash-flow problem.

Not only are fee-collection procedures inadequate, they are not clearly specified. For example, patients normally do not receive a written policy statement and instructions for paying fees. Therefore, patients may not completely understand their financial obligations. Further, some programs are inconsistent about prompting patients to pay their fees. These procedures cause confusion for the patients, particularly when the patient is asked to pay more towards the balance of the bill. For example, the patient is told, "Mrs. Smith, you are not meeting your responsibility towards paying your bill. I will have to inform your therapist of this problem." This situation could have been avoided if Mrs. Smith had previously been made aware of the fee-collection policies and the consequences of not following those procedures.

Before attempting to describe a more appropriate fee-collection system, it is necessary to point out that outpatient services characteristically have a high drop-out rate. If your organization reports such a problem, this is a case of lost revenue, not an additional fee-collection problem, because it is difficult to collect fees after termination.

CREDIT CRITERION MODEL.   Fee-collection procedures should clearly state the organization's policy for fee payment, and be given to each patient at the first visit. If the patient understands the procedures and the consequences beforehand, some misunderstandings will be avoided. The system will be effective as a result of its inherent social consequence, since most people are concerned about their financial credit. The procedures should be routinely followed as specified, and applied to everyone (exceptions to the rule should be in writing). Also, the procedures should not exclude anyone from services because of their inability to pay a fee. In light of the patient drop-out problem, patients should be instructed to pay the fee upon each visit during the early phase of their involvement with the organization. By instructing patients to pay their fees, the organization is assisting them in being responsible for their own behavior. Responsibility for one's actions is an important therapeutic principle. Further, Hurst, Davidshofer, and Arps (1974) and Roback, Webb, and Strassberg (1974) have found that patients who pay their fees appear to be more motivated, cooperative, and goal-oriented.

At the initial phase of the client's visits to an organization, a fee-collection system called the *Credit Criterion Model* would include the following procedures:

1. The patient receives a copy of the agency's billing policy which instructs the client to pay cash for each of the first three office visits in order to establish billing credit with the agency.
2. A financial interview is conducted with the patient to determine a sliding-fee rate, and also to answer any questions the patient might have about the billing policy.
3. The patient is prompted by the business office staff to pay his fee after each visit.
4. If the patient cannot pay after the first office visit, he or she is given a stamped envelope and is asked to mail his or her fee before the next office visit.
5. If the patient fails to pay after the second visit, a meeting is arranged with the business manager to work out any problems that might be preventing the patient from paying.
6. When a patient needs emergency treatment, services are rendered, regardless of the extent of payment.

Once the patient has established billing credit with the organization by paying cash for each of the first three office visits, it seems reasonable for the organization to allow the patient to assume the responsibility of paying a monthly bill. Therefore, the next step would be to develop a set of fee-collection procedures for the patient who continues beyond three visits and has established credit. The procedures would include the following:

7. Upon paying the fee for three consecutive visits, the patient is reinforced by verbal feedback from the business office personnel.

8. The patient is given a copy of the billing policy which states that the patient has the option to pay cash at each visit or request a monthly billing.

9. Upon each billing, the patient pays at least fifty percent of the monthly bill.

10. If the patient fails to pay his or her monthly bill, he or she is returned to the previous set of procedures for the purpose of re-establishing credit.

11. The balance of the patient's bill should be paid in full within three months after termination.

12. If unforeseen financial difficulties should arise, the patient should contact the business manager.

To assist the patient in following the Credit Criterion procedures, business office personnel meet with the patient during the first office visit and when the patient establishes credit and chooses to be billed monthly. During this meeting, the staff discuss the procedures. In this manner, the business office has invested some additional time with the patient to insure that the patient clearly understands the responsibilities for fee payment.

It is important to note that Credit Criterion procedures are designed to include efficient business office procedures, such as:

1. An accurate patient billing record system.

2. Business office hours coinciding with the office hours of service staff.

3. A business office staff member always being present to assist the patient.

4. When possible, the business office staff being involved in establishing the patient's fee.

The business office personnel should be monitored routinely by the business manager and receive frequent feedback. This will help to correct small problems before they develop into crises. New business office employees should be trained to mastery of the Credit Criterion billing procedures.

The effects of the Credit Criterion procedures were evaluated in an urban community mental health center. Results (see Figure 6-1) indicated that the percentage of fee payment for the first three office visits increased from a baseline average of 21.8 percent and 33 percent to a Credit Criterion average of 92 percent and 86.5 percent.

Figure 6-2 is a cumulative representation of cash collected (solid lines) and the total collections that were possible (broken lines) for the first three office visits. During use of the Credit Criterion model, $804.25 was collected of the total $827.00 charged, while during the baseline conditions, only $558.75 of the total $1,189.75 charged.

Figure 6-3 shows that the increase of fee payment during the use of the Credit Criterion model continued after the third visit, resulting in an average of 90 percent while the average for baseline was 44 percent.

Consumer feedback data suggested that patients felt the fee-payment policy was fair and acceptable. Patient attendance data indicated that the Credit Criterion model did not inhibit attendance. Further, there were no additional administrative costs for implementing the model.

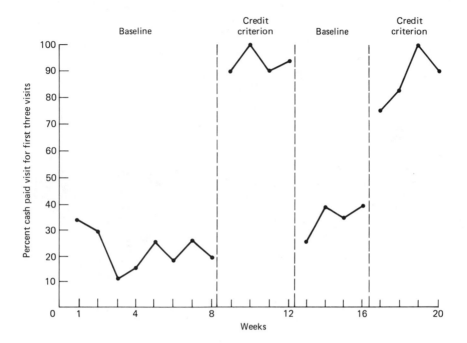

FIGURE 6-1   From G. T. Hannah and T. R. Risley, Experiments in a community health center: Increasing client payments for outpatient services. *Journal of Applied Behavior Analysis,* 1981, *14,* 141–151. © 1981 by the Society for the Experimental Analysis of Behavior, Inc. Reprinted by permission.

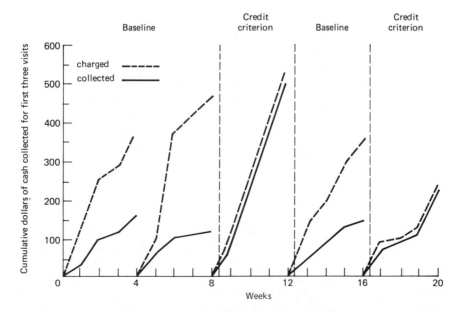

FIGURE 6-2   From G. T. Hannah and T. R. Risley, Experiments in a community health center: Increasing client payments for outpatient services. *Journal of Applied Behavior Analysis,* 1981, *14,* 141–151. © 1981 by the Society for the Experimental Analysis of Behavior, Inc. Reprinted by permission.

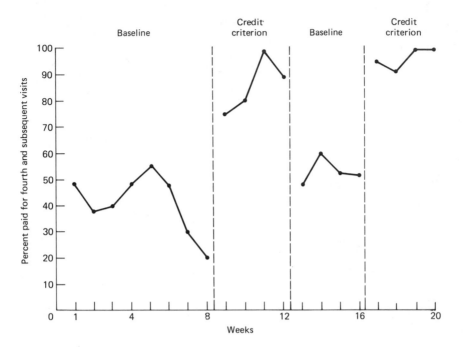

FIGURE 6-3 From G. T. Hannah and T. R. Risley, Experiments in a community health center: Increasing client payments for outpatient services. *Journal of Applied Behavior Analysis*, 1981, *14*, 141-151. © 1981 by the Society for the Experimental Analysis of Behavior, Inc. Reprinted by permission.

In summary, a human service organization can develop procedures for collecting patient fees that are efficient and effective, while at the same time keeping in mind the humanitarianism of such a system. Basically, a human service manager needs a fee-collection model and competent staff to implement it. Patients who are instructed to pay for their services should receive a copy of the fee-payment procedures and have the opportunity to discuss them for clarification. Thus, the human service organization and patient can both meet their financial obligations. The Credit Criterion model has been evaluated and the findings replicated in other community mental health centers and other types of human service agencies (Hannah & Risley, 1981).

Philanthropy Funding

Another way to increase and acquire revenue is to obtain philanthropy funds. These funds can be a significant resource for making up deficits in various program budgets. In 1976, the American Association of Fund-Raising Counsel, Inc. reported that the giving of philanthropy funds that year totaled $26.88 billion (Conrad, 1976). These funds come from four principal sources: individuals, bequests or deferred gifts, foundations, and corporations. Conrad's (1976) document indicates the following funding breakdown of the $26.88 billion: individual gifts,

$21.44 billion, or 79.7%; bequest gifts, $2.23 billion, or 8.3%; foundation gifts, $2.01 billion, or 7.5%.

Bequest gifts usually go to health agencies and educational institutions; foundation gifts are most often awarded to education and health/hospital projects. Individual gifts, therefore, are almost the best source of funds for a human service organization.

A human service organization wishing to increase its ability to collect philanthropy funds can establish a separate tax-exempt, non-profit corporation to receive grant funds for the advancement of human welfare, in this case through funding the organization's services. This is best accomplished by seeking the assistance of an attorney experienced in the development and operation of non-profit corporations. It is important that the corporation be established so that it is tax exempt and qualifies as a non-profit corporation under Section 501 (C) (3) of the Internal Revenue Code. Many private, non-profit human service programs are able to qualify for tax exempt status without the need to establish a separate corporation.

Once established, the corporation can encourage individual contributions from persons giving directly or through business, civic, and social organizations. It can also receive funds from corporations and philanthropic foundations in the form of contributions or grants. Such a funding system serves as a force for unifying the community and building a local constituency for the organization.

OBTAINING FOUNDATION GRANTS. When a non-profit, tax-exempt corporation has been established or when a human service program's tax exempt status has been determined (that is, when it has been determined that it meets Internal Revenue Code requirements), grant support can be requested from corporations and philanthropic foundations. A *philanthropic foundation* is a non-governmental, non-profit organization established to maintain or aid social, educational, charitable, religious, or other activities primarily through grants to other non-profit organizations. A foundation's funds typically come from a single source (individual donor, family, or corporation) and are managed by its own trustees and directors. There are approximately 26,000 foundations in the United States which award upwards of 400,000 grants each year. In recent years (1978–1980), foundation grants have totaled between $2.16 to $2.4 billion annually (Kurzig, 1981).

Most foundations are small (less than $1,000,000 in assets), oriented to local geographic areas, and award a large number of small grants (less than $10,000). The smaller, low-asset foundations are seldom equipped to respond quickly to proposals since they often have little or no full-time staff. Foundations in high asset categories are more likely to employ full-time program officers, evaluate proposals according to established guidelines, award larger grants, and publish annual reports. In general, foundations typically reject about 95% of the proposals they receive (Hillman & Abarbanel, 1975) and each foundation has its own special procedures and funding priorities.

A review of foundation funding patterns using periodicals such as *The Grantsmanship Center News* (1031 S. Grand Avenue, Los Angeles, CA 90015) or

Foundation News (1828 L Street, NW, Washington, DC 20036) indicates that foundations typically award three major *categories of grants:* to (1) individuals, (2) profit-making organizations, and (3) non-profit organizations. While the over-whelming majority of foundations fund nonprofit organizations, almost 1000 foundations award grants to over 40,000 individuals each year.

Foundations can also make grants to profit-making organizations. An exam-ple of this type of award is the "program related investment." Made by relatively few foundations, program related investments are loans for projects related to the foundation's stated purpose and interests. The foundation making such an invest-ment usually expects to receive this money back with interest.

Kurzig (1981) has noted that, since 1961, the *distribution of foundation grant funds by subject area* has remained stable with education ranked highest followed by social welfare, health, culture, sciences, and religion in that order. Education main-tains its high ranking (25-30% of the total grants awarded) since so many projects or programs funded through other headings (e.g., health, sciences) are channeled through educational institutions.

Identifying prospective foundations. The best strategy for finding prospective foundations is to thoroughly research foundations that have interests and funding priorities consistent with one's needs and to develop a list of about 25 prospects. Further research should then be conducted until the list is narrowed to about five to ten target foundations to which proposals will be sent. This is done by considering each foundation's giving patterns, geographic restrictions, application guidelines, submission deadlines, timetables for funding decision, and so on.

Two types of reference books are essential for success at this task: foundation grant indices and foundation directories. These are published by clearinghouses such as The Foundation Center (888 Seventh Avenue, New York, NY 10106 [212] 975-1120) and The Grantsmanship Center (1031 S. Grand Avenue, Los Angeles, CA 90015 [213] 749–4721). *The Foundation Directory* (Lewis & Gerumsky, 1981) is particularly useful since it is generally considered to be the most authoritative guide to the grantmaking interests of major American foundations. Its 1981 Edition in-cludes descriptions of the nation's 3,363 largest foundations which are the source of 93% of all foundation assets and 89% of total grant dollars. Entries include a description of giving interests, addresses, telephone numbers, current financial data, names of donors and key officers, and grant application information.

Approximately 40 states and several cities have their own foundation direc-tories. A bibliography of these sources has been provided by Kurzig (1981). Foundation directories are also available from commercial and nonprofit publishers. For example, the Public Service Materials Center (415 Lexington Avenue, New York, NY 10017) publishers *Where America's Large Foundations Make Their Grants* (1980); the Taft Corporation (100 Vermont Avenue, NW, Washington, DC 20005) publishes the *Taft Corporate Foundation Directory* (1979); and the Lawson Associates, Inc. (39 E. 51st Street, New York, NY 10022) publishes *Foundation 500; Index to Foundation Giving Patterns* (1978).

Developing the foundation grant proposal.   The most effective foundation proposal is characterized by adequacy, brevity, clarity, credibility, and a realistic budget. The best way to ensure that the proposal is adequate is to obtain as much information as possible from the target foundation concerning what it needs to know. If the foundation publishes an annual report, and/or proposal guidelines, these should be obtained. Telephone communication is usually best. If the foundation does permit personal interviews, and it is felt that it would help, it should be arranged (cost permitting). It is also a good idea to take along some highly credible associates such as members of one's Board of Trustees. Additional suggestions about personal interview/telephone communication strategies are provided by Somerville (1982).

In the absence of specific guidelines, the following format is recommended for the foundation grant proposal: [1]

1. Cover letter (2 to 3 pages)
    a. Analyze needs (the project and what it involves).
    b. Establish one's credibility and the capacity to carry out the proposed project.
    c. Describe qualifications of project staff.
    d. Summarize the costs of the project (start up as well as operating costs) and other sources of funding.
    e. Describe how the success of the project is to be evaluated.
2. Appendices
    a. Additional information about the applicant agency or individual (e.g., agency brochure, professional vitae)
    b. IRS certification that the applicant is a non-profit, tax-exempt corporation consistent with Section 501 (c) (3) of the Internal Revenue Code.
    c. Itemization of costs and other sources of funding for the proposed project.
    d. Copy of an audited financial statement for the last fiscal year of program operation.
    e. Evidence of support for the proposed project (e.g., letters from experts in the field, copies of participation agreements with other agencies).

The cover letter is obviously the most critical component of the foundation grant package. It must be concise, specific, and capable of capturing the interest of foundation reviewers. Dermer (1976) has provided a useful collection of successful fund raising letters; Abeles (1982) has offered a number of recommendations specific to the development of the scientific research proposal.

Submitting the proposal.   While each foundation has its own deadlines, there are two major research/proposal cycles that one can follow to meet the deadlines of most foundations. One calls for research and planning in January, proposal development in February, and submission of proposals in March. The outside application date for this cycle is April 15 so that foundation agendas can be complete and ready for a decision in June or July.

The second cycle calls for research and planning in July, proposal development in August, and submission of proposals in September with October 15 as the outside date. In this cycle, foundations plan agendas in November, vote in December, and reach a decision in January or February. However, it is important to reemphasize the importance of identifying the *specific submission deadline* for each foundation that one plans to approach (Christian, 1982).

In summary, we recommend the following steps in seeking foundation funding:[2]

1. Determine the needs to be addressed, the patients to be served, and the amount and type of support needed.
2. Develop a list of foundation prospects based on subject, geographic interest, and patterns of giving.
3. Consult the foundation's latest annual report, its IRS forms 990–PF and 990–AR or foundation indices and directories for more detailed grants lists and application procedures.[3]
4. Select the foundations which are most appropriate to approach in terms of the project's goals. Eliminate foundations whose limitations would clearly prohibit their funding one's program.
5. Develop a well-organized proposal which follows the foundation's specific guidelines (if available). Make sure that the proposal describes program's needs for the proposed project, establishes credibility and capacity to carry out the proposed project, and indicates the qualifications of individuals to be involved in the project. Include a sufficiently detailed budget, evidence of tax exempt certification, and describe how the success or failure of the proposed project will be determined.
6. Comply with the foundation's grant management and/or reporting requirements after a grant has been awarded.

Private Contribution Mailing System

Soliciting contributions through the mail is not new. The technique has been used for several decades. However, very few human service organizations are successful, mainly because they view soliciting private contributions as a waste of time, or because they lack the know-how. Nevertheless, people do like to give of themselves and their money if there is a justifiable cause and if they are approached correctly. (Individuals and organizations who donate funds and other resources usually support specific causes, programs, projects or new facilities, and typically prefer to contribute to *specific projects* as opposed to ongoing operating expenses or operating deficits.)

While the pay-off through donation by mail is not immediate, research shows that people who have donated by mail continue to do so consistently over the years (Fisher, 1978). Depending on the method of building a mailing-list, it takes three to four years for a mail campaign to become profitable. Our research led to our development of a private contribution mailing system. Our studies were conducted to determine who were good contributors and what type of funding-material package would yield the largest contributions.

We have found the following materials and procedures useful in developing a successful private contribution mailing system:

A.   *Materials*

1. Outer mailing envelope.
2. Donor card.
3. Letter.
4. Return envelope.
5. Digest.
6. Financial report.
7. Center brochure.

B.   *Procedures*

Procedures 1–5: Mailing Preparation

1. Each organization can best determine its potential contributors. In our case, the following groups responded best: physicians, accountants, a million-dollar-and-above business, an under-a-million-dollar business, lawyers, dentists. Of course, a special list of potential contributors prepared by the Board of Directors and staff should be included.

2. Keep addresses on a special Xerox copier. If you have more than three thousand names, a computer is recommended.

3. Designate a staff member (a bookkeeper or secretary who will spend approximately eight to twelve hours a month) to be responsible for implementing the system.

4. An area of approximately fifteen by twelve feet is needed for assembling the mail-out envelopes. We recommend that this space be a permanent area, where you can post graphs and various information about the results.

5. Have a professional printer print your material, because color, size, and type of print or paper are important. On the basis of our research, we recommend the following:
    a. Outside envelope.
        Color—warm earth.
        Size—personal note, invoice (6″–8″).
        Type—"clear-vu window."
    b. Letter
        Color—same as outer envelope.
        Size—small personal size.
        Type—heavy paper (24 or 28 lb.).
    c. Donor Card
        Color—warm earth.
        Size—difference size than other componets; also, avoid postcard shapes.
    d. Return envelope
        Color—warm earth.
        Size—large enough to insert donor card.
        Type—a business-like type-face.
    e. Brochure
        Color—warm earth.
        Style—avoid professional verbiage.
        Type—a business-like type-face.
    f. Financial report.
        Type—a business-like type-face
    g. Digest
        Color—warm earth.
        Type—professional printing.

Procedures 6–9: Mail-Out

6. The United States Post Office requires various procedures for bulk mailing. Ask your local post office for an instruction manual—Publication #13.

7. It is important that staff's schedule when assembling the mail-out envelopes is not broken up with other duties. Try to avoid incomplete envelopes.

8. Another staff member should check a sample of at least twenty percent of the letters to determine completeness.

9. Fall and spring mail-outs are recommended.

Procedures 10–13: Return Mail

10. Assign staff to check return envelopes to record funds received, and make a donor's list.

11. Forward contribution list to another staff for preparing thank-you note and tax receipt as soon as possible. A donor's interest wanes if he or she must wait a long time for a response.

12. Add name and address from the received envelope to the donors' mailing-list.

13. Keep track of the cost and response to your mail campaign, and evaluate its effectiveness.

Special Annual Fund Raising Project Model

Again, most human service managers feel intimidated about marketing their organization's services and soliciting community support. This is often due to their lack of confidence that their community will respond to their financial needs. If carefully planned, annual fund raising projects can be successful in increasing revenue and creating community interest in an organization.

Annual fund raising events should be planned by a special committee composed of individuals (not necessarily all board members) who have had experience in planning and conducting fund raising projects and who have close contacts with both the financial and business communities. We recommend two annual events that are conducted in the same month each year in order to get the community into the habit of attending. Winter and spring months are best. There is a wide range of possible special events, among them (a) an annual award dinner with special programs (for example, a speaker, a stage presentation) to which the public is invited and charged above cost (most restaurant owners will charge for such events *below* their actual cost); (b) an annual musical fund raising concern (if possible use a professional booking agency to solicit the musical group and place the concert); and (c) a week, or month, with a theme (for example, Mental Health Week) in cooperation with McDonald's, Burger King, etcetera, where you arrange for a percentage of the profit on a specific item sold.

Procedures

1. The Governing Board should appoint a special committee with members who have experience in planning and implementing fund raising events.

2. Similar fund raising events should be implemented during the same month each year.

3. At least one "big name" citizen or company should, if possible, sponsor one of the events.

4. The mass media should be relied on to promote the events. At least one feature newspaper story should be obtained before the event; radio announcements should commence two weeks prior to the event. There should be television coverage during the event and, later, a brief newspaper article describing the manner in which the funds raised will be used.

5. An event should not be scheduled during the local United Way season (September–November) or the summer months.

Community Service Group Sponsorship Model

Most human service organizations offer one or two unique services that the community is interested in seeing maintained. On some occasions, an organization has a one-time need, such as a new building or start-up expenses for developing a residential program. In these cases, most community service groups are interested in assisting an organization.

Various social and/or civic community groups, (Kiwanis, Rotary, Lions, Junior League, Women's Club, etcetera) can be approached to sponsor a particular program for a two to three-year period. Let us say, that you wish to develop a group home to serve mentally retarded adults and you need $40,000 over a two-year period to apply toward the total cost. A community group might serve as a sponsor for the project's start-up costs with operating costs to be covered by the program's budget or by funds from another sponsor.

Community groups are willing to assist human service organizations, but are usually interested in some tangible results from their involvement. That is, you need their assistance for a specific program or project for a specific time period and in return your organization will provide the community with a needed service.

Procedures

1. The Governing Board should appoint members to represent the organization when approaching social/civic groups. It is hoped that certain members will approach their own service groups, as a start.

2. The presentation to a community group should be conducted in a professional manner—that is, with a good speaker (board member) and, if possible, a film or slide-show telling the story of the organization.

3. When a group agrees to sponsor the organization, a board member should be assigned to serve as the liaison person between the organization and the community service group.

4. If possible, the group should be invited to conduct some of its meetings at the organization's facility.

5. Staff should conduct special educational classes for the group's members as a service to the service group.

6. An annual goal should be set—for example, to have four service groups sponsor your organization.

BUDGETING

The manager of an organization is the architect in the budget process, and usually the success or failure of the budget plan depends on the degree of his or her involvement. Most managers of human service organizations believe that the only requirement for success in budgeting is to have a competent business manager or budget director. Human service managers often rely too heavily on these support staff because their training in social work, psychology, or psychiatry was deficient in administrative content. However, they cannot afford to ignore the budgeting process. Every manager has goals for the operation of his or her organization; the budget system becomes the process for formalizing and implementing such goals and monitoring the performance of his or her staff.

The budget of an organization can be regarded as primarily a planning and control system. To regard budgeting as a progressive system is important, because it implies a continuing process throughout the year. Furthermore, it is a system with built-in feedback that allows management to monitor and direct the activities of an organization. Basically, a budget is a short-term (generally one-year) plan expressed in numbers—money, patients served, staff, performance measures, etcetera.

We have discussed what budgeting is, but what is budgeting not? First, budgeting is not a management function performed solely by the business departments and bookkeepers, although they play an important role by recording, analyzing, interpreting, and reacting to the development and implementation of the budget. Second, budgeting is not just forecasting, that is, predicting the outcome of events. Rather, it is planning for a result and maximizing the chances of achieving that result. If a budget is little more than a forecast prepared by the business department—rather than a well thought out plan prepared by the entire management and governing board—then the result may well be only a superficial set of figures (Jones & Trentin, 1971).

In this section, we will briefly describe four traditional budget models: the line-item budget, the incremental budget, the planning-programming-budgeting system, and the zero-based budget.

Traditional Budget Models

LINE-ITEM BUDGETING.   Line-item budgeting is one of the oldest models for budgeting government and non-profit organizations. It first appeared in the early 1900s. It is viewed as a budget model to monitor expenditures. Basically, expenses are grouped into certain categories, such as salaries, supplies, travel, equipment, and so on. However, line-item budgeting does not take into account the goals and objectives of the organization. The budget does not describe the services being rendered. As a result, there is a sharp dichotomy between service needs and expenditure data. In other words, the budget is developed to measure expenditure regardless of program outcome or needs.

Line-item budgeting is commonly used in small human service organizations with an annual budget under $75,000. The manager prepares and presents the budget as shown in Exhibit 1. Notice that the budget only describes expenditure items without indicating program expenses. A budget needs to describe the entire organization, that is, goals and objectives, programs, staff and equipment, and demographic data of patients and services based on a prior budget year.

Sunflower Agency's Annual Budget

I. Expenses		Total
1. Staff salaries		$32,000.00
2. Staff benefits		4,500.00
	Subtotal	$36,500.00
3. Office supplies		2,000.00
4. Equipment		1,000.00
5. Travel		1,500.00
6. Utilities		1,200.00
7. Telephone		1,000.00
8. Rent/Maintenance		4,000.00
9. Miscellaneous		500.00
	Subtotal	$11,200.00
	Grand Total	$47,700.00
II. Revenue		Total
1. Client fees		$20,000.00
2. Third-party insurance		10,000.00
3. United Way		15,000.00
4. Private grant		2,700.00
	Total	$47,700.00

EXHIBIT 1   Sunflower Counseling Center: Line Item Budgeting

INCREMENTAL BUDGETING.   In incremental budgeting, a new budget is actually the old budget plus a gradual increase. In other words, the main issue is not the total budget but rather the amount of increase in funding that is needed. It is commonly used in human service organizations because such organizations customarily ask, ''How much more money can we receive this year?'' Those who defend incremental budgeting explain that it is an appropriate budget process since managers usually expand and/or change an organization slowly. However, incremental budgeting offers few incentives for managers to reduce spending and/or determine program priorities.

Incremental budgeting is basically the same as line-item budgeting. It describes expenditures and revenues. Normally the budget document contains a brief description of an organization's services and administrative structure. Most non-profit human service organizations use incremental budgeting—especially organizations that seek governmental funding and solicit private donations and grants. In addition, most state governments use incremental budgeting for developing their budgets and issuing state funds. State funding budgeting guidelines usually only request an organization to describe its expenses and revenue items and describe *why* it needs more funds.

PROGRAM BUDGETING (PPBS).   The planning-programming-budgeting system (PPBS) became widely known in 1951 through its use in the United States Department of Defense under Secretary McNamara; it was later applied to all executive departments by President Johnson. It has also been used in various state governments (Pennsylvania and Vermont) and private industries (John Hancock Mutual Life Insurance Company of Boston and General Electric Company's Research Laboratory).

PPBS is designed to be a rational approach to the budgeting process and to organize an organization's budget by focusing on output grouping—that is, goals and objectives—instead of inputs like staff salary, equipment, and travel costs. It also involves cost-benefit analysis and the establishment of priorities (Doh, 1971). PPBS allows managers to recommend certain programs for full funding while eliminating low-priority programs. PPBS has ten major features. These are:

1. Definition of the organization's objectives, written in specific terms.
2. Determination of programs, including possible alternatives, to achieve the stated objectives.
3. Identification of major issues to be resolved in the formulation of objectives.
4. An annual period with appropriate subdivisions for the planning, programming, and budgeting steps to ensure an ordered approach and to make appropriate amounts of time available for analysis and decision-making at all levels of management.
5. Continuous re-examination of program results in relationship to costs and anticipated outcomes to determine need for changes in stated programs and objectives as originally established.
6. Recognition of issues and other problems that require more time than is available in the annual period so that they can be explicitly identified and set apart from the current period for completion in two or more years as the program and availability of personnel changes.
7. Analysis of programs and their alternatives in terms of probable outcomes and both direct and indirect costs.
8. Development of analytical tools necessary for measuring costs and benefits.
9. Development each year of a multi-year program and financial plan with full recognition of the fact that in many areas resource allocations in the early years (for example, years one through five) require projections of plans and programs and their resource demands for ten or more years into the future.
10. Adaptation of existing accounting and statistical reporting systems to provide inputs into planning and programming as well as continuing information on resources used in and actions taken to implement programs.

ZERO-BASE BUDGETING.   Zero-base budgeting was introduced by the Texas Instruments Company and later used by President Carter. Pyhrr (1972) defined zero-base budgeting as:

SUNFLOWER FAMILY COUNSELING CENTER

Program: Preschool

Objectives: To provide parents with specific training educational and counseling skills, that is, positive reinforcement, site-watch, and so on, in order to improve their engagement with their child and their child's engagement with others and immediate environment.

Description: This program involves professional and paraprofessional staff working with parents and parents' preschool-age children. The children's mean age is two years. They are referred by pediatricians, nursery schools, and churches. The children attend a five-day-a-week program (9:00 a.m.-2:00 p.m.) with parents attending three of those days.

Cost Units:

	Description	1983	1984	1985
(1)	Staff salaries	$400,000	$490,000	$565,000
(2)	Staff benefits	60,000	85,000	90,000
(3)	Office supplies	8,000	5,000	5,000
(4)	Travel and telephone	15,000	13,000	13,000
(5)	Utilities	5,000	6,000	7,000
(6)	Equipment	2,000	1,000	0,000
	TOTAL	$500,000	$600,000	$680,000

EXHIBIT 2 Sunflower Counseling Center: Program Budgeting (PPBS)

An operating, planning and budgeting process which requires each manager to justify his entire budget request in detail...The burden of proof is placed on each manager to justify why he should spend any money at all. This approach requires that all activities be identified in decision packages which will be evaluated by systematic analysis and ranked in order of importance.

In other words, zero-base budgeting requires a manager to assemble the annual budget into decision packages or long-range goals. Thus, each department supervisor must prove that his or her department is effective and efficiently operated in order to receive a high ranking in the final budget priority list. To maintain a department's operation, its supervisor must become a persuasive salesperson.

For each package, the manager may ask department supervisors to answer the following questions: (a) What do we want to accomplish? (b) How do we propose to accomplish it? (c) Are there other alternatives for accomplishing it? (d) How much will it cost? (e) How will it benefit the clients? and (f) What will happen if it's not done? The bottom line is, "What will the patient receive for this expenditure, will the service be effective, how will consumer satisfaction be measured, and can the organization afford it?"

The decision packages are then ranked in order of importance. The ranking may be based on cost effectiveness, legal mandate, funding available, and/or con-

| Activity name | Department | Prepared |
| Preschool | Outpatient | Ms. Smith |

| Purpose of activity: | Division | Approved |
| To provide services to pre-school children & their parents. | None | Dr. Brown |

	Expenditures	Current year	Budget year
	1) Staff sal.	$100,000	$110,000
	2) Staff ben.	10,000	12,000
	3) Supplies	3,000	3,000
	4) Travel	5,000	5,500
	Total	$118,000	$130,500

Description of activity:

The activity requires six professional and two paraprofessional staff. The activity is located at 100 Main Street and office hours: Monday thru Friday, 8:00 a.m. to 6:00 p.m. Referrals are from local physicians, churches, and nursery schools. The activity served 200 families last year.

Alternative ways of performing activity:

The agency could only provide traditional outpatient services.

Advantages of retaining activity:

The activity has proven to be successful as reported by referral groups and participating patients. The activity does generate revenue, approximately $3,000 of its total cost while government funds provide the remaining amount.

Consequences if activity is eliminated:

Clients will not be able to receive services from other community agencies.

EXHIBIT 3   Sunflower Counseling Center: Zero-Base Budgeting

sumer/community requests. Once the ranking has been agreed upon, the decision packages can be approved and funded.

Various researchers have found that zero-base budgeting has not had a major impact on reducing spending nor an impact on the way that organizations attempted to modify the format of zero-base budgeting, that is, do not start at zero in developing a budget, thus combining incremental and PPBS budgeting.

The financial future of human service organizations is dependent upon the ability to generate revenue and then implement a budget within the revenue amount. The four budget models described above are not designed to assist an organization in determining its revenue limits. Therefore, a new budget system is needed for the 1980s.

Revenue-Base Planning
Budget: A Model for the 1980s

The revenue-base budgetary system is different from previous systems. It places emphasis on projecting an organization's annual revenue rather than on developing its annual expenditure budget. Its use seems inevitable in a time of limited resources. The emphasis with line-item, increment, PPBS, and zero-base budgeting is placed on producing information about needs before determining the total revenue. The revenue-base budgetary system reverses that process (McCaffery, 1981). It *starts* with its revenue limits. This requires an organization to determine its priorities based upon a fixed annual revenue amount.

Revenue-Base Planning Budget has four principal concepts (Muchmore, 1981).

1. *Department Cost Centers.* A department is a collection of related activities designed and managed to achieve a purpose. Most organizations orient their budgetary discussions to entire departments. Developing department cost centers makes the budgetary process more useful as a framework for management and performance evaluation. Each department cost center includes department objectives, a description of department operations, and an analysis of long-term trends that will affect the department over a five-year period.

2. *Base Budget.* A base budget is the reference point for financial planning. In other systems, the base budget generally represents the prior year's expenditures. However, in revenue-base budgeting, the base budget expenditures will equal the available revenues. The revenue allocations will be distributed across departments within an organization so as to meet client needs with maximum efficiency and effectiveness.

3. *Budget Policy Papers.* A budget policy paper is a format for assisting a manager in soliciting information that describes the service needs of an organization's clients. The paper is a critical factor in determining agency needs.

4. *Alternative Service Levels.* Since most managers are not in total control of their revenue allocations, an alternative service level format allows a manager to develop expenditure plans at three different levels of an organization's projected revenue base. These are referred to as the A level, B level, and C level. The B level budget corresponds to the revenue base amount. The C level budget identifies program expenditures if additional revenue beyond the balanced base were obtained. The A level budget reflects the organization's plans if it were to receive revenue below the projected revenue balanced base.

IMPLEMENTATION STEPS. The revenue-base budgeting model consists of six basic steps.

Step 1: Governing Board of an organization appoints a revenue-base review committee in January (fiscal year budget) or June (calendar year budget).

Step 2: Staff prepare budget policy papers and submit to manager by March 1 or August 1.

Step 3: Revenue-Base Review Committee reports to the Governing Board who approves and announces the revenue allocation amounts for Budget Levels A, B, and C by April 1 or September 1.

Step 4:   Staff begin preparing the department cost centers and budgets for Levels A, B, and C by April 1 or September 1.

Step 5:   Manager submits Budget Levels A, B, and C to the Governing Board by May 15 or November 15.

Step 6:   After a total projected revenue amount has been re-analyzed, the Governing Board approves an annual Revenue-Base Budget by June 15 or December 15.

Step 1: Revenue-base review committee.   It is important that a process be designed to plan and review an organization's revenue potential. Most organizations wait until the end of the budget year to begin forecasting the revenue picture for the new budget period. However, with the use of the revenue-base budgeting, an organization must begin approximately six months before the new budget year starts. The projected revenue amounts set the stage for determining department priorities and the expenditure limits. It also forces an organization to be more conscious of its ability to obtain revenue.

Therefore, the Governing Board of an organization appoints a special committee to plan and review the revenue amount for the upcoming budget year. The committee begins meeting in January (fiscal year budget) or June (calendar year budget). The committee consists of members who are knowledgeable about the organization's funding sources and program structures, and about the financial community. The committee reviews the organization's efforts to earn revenue, meets with current funding agencies to discuss funding possibilities for the upcoming year, and explores new ways to obtain funding.

Step 2: Preparing budget policy papers.   As shown in the sample Budget Policy Paper (Kansas Office of Mental Health/Retardation Services, 1981), the manager of an organization will rely upon the budget policy paper as a means to collect information regarding trends in service demand or other relevant factors that should be considered in order to determine the revenue allocation for budget levels A, B, and C. Budget policy papers are not expected to deal with details of the program or with financial detail. They should address the need for particular services, broad trends in patient composition, administrative issues and trends, and other issues that might lead to a reallocation of revenue from one department to another. A budget policy paper should be easy to read and not exceed five pages in length. Each paper should be organized under five headings:

1. *Policy Definition.* A short and clear statement of the policy or problem should be provided.

2. *Background.* The relevant facts bearing on the policy should be described. A statement should be made as to why the decision-makers should consider the policy.

3. *Possible Action.* Alternative approaches to the policy should be listed and explained, along with an assessment of the probable consequences of each alternative.

4. *Recommendations.* One of the alternatives enumerated should be selected and the criteria upon which the choice is based should be explained.

5. *Budget Impact.* Both short- and long-term effects should be described with as much precision as possible, and the methodology upon which impact estimates are based should be explained.

BUDGET POLICY PAPER

Issue Definition: Should community-based mental health and mental retardation centers receive additional state aid to: (1) offset reductions in federal funds; (2) increase services to accommodate individuals currently on waiting lists, individuals exceeding the age limit for receiving services through public school regular and special education programs, and individuals leaving state institutions for the mentally retarded?

Background: The 35 community mental health centers and the 28 community mental retardation centers provide a variety of services related to prevention and treatment of mental illness and mental retardation as an alternative to institutionalization. A major problem experienced by community-based mental health and mental retardation programs is limited sources of stable funds. The three primary sources of funds are county (mill levy), state (formula aid) and federal (Title XX & Title XIX). The current and proposed reductions in federal funds are forcing reductions in the number of individuals being served. The proposed increase in state formula aid (from 29% to 33% of funds generated by a center in fiscal year 1982) will not offset the reduction in federal funds. For example, in 1980 mental retardation centers had approximately 500 individuals on waiting-lists for services. A further complication is the presence of a large number of individuals (approximately 40,000) who are currently receiving special education services under the Education for All Handicapped Children Act (Public Law 94-142). Approximately 1,500 special education students reach post-school age annually. It is estimated that as many as 700 of these young adults will need services provided by community-based mental retardation centers and approximately 1,000 may require services from community-based mental health centers. Another factor that is placing increased demand for services from community-based mental health and mental retardation centers is the commitment on the part of federal and state agencies to provide services in the least restrictive, most normalized program possible. In 1980, there were approximately 1,318 residents in the four mental health institutions and approximately 1,600 residents in the four state hospitals and training centers for the mentally retarded. It has been estimated that perhaps as many as 60% of those in the mental health institutions and as many as 30% of those in institutions for the mentally retarded would be more appropriately served in community-based programs. In 1980, community-based mental health centers served approximately 64,000 clients and community-based mental retardation centers served approximately 3,200 clients. To meet the demand for services in fiscal year 1983, mental health centers will need to expand programs to serve approximately 72,000 clients and mental retardation centers will need to expand programs to serve approximately 5,200 clients. An inability to expand community-based mental health and mental retardation programs could lead to increased demands for often inappropriate institutional placement, increased demands on welfare programs, and increased numbers of mentally ill and mentally retarded individuals coming before the courts. For these reasons, the availability of an appropriate array of community-based services for mentally ill and mentally retarded citizens of Kansas is a matter of gubernatorial concern.

Possible Action:

A.   The Office of Mental Health and Mental Retardation can continue to promote additional county support for community-based mental health and mental retardation centers. While all 105 counties provide some financial support of mental health centers, eight counties have not levied taxes or appropriated other county funds to establish a mental retardation center or to formally join or contract with another center to provide services. In addition, only six counties were at the statutory maximum rate of 0.75 mill for mental health and only five were at the maximum rate of 0.75 for mental retardation.

B.   The Legislature, over a three-year period, can raise the per cent by which funds generated by local mill levies and other means are matched to 38.66% in fiscal year 1983, 44.32% in fiscal year 1984, and finally the 50% maximum permitted by statute in fiscal year 1985.

C.   The Legislature can authorize additional funds that can be used for direct grants to community mental health and mental retardation centers contingent on agreements to provide services to those on waiting-lists, those exceeding the age limits for receiving special education, and/or those leaving state institutions for the mentally retarded and for the mentally ill.

Recommendations: Possible actions "A," "B," and "C" above are all appropriate alternatives. Action "A" is already a high-priority objective for mental health and retardation services. However, most county commissioners have been reluctant to levy any additional taxes on county residents. Further, there is little incentive to do so. Mental health centers provide the same service to all counties in their catchment area even though one county may have a low levy and another the maximum. The same is true of mental retardation centers. In 1980, community mental retardation centers provided services to a total of 51 residents of counties that had no mill levy to support a mental retardation center. These same counties also had 52 residents who received services in State institutions for the mentally retarded. Since mentally ill and mentally retarded residents of counties with no or a very low mill levy have access to the same services as citizens of counties with the maximum mill levy, there is little incentive to levy taxes to increase support of community mental health and mental retardation centers, yet such support is required to expand the services needed and the number of clients that can be served.

Action "B" would eventually provide the needed services through additional state aid to the community-based mental health and mental retardation centers. Reduction in federal funds of up to 25% is anticipated. An increase to 38.66% match in state formula aid in fiscal year 1983 would partially offset the loss of federal funds and enable the centers to continue many services. An increase to 44.32% in fiscal year 1984 would permit the centers to offer some expansion and begin to serve those on waiting lists. Finally, the 50% match in fiscal year 1985 would permit the community centers to provide services to many of those inappropriately placed in institutional programs. If enough mentally ill and mentally retarded individuals currently in institutions can be served through community-based programs, it is possible that one mental health and one mental retardation institution could be closed or designated for an alternative use. This would be consistent with the legislative directive to study the feasibility of converting Norton State Hospital to a center for adjudicated youth. The Office of Mental Health and Mental Retardation, at this time, is considering the possibility that Norton State Hospital should be reduced to 100 beds in fiscal year 1985. If one or more institutions are reduced, the savings in funds formerly allocated to these institutions could be viewed as partially offsetting the increase in state aid to the community mental health and mental retardation centers.

"C" would provide the Office of Mental Health and Mental Retardation with the flexibility required to initiate specific services through the community-based mental health and mental retardation centers. It also would provide a mechanism to promote equal distribution of services across different client groups (for example, waiting-list clients and those currently in institutional programs).

Budget Impact: If all 105 counties raised their mill levy for community mental health centers to the full 0.75 authorized by state statute, this would generate approximately $4,000,000 in additional local funds. An increase to the 0.75 maximum for community mental retardation centers would generate approximately $6,000,000 in additional local funds. This represents an increase of 57% to mental retardation centers.

If mill levies are not increased and state formula aid remains at 33%, the approximate total of state matching dollars in fiscal year 1983 would be $4,703,948 for mental health centers and $2,834,402 for mental retardation centers. If formula aid is raised to 38.66% in fiscal year 1983, the approximate State match would be $5,510,746 for mental health centers and $3,320, 545 for mental retardation centers. If formula aid is raised to 44.32% in fiscal year 1984, the approximate state match would be $6,317,544 for mental health centers and $3,806,688 for mental retardation centers. Finally, if formula aid is raised to 50% in fiscal year 1985 the total state match would be approximately $7,127,194 for mental health centers and $4,294,548 for mental retardation centers.

Alternatively, any increase in state dollars above the current 33% match could be allocated to the Office of Mental Health and Mental Retardation to be used as direct grants to specific centers for specific purposes. This would amount to approximately $800,000 for mental health centers and $500,000 for mental retardation centers in fiscal year 1983; $1,600,000 for mental health and $1,000,000 for mental retardation centers in fiscal year 1984; and $2,400,000 for mental health and $1,500,000 for mental retardation centers in fiscal year 1985.

Step 3: Announcing revenue allocation.   As shown in the sample Memorandum, the decision-makers of an organization should announce the new revenue allocations for Budget Levels A, B, and C. This statement should be made sometime in April (fiscal year budget) or September (calendar year budget). Note that the sample Memorandum gives certain policy guidelines for preparing the budgets, and projected revenue amounts for each funding item. Thus, the manager is now ready to develop the expenditure amounts to match the revenue allocations for each budget level in A, B, and C.

Step 4: Preparing department cost centers.   In order for an organization to budget effectively, its manager and/or Board of Directors must be provided with information that enables them to judge the highest level of consumer needs. Given a limited amount of revenue, an organization must be in a position to evaluate in a meaningful way the departments that should be funded. Thus, the first step is to review all of an organization's services and group them in a program format.

As stated above, a department is a set of related activities that follows a planned course of action to achieve specified objectives. In other words, the department is a cluster of similar services (*the what*) delivered to a specific group (*the who*) for a legitimate reason (*the why*). To be useful for budgeting, a department must be defined in such a manner as to (a) include integrated activities; (b) be directed

TO: Ms. Mary Brown, Executive Director
            Sunflower Agency
FROM: Mr. Ralph East, Board Chairperson
DATE: April 1, 1981
SUBJECT: Revenue Allocation

Attached you will find a set of revenue allocations for preparing the fiscal year budget.

In addition, the Board indicated the desire that certain policy directions be taken as you prepare these budgets.

1. The children outpatient program to include a preschool program.
2. Clinic office hours to be expanded to three evenings and Saturday morning.
3. A management plan to be developed and implemented to increase the collection of client fees.

In preparing your budgets, the Board has established the policy that there will be no growth in staff positions except for the children's department and an increase in staff salaries will be set at nine percent.

Of the three levels, Budget B revenue allocation is the most important because it represents the projected base for a balanced budget. The A and C Budgets are designed to extract information that can be analyzed to determine what effects a greater or lesser level of funding will have on the performance and operations of the organization as well as the relative priority of programs within the agency. It should be noted that the analysis of alternative revenue levels may lead to the conclusion that some resource level between A and B or between B and C is desirable.

Please submit the budgets by May 15, 1981. Thank you for your cooperation.

FISCAL YEAR 1981 REVENUE ALLOCATIONS

	FUND	FY81	Level A	Level B	Level C
1.	Client fees	$276,000	$300,000	300,000	$300,000
2.	Private insurance	25,300	40,300	40,300	40,300
3.	Private contributions	15,000	10,000	15,000	15,000
4.	United Way	90,000	60,000	90,000	90,000
5.	Annual events	20,000	20,000	20,000	20,000
6.	State government	360,000	300,000	400,000	600,000
7.	City government	340,000	250,000	385,000	385,000
8.	Title XIX	150,000	150,000	200,000	200,000
	TOTAL	$1,276,300	$1,130,300	$1,450,300	$1,600,300

EXHIBIT 4   Sample Memorandum Announcing Revenue Allocation

toward a defined purpose; and (c) have impacts or effects that can be measured. Thus, the definition of a suitable set of departments meeting these criteria is of primary importance as an organization looks toward a new budget year. The department cost center will be the framework within which information is gathered and processed. As a result, a well-conceived department structure frequently results in good budget decisions.

As shown in the example, p. 148, the department cost center is used to classify services. It also provides a basic framework for revenue allocation decisions. For each department, a plan such as the one recommended by Muchmore (1981), should be formulated consisting of the following components:

1. *Department Title.* The department plans should be headed by the department title.
2. *Department Objectives.* Objectives are those tasks toward which all activities included in a department are directed. A satisfactory statement of objectives should specify results for which a department manager could be held accountable. In other words, the statements should be output-oriented rather than input-oriented. Objectives should indicate:
   a. the intended effect of department activity;
   b. the client group upon which the effect will be registered;
   c. a quantitative measure of the intended impact; and,
   d. the time frame within which the impact is to appear.
   Where a department is divided into one or more subdepartments, objectives should be presented for each subdepartment as well as for the department itself.
3. *Department Explanation.* This section of the department plan should be a clear and uncomplicated description of the manner in which department activities are conducted. The explanation should be brief but should include the major items needed to understand how the department operates.
4. *Department History.* A brief narrative summary should refer to the creation of the department and to the statutory or regulatory changes which have increased or decreased the department responsibility. Where appropriate, a statement explaining why statutory or regulatory changes were undertaken and indicating changes expected in the near future may be included.
5. *Proposed Budget Year 19— Operations.* This section should be used to present and justify major actions which will be taken during the new budget year to accomplish department objectives. A description of proposed actions should be given for each of the subdepartments.
6. *Long-Term Trends.* An organization should describe any major trends that affect services as projected through five budget years. Appropriate statistical indicators should be used to establish trends. Also, a brief description of department responses necessary to deal with long-term trends should be given.
7. *Performance Measures.* Performance measures are used to determine the cost-effectiveness of services provided. Impact measures are the best performance measures because they describe the degree to which objectives are being accomplished. Impact measures should be developed according to the following guidelines:
   a. The measures should be output-oriented. They should reflect the results of departments rather than the level of resources used for department purposes.
   b. The measures should clearly indicate the degree to which department objectives have been accomplished.
   c. The measures should be thoroughly defined so as to avoid misinterpretation.
8. *Performance Comparison.* A statement showing a clear indication of the differences in operations proposed at each of the Budget Levels A, B, and C should be made. A rationale for the difference in expected performance should be included.
9. *Expenditure Items.* This section comprises a summary of expenditures of the previous budget year, current budget, and projected Level A, Level B, and Level C budgets.

After the first year in using the Department Cost Center format, an organization could omit steps 3, 4, and 6, providing the department's goals and objectives

Cost Center

I. *Department Title:* Children Outpatient Services

II. *Department Objectives:* To provide individualized and/or family treatment for approximately 400 children and families who are self, school, court, or human service agency referrals, while maintaining an active therapeutic environment and ensuring the fundamental rights and dignity of each participant. Within three months of client termination the department will systematically seek consumer feedback. The objective is to obtain at least 85 percent satisfaction ratings from consumers and referral agencies. Satisfaction ratings should further indicate that 90 percent of the patient's treatment goals have been met.

III. *Department Explanation:* The department provides comprehensive evaluation, diagnosis, and counseling services to children ranging in age from four to twelve years. At the first appointment, an evaluation is made of the child and family. Then an individual treatment plan is developed, which may include individual and family therapy, play therapy, parents' groups, etcetera. The child's educational needs are also considered.

IV. *Department History:* The department was one of the original six services when the agency was created in 1965. It has experienced a gradual decrease in total client service (approximately 20%) since the local schools expanded their special education services. However, currently the local public schools are using the department's services to treat more behavior-problem and disturbed children.

V. *Proposed Budget Year 1981 Operations:* An annual case load of approximately 400 children is projected for next year. This represents a 10% increase, due to the local schools' recommendations for future referrals. The schools have reduced their special education staff by two. No new staff will be needed.

VI. *Long-Term Trends:* An increasing number of children under five years of age are being referred—in 1978, 15 or 11%; 1979, 22 or 18%; 1980, 31 or 27%. As a result, we need to study further our staff's skills and services for children of this age. Also, a preschool program including a facility site will need to be studied for future implementation.

VII. *Performance Measures:*

Measure	FY 1978	FY 1979	Estimated FY 1980	Lvl A	FY 1981 Lvl B	Lvl C
(1) Number of clients	362	370	375	400	400	400
(2) Consumer Satisfaction	88%	87%	90%	70%	92%	92%
(3) Appealed to the agency's human rights committee	1	1	0	2	0	0
(4) Completed treatment goals	83%	87%	90%	75%	90%	90%

VIII. *Performance Comparison:* Budget Level B—would allow for the continuation of current staffing (five full-time) and increase in client referrals. However, there would have to be a 10% decrease in staff travel which could impact staff's school and home visits. Other expenditure items would not be affected.

Budget Level C—would allow for an increase in one staff therapist and a 5% increase in staff travel. However, Level B, except for reduction in staff travel, has been determined to be the level of programming desired in maintaining a balanced budget.

Budget Level A—this level of funding would require the elimination of two staff, which would cause a reduction in the number of clients served. In order to keep three staff, a 50% reduction in staff travel and office supplies would have to be made. As a consequence of Level A funding, a large number of children referred by the courts and schools could not be served.

IX. *Expenditure Items:*

		FY 1980	Budget for FY 1981	FY81-A	FY81-B	FY81-C
(1)	Staff salaries	$80,000	$85,600	$59,304	$93,304	$93,304
(2)	Staff benefits	9,600	10,272	7,116	11,504	11,504
	Subtotal	$89,600	$95,872	$66,420	$104,808	$104,808
(3)	Office supplies	500	500	250	500	500
(4)	Equipment	200	000	000	000	000
(5)	Travel	2,000	2,300	1,150	1,700	2,500
(6)	Utilities					
(7)	Telephone	500	700	800	800	800
(8)	Rent/maintenance					
(9)	Miscellaneous	200	200	000	200	200
	Subtotal	3,400	3,700	2,200	3,200	4,000
	Grand Total	$93,000	$99,572	$68,620	$108,008	$108,808

and services do not change. However, we would recommend that steps 2, 3, 4 and 6 be updated every three years.

Step 5: Manager submits budgets. Upon completion of the department and budget documents, the manager is ready to submit the A, B, and C Level Budgets. In the process, the manager should schedule a meeting or series of meetings with the executive officers and/or finance committee for the purpose of discussing in detail the budget document. Once the subcommittee is comfortable with the document, the budgets are presented to the entire governing body.

Step 6: Final decision. After budgets A, B, and C have been submitted, analyzed and fully discussed, the governing board meets with the revenue advisory committee to determine the final projected revenue amount and to make the revenue allocations to each department and/or subdepartment. The revenue allocations could be made in several combinations, such as (a) the total of Level A, B, or C; (b) a slight increase above Level A or B; (c) a slight decrease below B or C; and (d) any other combination as described by the decision-makers. The manager of an organization is now ready to implement the new annual budget which will be a balanced budget representing the departmental priorities of the organization.

SUMMARY

Solving budget problems is not easy, but it can be accomplished. As manager, you can become more skilled in seeking a variety of funding while, at the same time, implementing a budget process that yields a balance-base budget. Remember the manager of an organization is the architect in designing a revenue-producing system and a balance-base budget. The manager must be involved.

We have described five revenue-producing models that can successfully be implemented in your organization. The *Credit Criterion model* is a model for increasing fee collections. *Philanthropy funding* comes from four principal sources: individuals, bequests or deferred gifts, foundations, and corporations. It is to a human service organization's advantage in collecting philanthropy funds to establish a separate non-profit corporation as a private foundation. A *private contribution mailing system* can be a successful way to solicit funds. Research shows that people who have donated by mail continue to do so consistently over the years. A *special annual fund raising project* can be successful, if carefully planned, in increasing revenue and creating community interest in your organization. Finally, the *community service group sponsorship model* allows community groups to assist human service organizations by sponsoring (funding) a particular program or building project.

It is important that a manager develop and implement a successful annual budget. The budget is the nervous system of an organization. We have described the budget model for the 1980s, the *revenue-base planning budget*. It places emphasis on projecting an organization's annual revenue *before* developing the annual expenditure budget. It also requires an organization to determine its departmental priorities based upon a fixed annual revenue amount. The financial future of an organization is dependent upon the ability to generate revenue and then implement a budget within the revenue amount.

7

Getting the Most
Out of Program
Evaluation Efforts

In previous chapters, we have attempted to establish the fact that evaluation is essential to effective human service management. Indeed, we are convinced that ongoing evaluation and feedback are critical to the success of any business. As Mace (1975, p. 22) has observed:

> When chief operating executives do not, as an integral part of their planning role, recognize realistically the status of their existing operations and fulfill the leadership role by adapting to changing conditions, they jeopardize current profits as well as the capacity of the organization to prosper in the future.

In other words, program evaluation is necessary to ensure effective, proactive performance by the human service manager. When a manager implements a procedure or makes some change in program policy, he or she must be able to obtain feedback from the program concerning the results of his or her performance. Without this type of information on an ongoing basis, the manager is unable to learn from experience or plan for the future.

Furthermore, it is only through evaluation that one's program can be *accountable*, and it is only through accountability that it can continue to be *functional*, much less effective. Case law has established the rights of patients to treatment (*Donaldson* v. *O'Connor*, 1974), regular evaluation of progress (*Morales* v. *Turman*, 1973), periodic re-evaluation of treatment or educational plans (*Pennsylvania Association for*

Retarded Children v. *Commonwealth of Pennsylvania*, 1971), and removal from a course of treatment that worsens his or her condition (*New York State Association for Retarded Children* v. *Rockefeller*, 1973). Each of these rights requires some form of ongoing evaluation on the part of the human service provider.

Despite these facts, many human service managers are not sufficiently committed to program evaluation. We have known managers to hire program evaluators and develop policy and procedure for program evaluation without ever proceeding to *obtain* reliable data or to *use* the data if obtained. Two of the major reasons for this lack of commitment are that managers are not always aware of the *criteria* for effective evaluation of a human service organization, and they are not equipped with *models and strategies* for effective program evaluation.

DESIGNING AN EFFECTIVE PROGRAM EVALUATION SYSTEM

The term "program evaluation" is typically used to refer to all procedures employed in determining the extent to which a program of services is meeting (or has met) its previously established goals and objectives. An effective system of program evaluation must therefore be concerned with *objectives* (what the manager wants the program to accomplish); *resources* (personnel, funds, materials that can be utilized in meeting objectives); *performance* (work performed, resources utilized in seeking to accomplish objectives); and *outcomes* (products resulting from performance). This suggests some general tasks and criteria for program evaluation: planning, goal specification, baseline assessment, follow-up assessment, and analysis of results.

Planning refers to the fact that program evaluation is systematic. It involves a sequence of procedures whereby the effect of a manipulation of independent variables (for example, the passage of time, the implementation of a staff training program) is determined by a measurement of dependent variables (for example, change in staff performance). Planning for effective program evaluation suggests the following tasks for the manager:

1. Identifying the *types of results* that program evaluation should yield (*What does the manager need to know?*). The human service manager is typically most interested in results that provide information concerning activity or performance, productivity, quality, efficiency (cost, effort), effectiveness, adequacy, publicity, morale (staff, patient), utility (resources), and legality.
2. Specifying *sources of data* for evaluation and determining *levels* at which the program will be evaluated (*From what sources will this knowledge be obtained? What areas or components of the program will be evaluated?*) Evaluation is needed at many levels of program operation. *Structure evaluation* involves an examination of the effectiveness of a program's organizational structure and its administrative policy and procedure. For example, evaluation at this level would be concerned with personnel management variables such as recruiting, scheduling, upgrading, and capital investment.
    System evaluation examines the effectiveness of various "pieces" or components

of the total program to determine their contribution. This kind of evaluation is designed to assess the specific systems of program operation that are responsible for the specific results that have been obtained. This is important, since not all of the positive and negative results of program operation are expected or even goal-related, and such unforeseen results should be evaluated and accounted for. For example, if the morale of staff in one department of a human service program is higher than that of staff in another department, it is necessary to evaluate the ongoing process responsible.

Outcome evaluation examines the program's outcomes or products. This requires that the adequacy (quality, quantity), efficiency, and effectiveness of program performance be evaluated relative to patient needs; resources (including materials, funding, personnel, etcetera); program goals and objectives; local and national standards for human service programming; and attitudes of staff and patients concerning program operation.

It is also important to evaluate the services provided *to the program* as well as those provided *by the program*. For example, if the manager contracts with outside consultants or businesses for services, the adequacy and cost-effectiveness of those services should be evaluated. This is greatly facilitated by contracts that clearly specify expected products and time-lines.

Finally, the manager must determine how these types of data will be generated. This involves *getting program structure, process, and outcome into measurable form.* Throughout this book, we have described the importance of specifying goals and objectives; defining performance operationally; and observing, recording, and graphing performance at baseline and follow-up. We have also recommended the use of certain forms and checklists to structure performance and to generate permanent product data for evaluation.

For example, in Chapter 5, we listed forms and procedures for use in evaluating staff performance and patient progress. Later in this chapter, we will discuss forms and procedures for internal and external peer review of program operations. Procedures for evaluating organizational structure, policy, and procedure (Chapter 3), staff orientation and training (Chapter 4), and staff scheduling (Chapter 5) have also been described. All of this takes place as part of the systematic planning for evaluation that was described in Chapter 2. In short, the manager is always working to ensure that his or her program is accountable by ensuring that its operation is measurable.

3.   Identifying and researching *systems and procedures* that are most effective in generating the types of data desired and in analyzing the results expected (*What strategies will be employed in an effort to obtain this knowledge?*). We have already described the criteria that any evaluation procedure should meet (see pages 108–09). Briefly, for an evaluation system or a particular evaluation procedure to be of any value, it should be standardized; be easily administered; yield reliable and objective data; provide results that are representative of program operation and interpretable by program staff; and provide both positive and negative feedback about program operation. The results of the evaluation should *pinpoint the program's deficits* in such a way as to suggest corrections. Most importantly, program evaluation systems and procedures should be designed primarily to serve a feedback function and only secondarily as a means of dealing with problems, or weeding out procedures or employees.

4.   Deciding how the task of program evaluation will be performed (*How will systems and procedures be implemented? Who will implement them?*). Specifically, the manager should contract with both internal and external evaluators for specific tasks, time-lines, and products. *Internal* evaluators might include a "program evaluation specialist" who is employed, trained, and supervised by program management to perform evaluation and feedback tasks. The training for this individual should be specialized and his or her work performance standards (especially products and time-lines) should be thoughtfully developed. Internal evaluation can also be provided by program staff

who may serve as inter- or intra-departmental peer reviewers and evaluators. For example, staff from one department might review the treatment procedures employed by staff in another department as preparation for an external review by the Joint Commission for the Accreditation of Hospitals. In-house evaluation and review can also be conducted by consultants who are employed by or work closely with one's program.

External review and evaluation can be provided by professional associations; regulatory agencies; consultants not involved with the program, who have expertise in some area of program operation; members of the public; representatives of social service agencies; and staff from other human service programs. External evaluation is essential if the manager hopes to obtain accurate, unbiased feedback about program operation. External evaluation also provides feedback useful in checking the reliability of in-house evaluation. In fact, this type of external "social validation" is essential if the program is to become accountable to the professional community as well as to the general public.

Decisions must also be made about the *materials and equipment* to be used in evaluation, the *costs* of manpower, materials, space, and equipment, and the ways in which resources and financial support are to be obtained, budgeted, and so on. For example, feasibility studies might be conducted to determine the potential value of computer storage and retrieval, word processing and duplication, and audiovisual and electronic recording capabilities. When these decisions have been reached, the manager must take the steps necessary to obtain the resources required.

The next task, *goal specification*, is required since program evaluation is ultimately concerned with the progress that a program is making toward its stated mission, goals, and objectives. As described in Chapter 2, *goals* must be understandable, practical, and achievable. They should also be defined in terms of observable, measurable components so as to facilitate their evaluation. Finally, they should be consistent with the program's mission and realistic with respect to the resources and technology required to achieve them. *Objectives* should be even more specific, identifying the key conditions under which a performance is expected to occur and indicating the criteria for successful performance. (We recommend returning to Chapter 2, pages 19–23 at this point for more information about specifying goals and objectives and for a review of Mager's (1972) "goal analysis" procedure.)

As previously described, *baseline assessment* is also an essential component of any evaluation effort. It involves determining the level of performance or status of program operation that exists before the implementation of a policy, procedure, and so on or the passage of a specific period of time. This type of assessment provides a picture of the program that can be compared to a later one so that progress or lack of progress can be determined. Baseline observations, ratings, and assessments must be representative and reliable if they are to be useful in program evaluation.

Follow-up evaluation involves the observation and recording of performance at some point after baseline assessment and utilizes the same sources of data and the same evaluation procedures that were employed at baseline. When follow-up data have been obtained, they should be represented chronologically relative to baseline data on graphs to facilitate visual inspection and analysis. The graphical representation of data should therefore reflect the *evaluation design* being employed.

(Examples of graphical representation were presented in Chapters 2 and 5.) As described in Chapter 2 (page 30), it is also important to check the reliability of follow-up data.

The scheduling of follow-up evaluation is determined by the passage of time and/or the implementation of some policy or procedure that is expected to have some effect on the baseline status of the program. For example, follow-up evaluation conducted in preparation for the program's annual report serves as baseline data for follow-up evaluation conducted prior to the next report. In some cases, the passage of time is not as important as the fact that some new procedure or policy has been implemented. In short, *ongoing evaluation requires ongoing follow-up*.

Analysis and dissemination of results involves the following procedures: (1) analyzing the level of performance (dependent variable) at follow-up relative to that recorded at baseline; (2) determining the apparent effects of each policy or procedure, period of time, and so on (independent variable) on level of performance; (3) considering why desired or predicted results were not obtained; (4) generating recommendations concerning future program structure and operation as well as sources of data, strategies, and so on for future evaluation efforts; and (5) submitting a written report (summary of results and recommendations) to program management, higher authorities, etcetera. Analysis of results is greatly facilitated, and is more likely to be valid and reliable, when outside consultation and in-house peer review of results and recommendations is obtained.

In addition to meeting these criteria, effective program evaluation must be *ongoing* and *coordinated*. As described in Chapter 4, effective personnel management and supervision requires the ongoing monitoring of staff performance and morale, and the tracking of patient progress. Similarly, ongoing evaluation is essential to effective budget management and resource allocation. As we will discuss in Chapter 8, ongoing evaluation is also necessary if patients' rights are to be adequately safeguarded and if the human service program is to operate consistent with applicable local, state, and federal regulations. Coordination is important if program evaluation activity is to be goal-oriented and productive. In addition, we have found that proper coordination makes evaluation much more efficient (for example, minimizing duplication of effort). The use of an *overall framework* for evaluation, supplemented by work performance contracting, is the best way to ensure this type of coordination.[1]

STRATEGIES FOR IN-HOUSE EVALUATION

In-house evaluation procedures are performed by program staff and consultants who are likely to have a vested interest in seeing the program portrayed in a positive light. The major advantage of in-house evaluation is that it is performed by individuals who know the program and, presumably, its strengths and deficits; the major disadvantage is that internal evaluation is more likely to be biased than evaluation performed by individuals with no vested interest in the program.

Nevertheless, we view ongoing, in-house evaluation as an important feature of proactive management. In addition, we have found that, by carefully training in-house evaluators, making them aware of the effects of bias and the importance of their remaining unbiased, and checking the reliability of their observations, recordings and recommendations, in-house procedures can provide the manager with much reliable and useful information.

The most commonly used form of in-house evaluation involves the collection and analysis of data considered to be representative of program operation. First, the manager specifies goals and objectives for each department or component of the organization and determines the types of data required to evaluate adequately the department's structure, performance, and productivity. Next, the manager develops work performance standards for each department supervisor that specify the evaluation procedures to be employed, (forms, checklists, assessment instruments), the timetable for their implementation, the types of data to be collected, and how the data are to be analyzed and reported.

At regular intervals, the manager should receive a written report of each department's activities and achievements during the previous evaluation period. The report should also include information concerning the department's plans for the next evaluation period (activities, achievements) as well as indications of its current and future needs (personnel, material resources). These evaluative reports from department supervisors, when checked for reliability, represent the major permanent product output of program evaluation. The overall framework for such a system is described in the final section of this chapter.

However, while the ongoing collection and analysis of permanent product data is the most essential component of the in-house evaluation system, it should not be the only component. We have found that, when permanent product assessment is supplemented by procedures designed to monitor patient progress and to obtain peer review of program structure and process, in-house evaluation can come to be viewed as an effective quality assurance procedure.

Patient Tracking Systems

In order to determine reliably the quantity, quality, and effectiveness of the services patients receive, it is critical that assessment occur not only at intake (baseline) and follow-up, but that periodic evaluations be made of the patient's progress. The purpose of the patient tracking system (Christian, Clark, & Luke, 1981) is to coordinate services for each patient, ensuring that the patient receives treatment based on his or her needs, periodic reviews of progress, and protections that are his or hers by law and by the standards of good professional practice. In effect, the patient tracking system prompts the service provider to attend to these activities in a timely manner.

We have used two types of tracking systems in human service settings. One involves the use of a *worksheet* which prompts the provider to complete various activities with a given patient or group of patients at particular times during the course of service delivery. For example, in the clinical counseling program of a community mental health center, the worksheet may prompt the therapist to complete an assessment of the patient's presenting problem during the first session and request that certain baseline data be kept by the patient (or his or her legal guardians) for presentation at the second session. During the second session, the worksheet may prompt the therapist to develop a preliminary treatment plan for the patient and begin its implementation. At this point, the worksheet might also prompt a review of the treatment plan by a Human Rights Committee (see Chapter 8).

After six sessions, the therapist in this example would be prompted to review the case in a professional staff meeting as a form of *in-house peer review*. The purpose of this review would be to determine the level of progress that is being achieved and to obtain recommendations for future treatment. A second review by the Human Rights Committee may also be prompted at this point. If adequate progress is not being made or if there is some risk to the patient's rights or welfare, an alternative treatment plan must be developed or alternative services sought for the patient.

After twelve weeks of service, the patient tracking system would prompt a *complete review of the patient's progress* and the goals of the treatment plan by therapist, patient, referring agency representatives, legal guardians, and others. (Human service project forms, see Chapter 5, are very useful in reviewing patient progress). The tracking worksheet would also prompt other progress reviews throughout the course of the patient's treatment to ensure that the therapist attends to all components of the transition from active treatment through termination and follow-up.

Another type of tracking system is to provide regular *overview* of all patients served by a particular service provider, housed in a particular unit or ward, and so on. The kind of information that is monitored in this system is situation-specific and depends on the type of service being delivered. For example, at regular intervals the unit supervisor of a nursing home would receive a form that includes the following information for each of the patients under his or her supervision: (a) date of admission; (b) date of current treatment plan; (c) dates of progress review; and (d) proposed date of patient's discharge. This type of information can also be included on patient status reports (Chapter 5, page 103) to provide the therapist, supervisor, manager, regulatory agency, and so on, with a clear picture of how the patient is progressing through the program or service system. At the very least, this type of tracking helps to ensure that the patient is not lost in the sequence of service delivery.

In short, both types of patient tracking system provide a method for evaluating the *process* and *outcome* of service delivery. We have also used these procedures to evaluate certain aspects of program *structure*. For example, the business office can include information on the tracking worksheet that indicates to the therapist whether or not the patient in counseling is paying his or her bill. The business office can use the overview form of patient tracking to indicate whether a therapist has completed the necessary forms to ensure timely Title XX reimbursement.

We have also used a combination of the overview and worksheet methods, although such a system is difficult to implement unless one has access to some form of computer storage and retrieval. When both tracking methods are used, the first system involves a form for each of the various types of service (for example, outpatient counseling, residential treatment) which prompts a sequence of events unique to that service. In this case, the worksheet can be viewed as an extension of the staff monitoring checklist described in Chapter 5 (page 102) with service delivery as the task to be performed and monitored. The second, overview, tracking system uses information stored in a memory typewriter or word processing unit. This information is updated and redistributed at regular intervals to service providers, supervisors, and the program manager, who in turn provide information to keep the overview current. In this way, information is always available concerning the current status of service delivery across patients, service providers, and departments. (An example of such an expanded overview tracking system is presented in Appendix F).

Peer Review

We recommend the use of three forms of in-house peer review: (a) treatment team meetings, (b) performance appraisal, and (c) evaluation of case record documentation. The use of *treatment team meetings* was described in Chapter 5 (page 104). Briefly, these meetings bring staff and their supervisors together each week to review the progress of a particular group of patients. We have also used this format to have staff from one department or unit review the progress of patients being served by staff from another department or unit.

Peer review of performance can be provided at both the direct service and supervisory levels. For example, a nurse may be asked to evaluate the performance of a co-worker. Forms such as the staff monitoring checklist and the employee feedback form (see Chapter 5) can be modified for use in this type of peer review. Supervisory-level, interdepartmental peer review can also be periodically conducted using a form such as that presented in Appendix F. Care should be taken to see that peer review and feedback procedures meet the criteria specified in our earlier discussion of performance appraisal (pages 108–21).

Case record review (Christian *et al.*, 1981) is a type of peer review and evaluation procedure that involves both meetings and performance appraisal. Case records provide a number of valuable sources of data for program evaluation. In many human service settings, it is the case record that includes documentation concerning patient contact with the program and the adequacy and effectiveness of the services that he or she receives. In addition, the case record generally reflects the extent to which human service personnel understand the patient's needs and his or her legal rights regarding treatment; the patient understands his or her rights; and the patient's rights are protected in prescribing and administering treatment procedures.

Case record review involves six general procedures: (1) establishing standards for case records; (2) developing forms and procedures for reviewing records;

(3) establishing the record review committee; (4) conducting record review; (5) providing feedback to staff (and to the patient, in the case of rights violations); and (6) conducting a follow-up review of records. *Case record standards* are determined by patients' rights (for example, standards concerning treatment plans and progress notes, evidence of informed consent, safeguards for confidentiality) as well as information required by the program and its state and federal regulatory agencies. A manual of these standards should include forms, procedures, and specific instructions concerning how to locate items in the record, add items to the record, and maintain the record in its required form. Samples of acceptable case notes should also be provided. Staff should be required to read the manual and become thoroughly familiar with its contents as part of their orientation to the program. Changes in the standards manual should be accompanied by in-service training for staff in the use of new forms or procedures.

The *record review form* should be easy to use but comprehensive enough to address both the quantitative and qualitative aspects of case record documentation. Quantitative ratings indicate whether a required item is *present* in the record and *signed* by the appropriate parties. Qualitative ratings indicate the record's internal *consistency* (for example, are progress notes consistent with the patient's plan of treatment and his or her presenting problems?) as well as the *appropriateness* of the program of services given the patient's needs (for example, is the patient receiving the appropriate types of services for the nature and severity of his or her problem? Is the patient making adequate progress in his or her present plan of treatment?). Therefore, record review is also useful in evaluating staff performance and their compliance with program policy and procedure.

We have also used the record review form to obtain input from the staff member reviewing the record—for example, what are the major strengths and weaknesses of this record?. This type of peer feedback is an important aspect of record review since it provides an opportunity for staff to make recommendations that may affect the program's future policy and procedure concerning case record documentation and maintenance. A sample record review form which we have used in a variety of human service settings is presented in Appendix F.

The *record review committee* should include members of the program staff (direct service, support service, supervisory level personnel) who are oriented, trained, and provided with standards for record review, and who serve on the committee for a limited period of time (for example, a three-month committee rotation). Membership on the committee can be identified as a special project on an employee's work performance standards and appropriate performance as a committee member can be rewarded with bonus rewards as described in Chapter 5. The program's patient advocate (or an individual with similar responsibilities) should serve as the committee's chairperson.

We recommend monthly or bimonthly committee meetings with each committee member being responsible for reviewing up to three case records in advance of each meeting. The number of committees, the size of each committee, and the frequency of committee meetings are determined by the number of patients served by the program and the program's goals and objectives for record review. When more than one committee is used, chairpersons should meet regularly to coordinate review activity.

The actual *tasks of record review, evaluation, and feedback* involve the following procedures:

1. Cases are randomly selected for review from patient files by the chairperson of the record review committee.

2. Cases are assigned to committee members one week prior to committee meeting by the committee chairperson.

3. Committee members complete a record review form for each case assigned to them, having no contact with program staff involved in the case.

4. A copy of each completed review form is presented to the committee chairperson the day before the scheduled committee meeting. (We strongly recommend checking the reliability of record review ratings.) At the meeting, members present the cases assigned to them, going over the completed form. The committee agrees as to the nature of the feedback that the case manager should receive (for example, praise for an acceptable record, corrective feedback for an unacceptable record). In addition, the committee agrees as to apparent violations of patients' rights (for example, no progress review, no signed plan of treatment).

5. In the event that there are no rights violations, the committee chairperson or the case manager's supervisor provides feedback concerning record-keeping performance and discusses any instances of noncompliance with agency standards.

6. Committee chairperson submits a written report concerning each client rights violation as well as any extenuating circumstances to the program manager and to the program's Human Rights Committee (See Chapter 8). At this time, the committee chairperson and the case manager decide on procedures for notifying the patient (legal guardian) concerning rights violations and informing the patient concerning grievance procedures. This meeting is documented in the form of a case note and is initialed by the patient.

7. Program manager files report on rights violations to higher authority (for example, Board of Trustees, Governor's Advisory Board).

8. Follow-up record review is conducted by the committee to see that the rights violation was reported to the patient and the situation (and any instances of non-compliance with program standards) has been improved to the extent possible.

9. Performance feedback (and disciplinary action if applicable) is provided to the case manager and in-service training is conducted on patients' rights issues, compliance with case record standards, and so on.

10. Written records are maintained of all committee activity for review by the Human Rights Committee, professional peer reviewers, regulatory agencies, etcetera.

STRATEGIES FOR EXTERNAL EVALUATION

As we have already mentioned, evaluation conducted by individuals from outside the program is more likely to provide the manager with candid, unbiased feedback concerning program operation. External evaluators and reviewers can also serve to validate or check the reliability of the methods used and results reported by in-house evaluators. Further, going outside of the program for review and evaluation services affords the manager the necessary flexibility to select individuals with special expertise in human service programming and evaluation.

There are two general sources of external evaluation for the human service program: consumers and consultants. *Consumers* are individuals (and their legal guardians) who have received or are receiving services from the program, and representatives of agencies that are involved with patient referral and funding. *Consultants* are individuals who are neither consumers of services nor employees of the program. Consultants provide services to the program in the form of evaluation, review, and consultation.

Consumer Evaluation

Consumer evaluation should be conducted on an *ongoing* basis (as services are being received) and at *follow-up* (at some point after services have been discontinued). This type of evaluation is best accomplished by the use of written questionnaires or surveys designed to elicit feedback concerning the following aspects of service delivery:

1. Planning for service delivery (goals and objectives for treatment, needs assessment, and so on).
2. Procedures utilized in service delivery.
3. Personnel providing services.
4. Facilities in which services are delivered.
5. Cost of services.
6. Effort required for participation in service program or procedure.
7. Effectiveness of services received.
8. Feedback from program concerning services received (progress reports).
9. Communication with referring and funding agencies (for example, completion of reports to ensure reimbursement for services, progress reports).
10. Overall impression of program and services received.
11. Recommendations concerning ways in which services can be improved.
12. Additional comments.

For example, patients can be asked to complete a questionnaire which addresses these issues at the time of their three- or six-month progress reviews, and again shortly after services are terminated. Suggestion boxes can also be provided so that patients and visitors to the program can submit anonymous feedback in the form of completed questionnaires or notes. A questionnaire can also be used to structure telephone interviews with former patients. An example of a consumer evaluation questionnaire for use with patients is presented in Appendix F.

Evaluation can also be provided by agencies responsible for referring the patient to the program and/or funding the services he or she receives. A questionnaire developed for this purpose should include items which elicit feedback concerning the agency's satisfaction with the services provided the patient and with the extent to which program staff were cooperative, professional, diplomatic, and so on in their interactions with representatives of the agency.

We have included an example of a form for use in obtaining feedback from a social service agency in Appendix F. This form can be adapted for use in obtaining feedback from other agencies involved with one's program, such as courts and school districts. Modifications of this form can also be used to obtain evaluative feedback from the Board of Trustees, and from the local community.

Consultant Evaluation

In our experience, human service managers typically make neither adequate nor effective use of outside consultants. The probable reasons for this are that managers do not always know when they *need* a consultant, how to *get* a consultant when they need one, and how to *manage* the consultant when they get one. Regarding the question of need, our position is firm and unequivocal: *Outside consultants should be utilized on an ongoing basis by every human service manager.* Frequent, unbiased review and consultation is essential to ensure that the manager is receiving valid, reliable feedback about program operation.

Obtaining and managing the services of a consultant require careful planning. *Selecting a consultant* is very similar to recruiting supervisory personnel. The prospective consultant should pass the following qualifications: (1) good interpersonal skills; (2) training and expertise in the specific areas of program operation for which consultation is needed; (3) previous experience in the evaluation of human service programs with similar patient populations, services, personnel, and consultation needs; (4) ability to observe, record, evaluate, and report change in staff performance and program operation; (5) good writing skills; (6) ability to model appropriate behaviors for staff, patients, board members, local citizens, and so on; and (7) ability to work effectively in a contract-for-service situation—that is, the ability to work independently as well as to accept direction. In addition, it is always a good idea to obtain information concerning previous work performed by the prospective consultant.

Managing the performance of the consultant is similar to managing staff performance with one important exception: care should be taken to afford the consultant sufficient flexibility to conduct a comprehensive evaluation. The manager should avoid temptations to control or bias the consultant's findings and recommendations. A *performance contract* should be negotiated with the consultant in advance of his or her visit to the program, specifying on-site agenda, tasks, time-lines for completion, and products. (Of course, consultant services can also be provided by written correspondence and telephone contacts. In this case, written documentation should be sent to the consultant to ensure that he or she will be adequately informed when making his or her recommendations.) While the consultant should be afforded flexibility in his or her choice of procedures, the manager should possess a knowledge of program evaluation sufficient to determine the appropriateness of the procedures selected.

We also recommend contracting with the consultant for a *brief presentation to program staff*. The consultant should use this opportunity to praise staff for the positive aspects of their performance, brief them concerning the purposes and findings of the consultation, and encourage their effective performance in the future. The consultant should also be asked to give a brief statement of his or her area of expertise, professional affiliation, research interests, and so on, and to provide a short presentation on a topic within his or her area of expertise. Staff should be given a period in which to question the consultant. In this way, in-service training is supplemented and the work environment made more stimulating.

The contract should specify that payment of any fees to the consultant is contingent upon the timely submission of a *written report* summarizing his or her findings and recommendations. This is an important contingency since the report represents the most important product of consultant performance. If this report is properly developed, it can provide several important functions for the manager. As previously stated, it can be used to validate the results of in-house evaluation. It can also be used as a vehicle for debriefing program staff following the consultant's visit, promoting good public relations for the program (for example, sharing reports with the program's Board of Trustees, and potential referring agencies), and for advocating increased funding and resources. Most importantly, it provides follow-up data for program operation in the past and baseline data (and needs assessment) for program operation in the future.

Given the importance of the consultant's evaluative report, we recommend developing a standard format for the report that can be included in the consultant's performance standards. We have found the following format quite useful in this regard.

Outline for the Consultant's Evaluative Report

1. Summary
   a. Purpose of the consultation.
   b. Findings.
   c. Recommendations.
2. Table of contents
3. Consultant(s)
   a. Affiliation.
   b. Expertise.
4. Acknowledgements
5. Body of report
   a. Purpose of consultation.
   b. Focus (areas of program evaluated).
   c. Procedures employed.
   d. Description of the program.
   e. Exemplary aspects of the program.
   f. Recommendations for improvement.
   g. Plans for follow-up.
   h. Concluding comments.
6. References (for publications cited in report)
7. Appendices

Reimbursement for the consultant's services should be provided as soon as possible after the submission of the evaluative report. Reimbursement should include payment for expenses incurred by the consultant in traveling to the program and conducting the evaluation (air fare, hotel accommodations, meals) and a fee for the consultant's services. Some consultants charge a fee for their time (by the hour or by the day); others may be willing to have their fee based on some product of their effort, independent of the time taken to produce it (that is, a project cost). Manager and consultant should therefore negotiate a fee and payment schedule, in advance, as a part of the performance contract. We also suggest providing a bonus payment contingent upon above-standard performance by the consultant (for example, early submission of the summary report). This bonus contingency should be carefully specified in the performance agreement.

A final word about the utilization of consultants. The manager must remember that a good consultant should provide frank, objective feedback that will not always be positive. It is often the case that managers obtain consultant services, only to be defensive when presented with the results. In short, the manager should follow the rules for providing and receiving feedback that we presented in Chapter 5 (page 116). In addition, the manager should provide feedback to the consultant concerning his or her performance in evaluating the program and reporting results and recommendations.

We also recommend the utilization of Professional Advisory Boards and professional peer review. The *Professional Advisory Board* is a means of obtaining *ongoing, informal* evaluative feedback with a minimum investment of time, effort, and money. The membership of a Professional Advisory Board for a human service program should include individuals with demonstrated expertise in various areas of programming and administration. At a minimum, such a board should consist of a physician (M.D.), psychologist (Ph.D.), attorney, management consultant, and accountant.

Professional Advisory Board members should be appointed to renewable one-year terms and, if possible, should visit the program (as salaried consultants) prior to, or soon after, their appointment. This visit provides each member with a basis for making recommendations and providing feedback to the manager as well as a ''baseline view'' of the program for use in evaluating change and progress during his or her tenure. However, it is important to note that Advisory Board members do not engage in frequent on-site consultation during the year. Frequent visits would be too costly and too taxing on the individual's time. The manager shares information with, and receives feedback from, Advisory Board members via written correspondence and telephone conversation. This informal aspect of Professional Advisory Board operation is what distinguishes it from the more formal use of salaried consultants and professional peer reviewers.

Professional Advisory Board members do not receive a retainer, and are only reimbursed if they provide formal on-site consultation and submit a written evaluative report of their results and recommendations. Professionals are willing to serve in this capacity for several reasons: they enjoy the prestigious role of consultant and appreciate that the demands put on them are limited; they are involved in a public service for which they obtain reinforcement from their employers and professional colleagues; they enjoy the opportunity to help others; and they find the human service environment a stimulating one.

Other rewards for Professional Advisory Board membership can be provided by the program manager: (1) maintenance of communication concerning program operation (for example, annual reports); (2) presentation of certificates of appreciation for service on the Advisory Board; (3) publication of Advisory Board membership in program brochures and on program letterhead; and (4) communication of positive feedback from program staff, management, Boards of Trustees, and so on. However, the most important reinforcer for these individuals is *consideration*. The manager will not take advantage of their willingness to assist the program.

Professional peer review differs from the Professional Advisory Board in that it is more *problem-oriented* in its focus and more *formal* in its operating procedure. In addition, professional peer review, as we will describe it here, is performed by individuals who have neither any association with, nor a vested interest in, the program.

It is important that the human service manager understand how *professional peer review* is conducted because, in some cases, he or she may have little control over the actual conduct of the review. For example, a state may ask a professional association (for example, the American Psychiatric Association) to conduct a peer review of a service program (for example, a psychiatric treatment center) suspected of some controversial practice. In this case, the manager of a state-administered human service program can do little more than be cooperative and informative.

We have been involved with a number of professional peer reviews—as both reviewers and reviewees—and have found a number of procedures useful in preparing to be reviewed as well as in contracting for peer review services. *Preparing to be reviewed* involves several steps:

1. Obtain as much advance information as possible about *why* the review is being conducted (problems, goals); *what* specific areas of program operation will be reviewed; *how* the review will be conducted (for example, on-site review of program and/or off-site review of documentation); and *who* will be conducting the review (names, affiliations, areas of expertise).
2. Obtain a detailed list of written materials (case records, audited accounts, and so on) that reviewers will need to examine. If possible, send this information in advance of their visit and have it readily available for inspection when they arrive on site.
3. Obtain a detailed agenda for the review (days, times, program staff to be interviewed, topics, etcetera) and have office space reserved for the reviewers.
4. Prepare staff for the review by explaining purpose and agenda; identifying their roles in the review; reviewing the guidelines for giving and receiving feedback (page 116); and rehearsing review procedures, and providing feedback for staff performance.

Contracting for professional peer review is an excellent example of proactive management. As noted by Risley and Sheldon-Wildgen (1980, p. 5): "With the increasing tendency of the public to question professional therapeutic practices, it has not been surprising that therapists and administrators of therapeutic programs have begun to initiate a review of their own programs and practices, either as a response to present criticism or in an attempt to avoid potential problems'' In short, while professional peer review can be very threatening to the reactive manager, it can prove to be a useful evaluation procedure for the proactive manager.

There are two forms of professional peer review: case consultation and program review. *Case consultation* involves a review of service programming for a particular patient. In this case, the manager would contract with a professional who has had considerable experience working with that particular type of patient or presenting problem. This type of peer review should produce (1) an assessment of the patient's present treatment plan (what it includes and why it is or is not effective); (2) a revised treatment plan (if necessary); and (3) a method for evaluating, and providing a follow-up review of, the revised plan. Case consultation may include a visit to the program or may be conducted off-site via telephone conversation, review of case records and related documentation, and written reports and correspondence.

Case consultation is designed to protect patient, therapist, and manager from the obvious limitation of every human service program, that is, that service providers cannot be trained and experienced in the treatment of every presenting problem. In addition, there are times when referral to an appropriate specialist is not possible.

Program review is more comprehensive than case consultation and, therefore, more useful in program evaluation. In fact, case consultation is often conducted as a component of program review. Program reviews typically involve an off-site examination of written materials (for example, policy and procedure manuals, organizational charts, annual reports) followed by an on-site review of the program. The most informative and effective program review is conducted by *peer review committees*, groups of individuals with extensive expertise specific to the program to be reviewed.

Contracting and planning for program review involves the following steps:

1. Identifying Goals and Objectives for Program Review
   a. Type of review needed.
   b. Areas of program to be reviewed.
2. Identifying Standards or Criteria for Program Review
   a. Legal policy.
   b. Regulatory guidelines.
   c. Research literature indicating the current state-of-the-art of human service programming.
   d. Program's goals and objectives.
   e. Program's patient population.
3. Establishing the Peer Review Committee
   a. Specifying areas of expertise needed.
   b. Identifying and contacting potential reviewers with the necessary expertise (through professional organizations, colleagues, local universities, and so on).
   c. Specifying performance standards for each reviewer (program area and task assignment.
   d. Negotiating performance agreements and completing contracts for service.

4. Planning for On-Site Activity
    a. Developing an agenda.
    b. Collecting written materials.
    c. Preparing staff.
    d. Developing review forms and guidelines.

Forms and guidelines function to structure the program review by providing prompts for the reviewers. Depending on the comprehensiveness of the review, the following areas of the program might be reviewed:

1. Administrative organization and personnel management.
2. Service programming.
3. Budget/accounting operations.
4. Case records.
5. Patients' rights.
6. Program evaluation.
7. Maintenance and security of buildings, grounds, equipment and supplies.
8. Public relations and consumer evaluation.
9. Fund raising.
10. Applied research.
11. Utilization of consultants
12. University affiliation.

For each of these areas, the reviewer should be provided with a list of "what to look for" in determining if the program is operating consistent with pertinent standards and criteria. The program manager's work performance standards (see pages 60 to 67) are useful in this regard. For example, the following performance standards might be used as criteria to structure a review of administrative organization and personnel management.

Program Area: Administrative organization and personnel management

    General: Administrative structure and staffing sufficient to support a progressive, comprehensive program of services designed to meet the special needs of the target population; administrative, direct service, and support service staff with education, training, and certification (if applicable), and in numbers sufficient to meet or exceed the requirements of pertinent state and federal licensing and funding agencies concerning personnel and the quality and quantity of services provided.
  A. Effective recruitment, orientation, training, supervision and evaluation of appropriately qualified administrative staff (for example, program manager and department supervisors) and support staff (for example, occupational therapist, activities coordinator, social worker, health care coordinator, language development specialist, and parent training specialists). Effective recruitment, orientation, training, supervision and evaluation of appropriately qualified direct service (nurses, health care specialists, teachers, teacher aides, and residential staff) and support service staff (for example, clerical, food service, maintenance personnel).

1. Orientation of new personnel completed within first week of their employment.
2. Training for new personnel completed within first month of their employment. Utilization of training model and methods which have been shown to equip staff with skills necessary for effective management and education of the patient population.
3. Maintenance of staff-to-patient ratio appropriate to the special needs of the patient population.
4. Written work performance standards for each employee appropriate to the needs of the program, the skills of the employee, and pertinent regulatory and licensing requirements of supervisory agencies; standards signed by the employee, his or her direct supervisor, and the program manager, within the first six weeks of an individual's employment. Review and/or revision of an employee's work performance standards when necessary *and* at the anniversary date of an individual's employment; written agreement of employee, direct supervisor, and program manager required for revision of standards.
5. Written evaluation of each employee's performance relative to the standards specified for his or her position, completed and approved in writing by the employee, his or her supervisor, and the program manager at six-month intervals from date of employment.
6. Weekly meetings of department supervisor with departmental staff; bimonthly meetings with the general staff to provide consultation, ongoing communication, inservice training, and/or clarification of program policy and procedures.
7. Daily monitoring of staff performance by visits to hospital, residential, classroom, and other areas of the physical plant.

B. Comprehensive manual of personnel policy and procedure describing all aspects of program operation.

C. Current chart of administrative organization showing staff positions, lines of authority, names of supervisors, and so on available for inspection by each employee.

D. Maintenance of current and complete personnel files for each employee as per regulatory agency requirements and in-house standards.

E. Competitive salaries and benefits for all staff within the limits of the program budget.

F. Current profile of the program staff available for inspection, including positions; name(s) of employee(s) at each position; salary range for each position; and employee's highest academic degree and certification (if applicable).

G. Adherence to Equal Opportunity/Affirmative Action and regulatory agency/state guidelines concerning all aspects of personnel management.

A form can also be used to facilitate the reviewer's task and to ensure that he or she obtains the kind of information most likely to result in a satisfactory evaluative report. (See Appendix F for an example of a peer reviewer's evaluation form.)

On-site peer review involves the following procedural steps:

A. Initial Conference with Key Program Staff
   1. Introduction of reviewers and program staff.
   2. Discussion concerning purpose, goals, and objectives for review.
   3. Review of agenda.
   4. Questions and answers.
B. Review Activity
   1. Examination of written materials.
   2. Examination of Human Rights Committee minutes (see Chapter 8).
   3. Tour of facility.
   4. Observation of staff performance and patient behavior.
   5. Interviews with key staff.
   6. Interviews with patients, representatives of local social service agencies, members of the local community, and others.
C. Wrap-up Meeting of Review Committee
   1. Brief summary by each reviewer.
   2. Preparation for debriefing program staff.
D. Debriefing Program Staff
   1. Purpose.
   2. Findings.
      a. Exemplary areas.
      b. Areas in need of improvement.
   3. Recommendations.
E. Preparation and Dissemination of Written Report
F. Follow-up
   1. Obtaining satisfaction ratings from key staff of program reviewed.
   2. Feedback from reviewers concerning how to improve future reviews.
   3. Monitoring program concerning follow-through on reviewers' recommendations.
      a. Written reports.
      b. Telephone contact.
      c. Additional on-site review.

The development of the summary report of professional peer review should follow the guidelines listed earlier in this chapter (see page 163). The importance of this report and its many uses have also been described.

A FRAMEWORK FOR
PROGRAM EVALUATION

To ensure that evaluation efforts occur on an ongoing basis, and that they are sufficiently comprehensive and coordinated, we recommend the use of a framework for program evaluation. A framework that we have found particularly useful in human service settings is one that is based on the development and dissemination of biannual progress reports to the program's ultimate supervising authority, that is, Boards of Trustees or supervising state officials.

First, the manager *develops a format for the biannual report* based upon feedback from staff, consultants, and the supervising authorities themselves. The format should include data documenting the program's efforts to meet its mission, goals, and objectives as well as its adherence to pertinent legal guidelines, regulatory requirements, and so on. The format should also include whatever additional information board members and state officials may require. In our experience, these individuals are particularly interested in information concerning program stability (for example, finances, licensing, patient enrollment), while also wanting to keep up with "what is happening to the patient."

Sample Format for Biannual Progress Report [2]

1. Administrative organization
   a. Changes in administrative organization during evaluation period.
   b. Current administrative organization chart.
2. Staffing
   a. Demographic data including current number of personnel by department and mean/range age, sex, educational level.
   b. New staff (by position) during the past six months.
   c. Current staffing ratios by shift.
   d. Staff turnover during past six months.
   e. Results of staff training conducted during past six months.
   f. Current work performance standards for each staff position (in each year's first biannual report).
   g. Current profile of the program staff—positions, names of employees at each position, salary range for each position, highest academic degree and certification, if applicable, for each employee (in each year's first biannual report).
3. Services
   a. Changes in existing service programs during evaluation period.
   b. New service programs.
   c. Plans for next evaluation period.
4. Patients served
   a. Mean operational capacity during past six months.
   b. Demographic data for population including mean/range age, sex, length of stay, etcetera.
   c. Demographic data for new admissions including number; mean/range age, sex; in-state versus out-of-state; source of payment for treatment.
   d. Number of inquiries concerning admission.
   e. Number of completed applications for admission.
   f. Number accepted and awaiting admission.
   g. Sources of referral.
   h. Demographic data for patients discharged during past six months including number, age, length of stay.
   i. New placements for patients discharged (if applicable).
   j. Discharges scheduled during next six months.
   k. Information concerning follow-up status of patients discharged from the program (if applicable).
5. Patients' rights

    a.   Any violation or potential violation of patients' rights discovered during past six months.

    b.   Description of action taken to remedy situation.

6. Parent involvement (if applicable)

    a.   Description of correspondence sent to parents during past six months.

    b.   Progress of parent training and in-home observation/consultation activities.

7. Program evaluation

    a.   Evaluation of services delivered to patients during past six months to determine progress being made toward patients' treatment objectives.

    b.   Results of consumer satisfaction surveys.

    c.   Results of case record review.

    d.   Results of any outside evaluation and site reviews (for example, visits by regulatory agencies, professional peer reviews) completed during past six months.

8. Applied research

    a.   Research projects in progress or completed during past six months.

    b.   Research projects planned during next six months.

9. Budget and accounting

    a.   Report on budgetary status using format developed by the Board Treasurer or the appropriate state official.

    b.   Proposal for budget revisions (if any).

    c.   Tentative projected budget for the next fiscal year (included with each year's second biannual report).

10. Renovation

    a.   Report on renovation projects in progress or completed during past six months.

    b.   Renovation project(s) to be initiated during next six months.

    c.   Analysis of projected costs versus actual expense for each renovation project using forms developed by the Board Treasurer (or appropriate state official).

11. University affiliations.

    a.   Status report for existing affiliations

    b.   Affiliations to be developed during next six months.

12. Professional Advisory Board

    a.   Present membership and any change in membership either occurring during past six months or anticipated for coming six months.

    b.   Schedule of visits made or planned by members of the Professional Advisory Board.

    c.   Copies of any evaluative reports completed by outside consultants during the past six months.

    d.   Copies of newsletters/progress reports sent to members of the Professional Advisory Board.

13. Policy and Procedures

    a.   Any changes made or anticipated in program policy and procedures manual.

14. Public relations

    a.   Public relations activities conducted during past six months and those scheduled for next six months.

b. Manuscripts submitted and/or accepted for publication during the past six months.
c. Conference presentations made and/or papers accepted for conference presentation during the past six months.
d. Professional activities of program staff during past six months that contributed to the program's positive public image.
e. Description of media coverage during past six months; copies of newspaper articles concerning program.

15. Fund raising
a. Local contributions during past six months.
b. Grants funded and/or proposals submitted during past six months.
c. Grant proposals to be submitted during the next six months.
d. Funding from other sources (for example, rate adjustment, CETA) obtained during last six months or anticipated during next six months.

16. Communication with Board of Trustees/State Officials
a. List (brief description) of written communications with the Board of Trustees/pertinent state officials during the past six months.
b. Description of special interim reports to Board/state officials during reporting period.

Second, the manager *prepares and disseminates the report.* The efficiency with which data are assimilated for the report, as well as the quality of the data, will be determined by the program's administrative organization and personnel management strategies. The report procedure will be most successful when the program manager employs the organizational structure and management methods that we have recommended in this book. These include (1) "adaptive" organizational structure; (2) orientation and training for staff in program policy and procedure; (3) work performance contracting; (4) utilization of teams for special projects; and (5) communication and feedback mechanisms to ensure consistency and generalization of program policy and procedure.

The delegation of specific assignments for preparation of the report is accomplished via work performance contracting. Each of the program's key administrative personnel should have work performance standards or objectives that specify his or her responsibilities in program evaluation and progress reporting. (We recommend returning to Chapter 4 at this point to see how this is accomplished in the sample work performance standards we presented.) These key staff work with the program manager as a "project team" that meets at regular intervals to coordinate program evaluation, data compilation and analysis, and preparation of the progress report. Figure 7-1 presents a flow chart which illustrates the responsibilities of the members of a biannual report project team.

When the report is disseminated to board members and program staff it is advisable for the program manager and his or her key staff to be available to provide explanation and clarification. This is best accomplished by circulating copies of the report among program staff and mailing copies to board members at least one week prior to a general staff meeting or board meeting. We have found that more interest and feedback is generated by providing staff and board members with the written report prior to discussing it with them.

Finally, the manager *obtains feedback concerning the report* from board members,

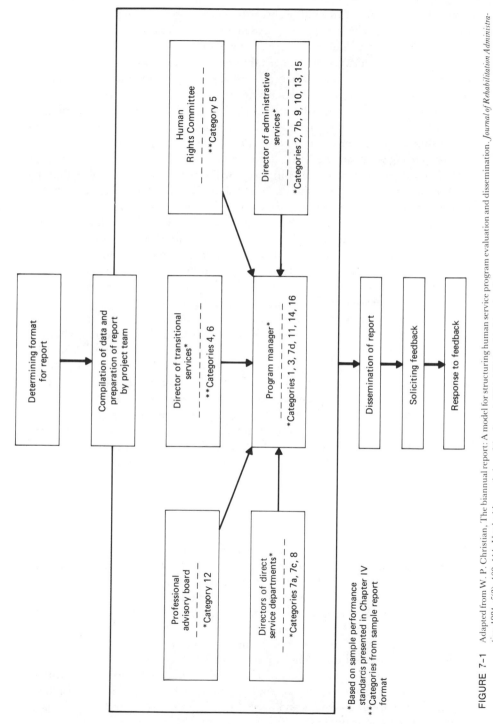

Determining format for report

Compilation of data and preparation of report by project team

Director of transitional services*
** Categories 4, 6

Human Rights Committee
**Category 5

Director of administrative services*
*Categories 2, 7b, 9, 10, 13, 15

Program manager*
*Categories 1, 3, 7d, 11, 14, 16

Professional advisory board
*Category 12

Directors of direct service departments*
*Categories 7a, 7c, 8

Dissemination of report

Soliciting feedback

Response to feedback

*Based on sample performance standards presented in Chapter IV

**Categories from sample report format

FIGURE 7-1   Adapted from W. P. Christian, The biannual report: A model for structuring human service program evaluation and dissemination. *Journal of Rehabilitation Administration,* 1981, *5*(3), 108–114. Used with permission of the *Journal of Rehabilitation Administration, Inc.*

state officials, and program staff to ensure that (1) progress reporting is effective in maintaining interest in and approval of manager performance and program operation; and (2) that necessary revisions are made in future progress reporting. The best way to ensure this type of feedback is to ask for it, for example, by including a letter requesting feedback from board members, or by contacting them by phone for feedback about the report. Furthermore, when changes in reporting format and content are suggested by board members, revisions should be made accordingly.

The rationale for biannual reporting is simply that more frequent preparation of such a comprehensive report is neither time-nor cost-efficient, and less frequent reporting would not be adequate to maintain the continued interest and support of board members and state officials. This does not mean, however, that the types of data included in the biannual report should not be made available to board members and staff on an ongoing basis. As previously stated, ongoing evaluation and feedback are important to staff and must be provided via regular meetings with supervisors, written performance evaluations, preparation of progress reports concerning client progress, and so on. In addition, board members and state officials should receive ongoing feedback via meetings with program staff and written correspondence. *The biannual report does not take the place of ongoing evaluation and feedback activities; it provides an organizational structure for these activities.*

The biannual report can serve a number of functions in addition to sharing feedback with one's board and staff and providing structure for program evaluation efforts. For example, managers of private human service programs can use the report to provide important information to their funding agencies, regulatory boards, and concerned state agencies. The biannual report is also useful in (1) providing outside consultants and professional peer reviewers with information to aid in their evaluation of the program; (2) preparing applications for grants, tuition rate increases, loans, and so on; and (3) providing feedback to professional advisory boards, Human Rights Committees, and the general public. (In cases where the report is shared with the public, care must be taken to see that confidential information is not included.)

SUMMARY

Program evaluation is essential to effective human service management. It includes all procedures employed by the manager in determining the extent to which his or her program is meeting (or has met) its previously established goals and objectives. In designing an effective program evaluation system, the manager is faced with the tasks of planning, goal specification, baseline assessment, follow-up assessment, and analysis of results. Effective planning involves identifying the types of results that evaluation should yield; specifying sources of data for evaluation; determining levels at which the program will be evaluated (structure, system, outcome) and getting levels and systems of program operation into measurable form (for example, through the use of forms and checklists to generate permanent product data); identifying and researching systems and procedures for evaluation; and deciding how the task of evaluation will be performed.

There are three basic components of program evaluation: in-house evaluation activities; external evaluation; and the overall coordinating framework for
evaluation activity. A frequently employed method for *in-house evaluation* of the program involves the collection and analysis of data considered to be representative of
program operation. Other forms of in-house evaluation are the use of a tracking
system and in-house peer review. One type of patient tracking system involves the
use of a worksheet which prompts the service provider to complete various tasks
with a given patient or group of patients during the course of service delivery.
Another type of tracking system is to provide a regular overview of all patients
served by a particular service provider, housed in a particular unit or ward, and so
on. Each type of tracking system assists the manager in evaluating the process and
outcome of service delivery.

There are three types of in-house peer review: treatment team meetings, performance appraisal (for example, interdepartmental review), and case record
review. Case record review involves the following general procedures: establishing
standards for case records; developing forms and procedures for reviewing records;
establishing the record review committee; conducting record review; providing
feedback to staff (and to the patient, in the case of rights violations); and conducting
a follow-up review of records. Case record review, as well as any in-house evaluation procedure, is most likely to be effective when in-house raters and reviewers are
carefully trained in how to use the necessary systems and procedures and how to remain unbiased in the collection and analysis of data concerning the program.

Consumers and consultants are the two general sources of *external evaluation*.
Forms and questionnaires can be used to obtain consumer evaluation, that is,
evaluative feedback from patients, representatives of agencies responsible for patient referral and funding, and other sources such as courts and schools in the local
community. Consultant evaluation can be conducted by individual consultants,
Professional Advisory Boards, and professional peer reviewers. To ensure the effectiveness of the evaluation, the manager should select individuals with sufficient
expertise in the area of the program to be reviewed or evaluated; negotiate a performance contract with the consultant or reviewer specifying on-site agenda, tasks,
time-lines for completion, and products (for example, the preparation of a summary report as per the format provided by the manager); obtain evaluative feedback and act upon the feedback obtained; and provide performance feedback to the
consultant(s) or reviewer(s).

Finally, the manager should employ an overall framework or set of guidelines
to ensure that evaluation efforts occur on an ongoing basis and that they are comprehensive and coordinated. One such framework is based on the development and
dissemination of biannual progress reports to the program's ultimate supervising
authority (Board of Trustees, state officials). The *biannual reporting framework* involves developing a format for the report; preparing and disseminating the report;
obtaining feedback concerning the report; and revising the reporting format as
necessary. The biannual report does not take the place of ongoing evaluation and
feedback activities; it provides an organizational structure for these activities.

8

Safeguarding
Patients' Rights

For many years, the treatment of the human service consumer was left to the discretion of service providers and program managers. More recently, however, the courts recognized that patients in human service programs are citizens and possess the constitutional rights to due process, privacy, and freedom from harm. Once these basic rights were recognized, courts began to inquire into the nature of the treatment that patients receive; their decisions have delineated a comprehensive "bill of rights" for patients. These legal developments have been accompanied by increasing public skepticism about human service programs, by changes in the requirements of regulatory agencies and certifying groups, and by the increased activity and vigilance of advocate groups such as the American Civil Liberties Union.

This critical attention and increased public awareness suggest additional responsibilities and concerns for the human service manager. Virtually every area of program operation must have goals, objectives, performance standards, procedures, and evaluation systems that protect patients' rights in conjunction with the delivery of the highest possible quality of services. It has become increasingly ob vious that if this type of commitment is not made, the program will fail and the manager may become the target of litigation and professional censure.

The challenge facing the human service manager can be operationalized to include the following tasks: (1) understanding the patient, that is, his or her rights as an individual as well as his or her special vulnerability as a function of age, handicap, or presenting problem; (2) educating the patient about his or her rights, about the treatment process, and about the provider's and manager's recognition of patients' rights and their efforts to protect those rights in providing services; and (3) safeguarding patients' rights as an integral part of service delivery, by means of program evaluation and accountability systems, ongoing staff training, and so on. Most importantly, however, as noted by Martin (1981, p. 13): "Practitioners and administrators alike must come to understand that there is not a dichotomy between client rights and good treatment. Rather, therapeutic practices of good quality encompass a sensitivity to the rights of clients as individuals in a free society."

CRITERIA FOR LEGALLY SAFE
HUMAN SERVICE PROGRAMMING

As previously noted, in recent years the human service field has seen a large amount of policy-making and litigation regarding the protection of patients' rights. There are now constitutional safeguards, defined by the courts, that are applicable to those persons being served by human service organizations. Professional organizations have specified ethical standards for human services (for example, Association for the Advancement of Behavior Therapy, 1978) and codes of ethics for their members (for example, American Psychological Association, 1977). In addition, human service programs are subject to the standards and guidelines of national and/or state regulatory and licensing agencies. The manager must know what is expected in this regard and take the necessary steps to develop the appropriate policies and procedures to ensure that the program is accountable.

The first step in creating a legally safe environment for human service programming is to *identify the criteria* or standards for "legal safety." For example, a review of patients' rights litigation reveals a number of standards for human service delivery (Hannah, Christian, & Clark, 1981). Each patient must be provided with an effective, least-restrictive, individualized program of services based on an assessment of his or her special needs. Regular progress reviews must indicate the effectiveness of services provided to the patient or must prompt a revision of the patient's service plan. Procedures utilized in providing services should have a documented history of effectiveness with individuals having problems and needs similar to the patient's. The individual's rights as a patient (for example, informed consent, the right to receive and refuse treatment, confidentiality) and as a human being (for example, dignity, privacy, the right of life) must be safeguarded in providing services. In order to preserve the rights of patients, a human service organization must ensure that its staff and patients are aware of these rights and the program's responsibility to protect them.

Griffith (1980) has identified a number of policies and procedures that are characteristic of the legally safe human service program. These include the following:

1. *Statement of Policy.* The manager should define the program's philosophy of service delivery, indicating the program's commitment to utilize procedures which are appropriate to the patient's needs and most likely to be effective in meeting those needs. The policy should also reflect the program's commitment to the use of the least drastic or intrusive means of reaching a particular treatment or service goal.

2. *Development of Treatment Procedures.* Procedures recommended by staff should be consistent with program policy and procedures. These recommendations should be reviewed and approved by the patient and/or his or her representative. The use of "at risk" procedures is legitimate only when the staff has supporting data showing that less restrictive approaches have been ineffective.

3. *Peer Review.* Professional peer review should be obtained for any controversial procedure to determine whether or not it places the patient at some risk. This ensures an objective assessment of the proposed treatment procedure in conjunction with program policy, as well as a review of the procedure's appropriateness and potential effectiveness.

4. *Informed Consent.* A procedure that involves a potential risk to the patient should not be initiated without the patient's informed consent. The patient or his or her representative should be capable of making reasonable decisions and should be informed as to the nature and potential benefits of the proposed procedure as well as its risks. This information should be communicated to the patient in such a way as to ensure that he or she gives consent without coercion.

5. *Human Rights Committee.* A Human Rights Committee should provide external review sufficient to protect the patient against improper treatment and to ensure that appropriate services are delivered. The committee should serve in an advisory role to program management, by representing the "conscience" of the local community.

After identifying the standards or criteria for legally safe programming, the manager should *assess the current status of his or her program relative to those criteria*. For example, the manager might evaluate his or her program using questions such as the following:

Patients' Rights Review Questions for Managers

1. Does the program provide a pamphlet for each new patient that lists and explains his or her rights as a human service consumer? Is this information written in language that the patient can understand?
2. Have procedures been established for protecting the patient's privacy and the confidentiality of his or her involvement with the program?
3. Is written consent obtained from the patient (or proper representative) to seek and/or give referral information from/to other agencies?
4. Is feedback obtained from the patient regarding his or her own perception of needs, strengths, and treatment goals?
5. Is there an opportunity for a hearing to air any dispute about procedures?
6. Have specific, measurable intermediate and long-range goals and objectives been specified regarding the patient's needs and strengths?
7. Does a method of evaluation exist for each goal and objective?
8. Has there been a full assessment of any medical, neurological, physiological, or psychological causes for the patient's presenting problem that might suggest an alternative approach?

9. Does the patient have access to his or her plan of service (treatment plan)?
10. Does the patient receive services as part of an individualized plan based on his or her special needs?
11. Have procedures been established for periodic review of the patient's plan of service (treatment plan)?
12. Does placement of the patient in the program subject him or her to unequal or unfair circumstances?
13. Have staff received in-service training regarding new developments in legal policy, human service technology, and evaluation strategies?
14. Does the program have a functional Human Rights Committee?
15. Does the Human Rights Committee function to provide an external, unbiased peer review of the services each patient receives?
16. Have policies and procedures been established that regulate the use of seclusion, restraint, physical isolation, and other coercive or restrictive treatment procedures?
17. Have due process procedures been established to ensure that each patient is served using the least restrictive alternative possible?
18. Are adequate written records maintained?
19. Are allegations of abuse investigated?
20. Are program staff sensitive to patient's rights issues, attempting to improve services while minimizing possibilities for abuse?

STRATEGIES FOR ENSURING LEGALLY SAFE HUMAN SERVICE PROGRAMMING

Every human service program can do a better job to ensure that the rights of its patients are protected. Furthermore, the procedures involved in safeguarding rights must be as ongoing, systematic and coordinated as any other management procedures. Therefore, after the manager has assessed his or her program's strengths and weaknesses in this area, we recommend the implementation of a package of procedural strategies that we have found effective in informing both patients and program staff of patients' rights, and ensuring that rights are protected in service delivery. This package includes procedures for (1) educating the patient; (2) protecting the patient's rights to informed consent and confidentiality; (3) obtaining peer review and consultation concerning rights issues; and (4) training staff and monitoring their performance to ensure that rights are protected.

Educating the Patient

The patient's first contact with a human service agency is usually by telephone. This occasion presents the first opportunity to protect the patient's rights. Potential consumers are seeking information regarding availability of services, cost, and appointment scheduling. After answering the patient's questions, the staff member should explain the program's policies concerning privacy and confidentiality. After a patient has indicated his or her understanding of these policies, the staff member should ask the patient to provide additional information for the program's records (name, address, phone number and so on). Finally, the program should obtain permission to contact the patient, if needed, and schedule a specific time during the day or evening when the patient can be reached. It should be the program's policy that a staff member never identifies himself or herself or the name of the service program when attempting to contact the patient.

The first office visit should be used as an opportunity to educate patients and assist them in understanding and preserving their rights. One easy way to inform patients is by providing materials designed to enable them to determine when their rights are being infringed upon, and how to exercise options to protect them. For example, descriptive material may be sent to patients prior to the intake interview, written material and audio-visual presentations may be provided, and verbal explanations may be given. We recommend using a combination of these procedures.

Whatever the procedures used, patients should be fully informed of their rights as human services consumers and should be required to sign a written statement to that effect before services are initiated (see patients' rights form in Appendix G). This written statement should include the following ''bill of rights'':[1]

1.   To be fully informed of the staff's qualifications to practice, including training and credentials, years of experience, etcetera.
2.   To be fully informed regarding the staff's therapeutic orientation.
3.   To be fully informed regarding the staff's areas of specialization.
4.   To ask questions about issues relevant to treatment, such as the staff's values, background, attitudes, and life experiences; and to be provided with thoughtful, respectful answers.
5.   To be fully informed of the limits of confidentiality in the treatment setting.
6.   To be fully informed of the extent of record-keeping regarding the treatment, in both written and taped form, and to be informed concerning how to gain access to those records.
7.   To be fully informed regarding the staff's estimation of the approximate length of treatment required to meet your goals.
8.   To be fully informed regarding specific treatment strategies employed by the staff (talking, body exercises, homework assignments, medications, etcetera).
9.   To be fully informed regarding potential risks and contra-indications for treatment.
10. To be fully informed regarding the format of the proposed treatment (individual or group therapy, etcetera).
11. To refuse any intervention or treatment strategy.
12. To be fully informed regarding the fees for treatment, and the method of payment (including acceptability of insurance).
13. To be fully informed regarding the staff's policies on issues such as missed sessions, vacation time, telephone contacts outside of the treatment hour, emergency coverage, and so on.
14. To know which ethics code the staff subscribes to.

15. To terminate services at any time.
16. To solicit help from the program's human rights committee or the ethics committee of the appropriate professional organization in the event of doubt or grievance regarding the staff's conduct.
17. To ask questions at any point.
18. To specify or negotiate treatment goals and to renegotiate those goals when necessary.
19. To be fully informed of your diagnosis (if the staff uses diagnostic categories).
20. To refuse to answer questions at any time.
21. To request that the staff evaluate the progress of treatment.
22. To discuss any aspect of your treatment with others outside of the treatment situation, including other staff.
23. To require your therapist to send a written report regarding services rendered to any qualified therapist or organization upon your written request and consent.
24. To be provided with copies of written files concerning your treatment upon your written request.
25. To give or refuse to give permission for the staff to use aspects of your case as part of a presentation or publication.
26. To get a written contract specifying the conditions of treatment, including the therapeutic goals.
27. To request, if you are seen in an agency setting, a specific staff member or type of therapist (for example, male rather than female).
28. To request, if you are seen in an agency setting, to speak with the agency's manager or administrator regarding any aspect of the program of concern to you.

Obtaining Informed Consent

The main reasons for educating the patients about rights and services are first, that services are more likely to be effective when patients are educated concerning the *how* and *why* of the treatment they are to receive; and, second, that the patient's consent to services is more likely to be truly *informed* the more he or she knows about rights and services.

Human service professionals tend to view informed consent as a process more for their own protection than for the protection of their patients. In fact, the primary purpose of informed consent is to ensure that patients (a) exercise control over the confidentiality of their case record and the type of treatment they receive; (b) approve the type of treatment or services they receive; (c) receive a fair and reasonable explanation regarding the program's assessment of their problems and the plan of service that the program has prescribed; (d) understand possible risks, if any, involved with the plan of service and with the specific procedures employed by the service provider; and (e) understand the alternatives to the plan of service that the program has prescribed.

In summary, informed consent includes at least three elements: competence, knowledge, and voluntariness. Competence refers to the patient's ability to make a well-reasoned decision, to understand the nature of the choice presented, and to give meaningful consent. Knowledge refers to the patient's understanding of the nature of treatment, the alternatives available, and the potential benefits and risks involved. Voluntariness refers to the patient's voluntary agreement to participate in treatment.

Standardized presentations using slide projection and videotape are particularly useful in introducing patients to rights issues, services, staff, and program facilities so that they become capable of making an informed choice. The advantage of standardized presentations is that information can be efficiently and effectively communicated to patients in a non-threatening way. Further, service providers are relieved of the necessity of presenting this information and the possibility of unclear or biased presentations is reduced. The standardized audio-visual presentation of material can also compensate for a patient's inability to read or comprehend material presented through a single modality. Different presentations and materials can be developed that are suitable for specific patient populations, including non-English speakers or people from a particular subculture. It is even possible to develop the materials that are suitable for direct presentation to children (see Christian, Clark, and Luke, 1981).

One disadvantage of standardized presentation of materials is the lack of certainty that the material is actually being attended to and, in fact, understood. It is therefore important that the service provider be available to ask and answer questions or to clarify topics, in order to ensure that the patient can effectively exercise his or her rights.

Standardized forms can be used to document (1) the patient's understanding of his or her rights and the steps taken by the program to protect them; (2) the patient's consent to, and authorization for, the services to be received; and (3) the contractual agreement to a particular plan of treatment, at a certain fee, and with certain rules regarding participation by the patient and the service provider. We recommend the use of three forms to provide this kind of documentation. They should be completed and signed by the patient (or his or her representative) and a member of the program staff. These are the (1) Patient's rights form (already described); (2) authorization for service form; and (3) contractual service plan. Samples of these forms are included in Appendix G. Case record review procedures and patient tracking systems such as those described in Chapter 7 can be used to ensure that these forms are completed in a timely manner and contain the necessary information, signatures, and so on.

Maintaining Confidentiality

Confidentiality is the most commonly known and used procedure for protecting patients' rights. It is viewed as the patient's right to privacy and as a process that prevents the public from obtaining certain information without permission from the patient. In other words, information regarding the patient's involvement with a human service program should be available only to patients, their legal representatives, and authorized agency personnel, unless otherwise ordered by the courts, or consented to by the patient.

There are some exceptions to this rule, however, and patients should be informed of the conditions under which they cannot prevent disclosure of their records. Such conditions may include the following: (a) mental examination ordered by the court; (b) determination by program staff that involuntary hospitalization is necessary to prevent physical harm; (c) proceeding brought by the patient against the program or its staff; (d) necessary facilitation of guardianship; and (e) a patient's introduction of his mental condition as an issue during court proceedings. In light of the ruling in *Tarasoff* v. *Regents of the University of California* (1974), in which a therapist was held responsible for failing to disclose that his client had threatened to commit murder, it is also important for patients to be informed that confidentiality may be violated if there is good reason to believe that they may do harm to another citizen.

The manager must also recognize that the issue of confidentiality is becoming more and more complicated for human service agencies due to the increasing emphasis being placed upon the accessibility of budgetary and program information. There is a growing uneasiness among human service consumers and providers about possible intrusions on the rights to privacy, resulting from the collection and storage of patient data. For example, it is difficult for a manager to ignore requests for information from state and federal funding agencies, insurance companies, and licensing authorities. However, it is the program's responsibility to ensure that, unless ordered by the court, information is not released without written consent from the patient and that patient records contain accurate and necessary information. The authorization for service form (see Appendix G) can be used for the purpose of defining the patient's "limits of confidentiality."

Human service agencies must also be careful in the manner in which they diagnose and label their patients. In addition, while case supervision does require the staff to share certain information about the patient, staff should be discreet in their selection of clinical and/or social history information for discussions with their supervisor and with colleagues during staff meetings. Also, patients should be informed in advance that certain progam staff will need to review their record.

Finally, patient records should be carefully coded for filing and monitored whenever removed from a secure record file room. Standards for case record documentation should also be developed and regular reviews conducted of case records to ensure that they are in compliance with program policy and procedure and the requirements of regulatory agencies (see pages 158 to 160). Another point of concern is the accessibility of case records. Typically a large number of program staff have access to patient information—for example, file clerks, statisticians, business and clinical staff. Some programs feel that confidentiality can be protected when all employees have access to patient records. We disagree. Some staff are not under sufficiently stringent professional ethical obligations to keep such information confidential. Therefore, tightly monitored procedures should be adopted to safeguard patient information from internal and external demands or access.

Developing Human Rights Committees

The decision in *Wyatt* v. *Stickney* (1972) called for the development of Human Rights Committees by human service programs to review research proposals, service plans, and treatment procedures, so as to ensure that the dignity and human rights of patients were preserved. The primary purposes of a Human Rights Committee are to provide sufficient and adequate safeguards for human service patients to ensure that inhumane or improper treatment does not occur, and that appropriate treatment is accomplished in the least restrictive manner. We are convinced that, if a human service program is to be truly legal and accountable, it must utilize a Human Rights Committee to provide an ongoing review of the services its patients receive.

We recommend that at least 50 percent of the committee members should be from outside the human service program. In large urban areas, up to 80 percent of Human Rights Committee members may be external to the program. There should be at least one committee member for each ten to fifteen patients served by the program. Such a composition allows for objectivity and community input. It is important that the members of the committee be genuinely concerned about the care and treatment of patients and be willing to devote time and energy to their work. Members can be individuals from the legal, mental health, educational, or medical professions as well as lay persons who represent the feelings and attitudes of the patient's community, parents, and/or guardians. The committee's main function is to represent the community when decisions are made in regard to the justification for the patient's treatment plan and procedures.

Human Rights Committees should meet a minimum of once a month. At each meeting, a specified number of patient records should be reviewed as well as reports from the program's case record review committee (see Chapter 7). Each member should serve as a representative for certain patients and should present information obtained from each patient's case record and/or from his or her own observations of and interviews with the patient receiving services, providing of course the patient has given consent for the release of this information. In addition, a member of the program staff should present the rationale and justification for the patient's treatment. The Human Rights Committee must determine whether the overall treatment goals and procedures are appropriate and whether the goals are being reached.

The existence of a Human Rights Committee can benefit both the patients and staff. First, the committee can serve as an advocate for the care and treatment of the program's patients. Second, if a citizen or regulatory agency questions whether the agency's services are humane, appropriate and effective, the Human Rights

Committee as an independent observer, can provide unbiased feedback about the services rendered.

We recommend developing very specific policies and procedures for Human Rights Committees and providing each prospective committee member with training sufficient to ensure that he or she will perform consistent with procedural guidelines. We have found the following guidelines useful in this regard.

A Sample Policy for the Human Rights Committee [2]

I. Statement of Purpose
   A. Provide sufficient and adequate safeguards for the patients of a human service program to ensure humane treatment.
   B. Ensure that appropriate treatment is accomplished as quickly as possible in the least restrictive manner.

II. Specification of Goals
   A. Review (*number*) restrictive treatment procedures and/or program policies per meeting, following the functional guidelines for the review process. (See page 187).
   B. Observe all areas of the program facility (*number*) times a month, following functional guidelines for review processes. (See page 187).
   C. Set up specific guidelines for receiving patient, staff, and/or guardian concerns pertaining to patients' rights.
   D. Educate patients, guardians, staff, and members of the local community as to the purpose and fuction of the HRC.
   E. Additional goals to be determined by each HRC.

III. Members
   A. Composition
      1. Fifty percent of the membership from within the organization.
      2. Fifty percent of the membership from outside of the organization. (When possible, a higher percentage of external membership should be recruited).
      3. Patient membership
         a. Dependent upon functioning level and capability of patient.
         b. Additional to internal and external membership.
   B. Training
      1. Tour of facility, including overview of facilities program and goals.
      2. Suggested readings: Joint Commission on Accreditation of Hospitals (1978); Hannah, Christian, and Clark (1981); Risley and Sheldon-Wildgen (1980); Sheldon-Wildgen and Risley (1980).
      3. Overview of relevant rights issues, regulatory guidelines, and program policy and procedure (lecture).
   C. Appointing members
      1. Manager appoints internal members.
      2. Manager appoints external members from a pool of volunteers recommended by external sources (see Recruitment).
      3. Program manager appoints patients and/or their guardians or advocates to membership on the committee.
   D. Recruitment
      1. Internal members recruited by program manager.
      2. External members

          a.   Special interest groups (local chapters of professional associations, advocacy groups, and so on) are contacted to suggest names of interested members.

          b.   Advertisements are run in local newspaper to recruit volunteers from the community at large.

          c.   Community Advisory Board and Professional Advisory Board members are contacted for suggestions.

      3.   Patient members are recruited by staff and/or by a patient advocate, through verbal notification, posting signs, and memoranda.

E.   Committee size

      1.   Approximately 8 to 15 members (not including patient members).

      2.   Sub-committees are not necessary unless required for special projects.

F.   Membership time-limits

      1.   Suggested minimum time-period for active membership: two years.

      2.   Maximum time-period for active membership: five years.

G.   Visibility

      1.   Patients, their parents, spouses, and/or guardians, and staff are informed about the Human Rights Committee and its functions.

      2.   A written fact sheet, briefly describing the purpose and function of the Human Rights Committee with the name and address of the committee chairperson should be distributed to each patient/guardian upon admission to the program.

      3.   Articles are run in local newspapers explaining the function of the committee and its current membership.

H.   Compensation: Reimbursement for travel.

I.   Confidentiality

      1.   Statutes governing confidentiality vary state to state. Each manager should be aware of his or her state's particular statutes as well as applicable licensing and accreditation standards. In Kansas, for example:

          a.   Disclosure of any records to the Human Rights Committee requires the prior consent of the patient and/or guardian.

          b.   Committee members are required to sign a pledge not to disclose the name of any patient.

          c.   The program manager is required to issue a statement granting members who have signed a pledge of confidentiality access to patient records for the purpose of review.

      2.   If non-Committee members are present at meetings, pseudonyms should be assigned to each patient.

IV.   Access to Consultants

A.   Internal (consultants employed as members of the program staff)

B.   External

      1.   Professional Advisory Board (See Chapter 7) Leading experts in a variety of specialty areas are available for telephone consultations with Human Rights Committee members. They can inform members if procedures are professionally justified.

      2.   Professional peer review (See Chapter 7)

V.   Mechanisms for Internal Operations

A.   Quorum.

B.   Visitor (non-member) policy.

    C. Meeting frequency:
       1. called by manager;
       2. called by committee chairperson.
    D. Agenda-setting process.
    E. Decision-making process.
VI. Functional Guidelines (Review Process)
    A. Review of policy and procedures.
       1. Selection of *(number)* programs or procedures to review.
       2. Specific requirements by subtypes of programs.
          a. Develop list of procedures requiring no approval from the Human Rights Committee before, during or after use.
          b. Develop list of procedures which can be implemented prior to committee approval but require post hoc review.
          c. Develop list of procedures which require committee approval prior to implementation.
       3. Review programs or procedures
          a. Program staff presents rationale for procedure.
          b. Committee member plays "devil's advocate" suggesting either less restrictive alternative or more restrictive procedure. Staff member justifies the choice of procedure.
       4. Complete Human Rights Committee due process summary report (See Appendix G)
          a. Circulate report to program manager.
          b. File copy of completed report in notebook maintained by committee.
          c. Enter case note in patient's record.
       5. Grant permission for a specific staff member to "pilot" a specific procedure with an individual patient for a limited time period *prior* to filing a formal review for the procedure to be used with the patient by program staff.
          a. Allows procedure to be tested without delay.
          b. Allows parameters of procedures to be adjusted prior to full implementation by all staff.
          c. Once tested, approves/vetoes continued use of procedure based on data of initial trial period.
       6. Review program policies
    B. On-going monitoring of living environment and observation of treatment procedures, and patient/staff interactions.
       1. Each ward, unit, or therapy group is assigned to a "team" of one to three committee members (actual number of team members depends on size of facility and size of Human Rights Committee).
       2. Team randomly visits its assigned ward, unit, or therapy group. (Each Human Rights Committee determines what is an appropriate number of visits to make.)
       3. Team members complete checklist "sensitizing" them to areas of rights and "quality of life" issues.
          a. How does the unit look?
             i. What, if anything, makes it attractive?
             ii. What does it need?
          b. How do the patients look (for example, are the clothes socially acceptable)?
          c. If the patient was your child or relative would you be comfortable with the staff-patient interaction you saw?

        d.   Interview the patients (depends on functioning level of patient).

        e.   Did the staff members you observed respect the patient's privacy (for example, knock on the door and wait for a response)?

        f.   In your opinion is the staff behavior appropriate given the age and functioning level of patients?

        g.   Were toys, magazines, etc., accessible to all patients? Was a staff member's presence necessary to remove items from high shelves, locked boxes, etc.?

        h.   What percentage of the patients observed were engaged in appropriate activity when you entered the ward or unit?

    4.   Copies of checklist results are circulated to program manager and to the unit staff.

VII.   Committee members complete a summary report of the service plan for each patient reviewed. (A copy of this form is included in Appendix G).

VIII.   Other responsibilities

    A.   Exit interview with patient/guardian.

    B.   Exit interview with staff.

    C.   Grievances.

        1.   If complainant is not satisfied with the action taken by program management, a formal complaint is filed with the Human Rights Committee.

        2.   Committee makes recommendation.

    D.   Investigation of abuses.

       Manager substantiates (Committee does not coordinate or conduct investigation.)

Training Staff to Preserve Patients' Rights

There are several traditional methods that could be used to train staff in the criteria and strategies for the preservation of patients' rights, for example, lectures, classroom discussions, and question-and-answer sessions. However, we recommend the use of an alternative, task-oriented method of in-service training. This type of training clearly itemizes what staff *should do* rather than what they should not do. It also eliminates the need for staff to make their own judgments about how the principles of patients' rights apply to their daily work tasks.

Task-oriented training requires that staff be trained to mastery, and that mastery be demonstrated through performance. The scope and content of staff training will be largely determined by the types of services to be implemented by staff, by patients' characteristics and needs, and by the goals of treatment for each patient. However, as suggested by Favell, Favell, and Risley (1981), every task-oriented training program for patients' rights should include the following components:

1.   *Operational definitions* of all patient's rights pertaining to a particular environment are presented to staff. In addition, staff should clearly understand the role of peer review, the Human Rights Committee and their responsibility, if any, to it.

2.   Staff are given a set of *step-by-step instructions* that describe how each staff activity (intake interviews, disciplinary actions, case-planning, record-keeping, etcetera) should be conducted so that rights violations do not occur.

3.   Staff are given the *opportunity to observe* trained staff performing the procedures correctly and to ask questions.

4.   Staff are given time for *on-the-job practice* of procedures.

5.   Supervisors observe staff conducting the procedures and give them *feedback* based on evaluation checklists that itemize the critical aspects of each procedure.

6.   New staff are considered trained and certified on a procedure when they can perform with a *100 percent score* on the checklist.

7.   Sub-standard scores indicate a need for rereading the procedures and/or *additional observation and practice with feedback* from supervisors.

In developing a staff training program on patients' rights, managers might ask, "How do staff supervisors measure the extent to which staff are complying with program policy and procedure for safeguarding patients' rights?" and, "If staff performance is deficient, how can it be brought up to standard and maintained?" Supervisory feedback methods, such as those described in Chapter 5, are particularly useful for maintaining the quality of staff performance. By conducting periodic, unannounced evaluations of staff activities by means of evaluation checklists, supervisors can keep staff focused on goals that are critical for maintaining patients' rights. Since staff performance is evaluated along the same dimensions as those measured during training and certification, these post-training checks are usually occasions to commend staff for a job well done. The results of supervisor assessments can be posted on the staff bulletin board and, over several weeks' time, these data can provide a general picture of how well the rights' safeguards are being implemented.

In short, the task-based method of on-the-job training helps to ensure that staff learn to perform their safeguarding duties at a specified level of competency. Supervisory feedback by means of checklist evaluation constitutes an effective quality assurance system that can be utilized by front-line supervisors and/or external monitors representing a high authority.

SUMMARY

The human service manager must take the necessary steps to ensure his or her consumers are served in accordance with their rights as patients and individuals in a free society. The best way to accomplish this goal is to identify the criteria for legally safe human service programming, determine the status of the program relative to those criteria, and implement strategies effective in enabling the program to operate more consistently with those criteria. Standards or criteria for legal safety have been provided through patients' rights litigation, the ethical codes of professional organizations, and the guidelines promulgated by regulatory agencies and patient advocacy groups. The most important of these standards are concerned with the program's establishment of policies and procedures regarding service delivery and patients' rights protection, and with the utilization of peer review and Human Rights Committees.

Recommended strategies for ensuring that the program is legally safe include educating the patient about his or her rights and the responsibility of program staff to protect them; protecting the patient's rights to informed consent and confidentiality; obtaining peer review and consultation concerning rights issues; and training and monitoring staff performance to ensure the patients' rights are protected. Specifically, standardized forms and audiovisual presentations can be used to inform the patient, obtain his or her consent, and explain the limits of confidentiality. Confidentiality can be maintained by providing training for staff concerning what types of information must remain confidential, and by developing adequate record keeping and record review systems. In-service training of management and program staff is also conducive to the protection of patients' rights, especially when a task-based method of training is employed that clearly itemizes and instructs staff in what they *should do* rather than what they should not do. This type of training enables staff to adhere to patients' rights guidelines in their daily work performance.

Perhaps the manager's most important strategy is the establishment of a Human Rights Committee. A Human Rights Committee provides safeguards regarding the justification for the patient's plan of service and the specific procedures utilized in serving the patient, and ensures against inhumane or improper treatment. The committee's members should be individuals from inside the program as well as individuals from outside the program who are concerned about the care and treatment of patients. Committee members can include professionals, laypersons, and consumers.

The Human Rights Committee is most effective when operationally specific goals, policies, and procedures have been developed for its operation, and when its activity involves both a review of documentation (for example, a patient's case record) and an on-site review of program operation. The Human Rights Committee can benefit both patients and staff because the committee can be an advocate for appropriate treatment of patients while, at the same time, serving as an unbiased observer of the services being rendered by the staff. Basically, Human Rights Committees make managers of human service agencies more accountable for the services rendered to their patients and communities.

9

Working Effectively
with Boards

Millions of private citizens contribute innumerable hours each year to public service programs, schools, and churches. Private citizens are also an important resource for the human service program and it is the manager's task to see that they are effectively utilized. For example, individuals who volunteer to work as program personnel must be oriented, trained, supervised, and evaluated using procedures such as those described in Chapters 4 and 5. Given the legal issues pertaining to human services and the potential risk to the patient when staff are not sufficiently trained for the task they are to perform, the human service program is no place for the untrained volunteer.

Citizens may also volunteer to serve as members of advisory and/or governing boards of human service programs. *Governing* boards such as boards of trustees are legally responsible for program operation and are essential for the development of a private, non-profit human service organization. *Advisory* boards have no legal responsibility or governing authority over the program but serve important support and evaluation functions. One type of advisory board, the Professional Advisory Board, was described in Chapter 7. Governing and advisory boards are compared in Figure 9-1. In this chapter, the word "board" will be used to refer both to boards of trustees and citizen advisory boards.

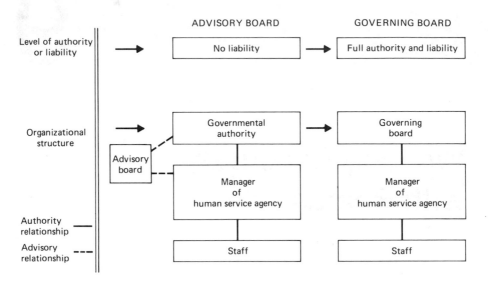

FIGURE 9-1 Comparison of Advisory and Governing Boards

BOARD DEVELOPMENT

The first task for the manager interested in developing a functional board is to understand the needs and interests of prospective board members and the steps required for getting them involved with the program. We have found the following criteria helpful in developing board membership and ensuring its involvement and productivity.[1]

1. *Board members are volunteers.* In order to develop and maintain a sense of commitment, volunteers need
    a. a clear sense of what is expected, and where opportunities lie for personal decisions;
    b. a feeling that activities have real purpose, and genuinely make a difference to the well-being of others;
    c. a sense of progress, followed by a sense of accomplishment; and
    d. the respect of associates, and confidence in fair treatment.
2. *Boards are an integral part of the program.* As such, board members should be able to expect
    a. information that is timely and expressed in language understandable to the lay person (for example, the biannual report described in Chapter 7);
    b. access to decision-makers;
    c. a climate that encourages initiative;
    d. early involvement in major policy and budgetary planning;
    e. indications from staff of opportunities for board impact;
    f. reimbursement for board-related expenses;
    g. staff assistance in obtaining information, keeping records, and communicating with each other;
    h. frankness in discussing issues and outlining priorities;

    i.   responses to issues and suggestions; and

    j.   a program-wide awareness of the board's purpose and activity.

3. *What is expected of board members needs to be made clear.* Managers should be able to expect board members

    a.   to be aware of the program's mandate and objectives;

    b.   to take an active part in board and committee meetings;

    c.   to respond to requests for advice and information;

    d.   to treat information shared with them as confidential if requested;

    e.   to suggest ways the board can interact with program issues;

    f.   to give staff a chance to respond, before concerns are aired in public;

    g.   to maintain visibility in the community so that channels of communication between the program and the public can be nurtured and used; and

    h.   to lobby local, state and federal leaders on issues of mutual concern.

The second step is to ensure that the membership of the board is appropriate to the program's goals and objectives, representative of the local and professional communities with which the board is associated, and capable of performing the tasks required. Nowlen (1981, p. 36) has suggested a number of variables that the manager should consider in developing or strengthening board membership.

1. Representative geographic distribution of board members throughout area served by agency.

2. Representative mix of age, sex, race, ethnic origin, income and level of education.

3. Special skills in management, health planning, "grantsmanship," accounting, public relations, languages other than English, adult education.

4. Connections with other community organizations and institutions, including churches, schools, recreation programs, political parties, banks, newspapers, public transportation, and major employers.

5. Effective leadership experience: solid interpersonal skills, effective chairing and interaction at meetings, record of productive committee work, success at fund raising.

6. Certain personal qualities, such as reasonable patience, even-temperedness, humor, confidentiality, and the shunning of gossip.

Specifying Roles

A critical indicator of effective human service management is the manner in which the program manager and board chairperson interact to achieve program goals and objectives. The manager is the instrument through which board policy is carried out; the board chairperson is the instrument through which board policy is communicated. Opportunities for effective communication and cooperation on the part of these individuals must therefore be provided on a regular basis. This requires that the manager and board chairperson understand the tasks they are to perform and provide each other with ongoing performance feedback. (In Chapter 4, we presented a sample list of work performance standards for the program manager; in Chapter 5 we described ways in which performance can be evaluated and feedback communicated; and in Chapter 7 we presented a format for a biannual report that can be used by the program manager to provide feedback to his or her board.)

It is also important that the board chairperson develop explicit standards for the tasks to be performed by each board member, negotiate with each board member for a level of performance consistent with those standards, and evaluate each member's performance relative to those standards and provide contingent feedback. As noted by Robins and Blackburn (1974, p. 38):

> ·. . . the effectiveness of boards is not insured by provisions regarding composition and constitutional authority; rather, effectiveness is probably a function of the clarity of objectives assigned to a board, the competence of a board to achieve the explicit objectives, formulation of objective criteria to measure achievement, and the tying of tenure of board members to achievement.

We therefore recommend the use of a form such as the following to assign tasks, products, and time-lines for completion to each board member.

1. Board member name _____

2. Address _____

3. Office telephone _____ Home telephone _____

4. Date of joining board _____

5. Committee/subcommittee assignments _____

    _____

    _____

    _____

    _____

6. Description of assignment (brief description of committee assignments, other assignments, products, and time-lines) _____

    _____

    _____

    _____

    _____

    _____

7. Description of how performance will be evaluated _____

    _____

    _____

    _____

    _____

8. Board member's signature _____

9. Board chairperson's signature _____

10. Date _____

Developing a Charter and Bylaws

The goals, objectives, and operational guidelines of the board should be specified in a charter and bylaws drawn up and formally adopted by the membership. Minutes taken at each board meeting can be used to determine whether board members are acting consistently with the charter and bylaws. The following sample charter and bylaws can be adapted for use by most boards of human service programs.[2]

Sample Board Charter and Bylaws
CHARTER

ARTICLE I: NAME AND OBJECTIVES
A. The name of this body shall be the Governing/Advisory Board of the __(program)__ .
B. The objectives are: To involve the community of __(program)__ service area in the governance of __(program)__ to help the community develop an effective human service system capable of meeting all the major human service needs of the community with the __(program)__ as the keystone of this system; to unite community members of all social groups in coming to grips with human service problems, so as to contribute to the development of a sound community.

ARTICLE II: MEMBERSHIP AND ELECTION
A. The Governing/Advisory Board shall be composed of twelve (12) members, who are eighteen (18) years of age or older, who are residents of the catchment area, and who are members in good standing of the community. Over half of the members of the Board shall be persons who are not providers of health care. The manager of the __(program)__ shall be a member of the board ex-officio.*
B. Election to the Governing/Advisory Board must be carried out no sooner than three (3) months and no later than two (2) weeks before the beginning of the term of office of the Board members. Names of the representatives elected shall be given in writing to the Board Secretary. No one shall be seated as a member of the Board until he or she attends a meeting of the Board, and does not become a member thereof until seated.
C. Governing/Advisory Board members shall be elected by the Board once every year, for a three-year term. The term shall start in September with the annual organization meeting. However, if for any reason the annual organization meeting cannot be held in September, the new members are not seated and the previously elected and seated members remain as Board members until the annual organization meeting is held. Such meeting must be held as soon as possible.
D. Vacancies in Board membership positions, however created, shall be filled by election, except that the Chairperson of the Board shall appoint a representative to fill the vacancy in case the Board fails to have a quorum at the meeting when the vacancy should be filled. The member filling the vacancy shall serve the remainder of the unexpired term.
E. Conflict of Interest: No paid employee of the __(program)__ may serve on the Governing/Advisory Board except that the manager of __(program)__ shall

---

*Whenever used in this document, ex-officio means membership without vote or the power to make motions from the floor, but without other restrictions (with the exception stated in Article II (H) of the Bylaws).

be an ex-officio member and other employees may serve on committees ex-officio as officially designated. Except for the manager of _(program)_ , no employee in an administrative position may serve on the Governing/Advisory Board.

F. A vacancy shall be created automatically in the event of a Governing/Advisory Board member resigning local membership or by not being reelected to the Board or by losing good standing. In any such case, the Secretary of the Board must notify the Governing/Advisory Board in writing.

ARTICLE III: OFFICERS

A. Officers shall be Chairperson, Vice Chairperson, Secretary, and Treasurer.
B. Duties shall be those usual to each office except that other duties may be assigned by the Board at its annual organization meeting.
C. Officers shall be elected by the Governing/Advisory Board at its annual organization meeting, once every year in September. The term of office shall be for one year, or until the election of new officers. In case the annual organization meeting cannot be held in September, for any reason, the previously elected officers shall continue to serve until the election is held. Members elected to office in the annual organization meetings shall take office immediately upon election.
D. No officer may serve more than two consecutive terms in any one office.
E. Vacancies in office shall be filled for the remainder of the term by the Governing/Advisory Board when such occur for any reason.

ARTICLE IV: MEETINGS

A. The Governing/Advisory Board shall hold its annual organization meeting in the month of September.
B. The Governing/Advisory Board shall have both regular and special (called) meetings as necessary.
C. Special meetings may be called by the Chairperson with the approval of one officer, in writing, and with at least forty-eight (48) hours notice. Also, the Chairperson with similar notice must call a special meeting upon the written request of at least four (4) members—within forty-eight (48) hours of such request.
D. An agenda shall be prepared for Governing/Advisory Board meetings by the Board Chairperson, or Vice Chairperson when necessary, in consultation with the program manager or his/her designee; however, the agenda may be amended by the Governing/Advisory Board in its meeting.
E. A quorum shall be constituted by the attendance of at least a simple majority. Vacant positions on the Board shall not be counted in establishing a quorum.
F. Guests, including staff members, may not be invited to Governing/Advisory meetings without the prior approval of the Chairperson.

ARTICLE IV: RESPONSIBILITIES

Aside from those inherent in Items I through III above, responsibilities are:

A. To give direction, suggestions, and recommendations to the program manager and/or the appropriate staff through meetings, committees, and otherwise.
B. To work to improve the program, based on the Board's specific authority to:
    1. approve the annual budget;
    2. establish general policies for the program;

3. approve the selection of manager for the program;
4. evaluate the performance of the program manager;
5. meet at least once a month.
C. To interpret the community to the program and the program to the community.
D. To monitor and champion the interests of the community as regards the provision of both preventive and treatment services—within the program, locally, and on the state and national levels.
E. To help In the assessment of community needs and problems relevant to human services.

BYLAWS

ARTICLE I: COMMITTEES
A. Ad-hoc Committee chairpersons shall be appointed by the Chairperson, with Governing/Advisory Board approval; ad-hoc committees are governed by the rules below (E through H) with the exception noted.
B. Standing committees may be created by the majority vote of the Board, provided a quorum is present. There shall be the following standing committees: Board Membership, Administrative or Management, Program, Personnel, Finance, Public Relations.
All standing committees shall be governed by the rules below (E through H).
C. The responsibility of dealing with the overall administrative operational issues of the (program) shall be exercised by the entire Governing/Advisory Board in its relationship with the program manager.
D. The Board through the above structure should deal with program-wide, community-wide, and service issues which concern priorities, policies, personnel, services, or other aspects of the program's functioning.
E. The Chairperson of each committee shall be designated by the Board Chairperson with the approval of the Board.
F. The Committee Chairperson chooses committee members subject to the approval of the Governing/Advisory Board.
G. Ex-officio: The Governing/Advisory Board Chairperson is an ex-officio member of each committee (and has no vote in the committee except in the case of a tie vote).
H. The (program) , in consultation with the Governing/Advisory Board, may assign staff consultants to the Board. Such consultants are not ex-officio and do not have the right to vote or to put a motion on the floor.

ARTICLE II: AMENDING PROCESS
A. The Charter may be amended by a two-thirds (2/3) vote of the Governing/Advisory Board in a regular or special meeting, provided there is a quorum.
Amendments may be proposed in writing by the Board Chairperson or by four (4) or more Board members.
Such proposals must be submitted in writing to the Governing/Advisory Board secretary and voted upon in the next regular or special meeting, provided that there is time for all members to receive amendments in writing no later than seven (7) days before the meeting. Otherwise, the vote must be taken in the next meeting. Such a meeting must be held no later than sixty (60) days after the Secretary has received the amendments.
B. Bylaws may be amended in any regular or special meeting by a majority

vote of the Governing/Advisory Board members present, provided there is a quorum. Copies of the amendments(s) to be offered must be included in the notice of the Board meeting, otherwise, no Board action may be taken.

ARTICLE III: BIANNUAL REPORT

A. A biannual (6-month) written report shall be submitted by the Governing/Advisory Board to the local community no later than two weeks before each biannual organization meeting.

BOARD ORGANIZATION

Human service boards vary in size, function, and structure. The operating rules (such as the charter and bylaws previously described) generally describe the structure and size of the board, members' terms of office, and so on. For example, the size of a board may vary according to the size of the organization, community, and/or the number of committees that are necessary to complete the board's functions. Terms of office also tend to vary. It has been our experience that boards for human service program typically range in size from ten to thirty members and feature a term of office of three years with provisions for renomination to a second full term.

Committee structure is also a key to the success of a board. Committees should be organized around the board's major goals and objectives. There are generally four types of committees:[3]

1. *Executive Committee*. This committee is composed of board officers, committee chairpersons, and a few members at-large. It serves as an overall planner and monitor of committee and board functioning. It is usually authorized to deal with situations requiring board action which occur between board meetings.
2. *Standing Committees*. These committees are generally defined in the bylaws as permanent committees and may include the following:
    a. *Board Membership Committee*, concerned with issues related to selection of board candidates, recruitment, and appointment of new members, etcetera.
    b. *Management Committee*, concerned with issues related to legal matters, legislative issues, building maintenance, etcetera.
    c. *Program Committee*, concerned with issues related to the development of new services, assessment of community needs, patients' rights, program evaluation, etcetera.
    d. *Personnel Committee*, concerned with issues related to staff salaries/benefits, grievance and termination policies, staff recruitment and in-service training, etcetera.
    e. *Finance Committee*, concerned with issues related to financial planning, development of the annual budget, audits, fund raising, grant solicitation, etcetera.
    f. *Public Relations Committee*, concerned with issues related to mass media, biannual reports (to consumers and the general public), community workshops, etcetera.
3. *Subcommittees*. These committees are established within one of the standing committees by a committee chairperson. They are delegated responsibilities for specific tasks.
4. *Special committees*. These are temporary committees responsible for fulfilling a specific, time-limited project. They are usually appointed by the board's chairperson.

BOARD TRAINING

We have already mentioned the importance of orienting and training board members in preparation for the tasks they must perform. Ongoing evaluation and feedback for their performance is also necessary. Unfortunately, there has been little research on orientation, training, and performance appraisal for board members. Perhaps this is due to the assumption that many of the strategies developed in studies concerning staff performance are readily generalizable to board members. This assumption is not justified, however, since the contingencies in operation for board members are vastly different than those for program staff. Most notably, program staff are under the control of contingencies established by the program manager. Board members, especially members of governing boards, are under no such control, often being totally removed from the program environment. In addition, board members have seldom received any prior training for their roles and many managers may find it difficult to suggest, much less provide, such training.

There are at least seven objectives for training board members of a human service program:

1. To orient the members to the program's patients, services, and staff.
2. To inform members of the functions, tasks, and authorities of the board.
3. To orient the members to the program's budget format and process, budget expenses, and funding sources.
4. To orient members to the issues related to patients' rights, program evaluation, and consumer needs.
5. To give them information related to governmental regulations and policies.
6. To develop a team (as opposed to a group of inundated individuals).
7. To give them a common vocabulary—the professional language and concepts.

An example of a curriculum for training board members that can be completed in a one and one-half day weekend session is provided in Figure 9-2. In addition, in Chapter 7 we described strategies for soliciting feedback from, and providing feedback to, board members via biannual reports. In Chapter 8, we described how individuals external to the program can provide an important monitoring and quality assurance function.

EVALUATING BOARD PERFORMANCE

The goal of these efforts is development, organization, and training is a board which will be an asset to the human service program and an aid to the manager in his or her efforts to meet the program's goals and objectives. The actual performance of the board can be evaluated in much the same way that staff performance is evaluated (observation and recording, measurement of permanent products, par-

TOPICS	METHODS/MATERIALS	PERSONNEL	TIME
1. Introductions: members spend these five minutes each describing their work, family, etc.	Group discussion	Board chairperson	1 hr.
2. Overview: board responsibilities, services, patient characteristics, staff, by-laws, committees, etc.	Program handbook (loose-leaf format)	Board chairperson	2 hr.
3. Overview: program responsibilities, services, patient characteristics, staff, budget, etc.	Program handbook (loose-leaf format)	Program manager	2 hr.
4. Special workshop: leadership, communication, and policy decision making skills	—Professional lifestyle —Role play	Professional consultant	3 hr.
5. Financial overview: long range financial plans	Program handbook (loose-leaf format)	Board chairperson	1½ hr.
6. Overview: patients' rights issues and function of human rights committee	Professional literature	Program manager	1½ hr.
7. Overview: governmental and other human service programs	Program handbook (loose-leaf format)	Program manager	1 hr.

FIGURE 9-2 Sample of Board Training Curriculum (one and one-half days)

ticipation ratings, satisfaction ratings, and so on). We recommend reviewing Chapter 5 for information concerning performance appraisal.

Nowlen (1981) has provided a number of criteria that can be used to evaluate board performance. He suggests that the successful board (p. 42):

1. possesses a clear understanding of its own nature and purpose;
2. sets objectives against which it regularly measures its progress;
3. identifies to whom it is accountable and regularly communicates with such persons;
4. works primarily through smaller groups such as task forces, which are assigned concrete, specific projects for completion within a reasonably short time;
5. never meets for the sake of meeting;
6. regards recruiting and retaining effective board members as a year-round activity of prime importance;
7. uses the secretary's minutes, the treasurer's report, and the like as action aids, not as oral history;

8. includes members who value time, that is, who don't waste other people's time and don't want their own time wasted.

Kappal (1960) has provided a number of questions that can be used to evaluate the "vitality" of one's board and to indicate the need for increased orientation and training of board members, recruitment of new members, reexamination of the board's goals and objectives, revision of charter and/or bylaws, and so on.

1. Do your board members cling to old ways of working after they have been confronted with new situations?
2. Are your older board members adhering rigidly to the ideas, methods, and approaches of the past and passing this kind of thinking along to your younger board members?
3. Are the board members failing to define new goals that are meaningful and challenging?
4. Has your board developed a low tolerance for criticism?
5. Has there been a decline in reflective thinking about the adequacy of current operations and the needs of the future?
6. Has institutionalism begun to set in? That is, has the board come to be something apart from the program's goals and objectives?
7. Does your program have a reputation as a secure and stable organization, but not a venturesome one?

SUMMARY

Governing boards, such as boards of trustees, are legally responsible for program operation and are essential for the development of private, non-profit human service organizations; *advisory* boards have no legal responsibility or governing authority over the program but serve important support and evaluation functions. The first task for the manager interested in developing a functional board is to understand the needs and interests of prospective board members and the steps required for getting them involved with the program. The manager must therefore understand that board members are volunteers, that boards are an integral part of the program, and that board members must clearly understand what is expected of them. The manager must also understand his or her role in carrying out board policy and the role of the board chairperson in communicating policy.

The board chairperson should develop explicit standards for the tasks to be performed by each board member, negotiate a performance agreement with each member, and evaluate each member's performance and provide contingent feedback. Each board should develop a charter and a set of bylaws that are consistent with the program's mission, goals, and objectives. The board should be organized to include an executive committee, standing committees (for example, membership, management, program, personnel, finance, public relations), subcommittees, and special committees. Each board member should also receive orientation and training specific to the tasks he or she is required to perform.

10

Effective Management in a Nutshell

In this book, we have identified the most important aspects of human service management and have recommended specific procedures for implementation by the individual who wishes to manage his or her program more effectively. The present chapter is not an attempt to oversimplify the manager's task, but rather to provide an overview and a list of criteria that the manager can use to evaluate his or her present and future efforts. While we have provided much of the information that follows in chapter summaries, we consider it beneficial for the reader to look at the strategies we have recommended in the context of a systematic, well-coordinated approach to the management of a human service program.

The Essential Tasks of Effective
Human Service Management

I.   *Preliminary Considerations*
    A.   Understanding the major issues and problems characteristic of human service management
        1.   Cost effectiveness.
        2.   Financing.
        3.   Consumer demand.
        4.   Legal pressure.
        5.   External regulations.

6. Personnel management.
7. Organizational structure.
8. Program evaluation.
9. Authority.
10. The individual manager.
B. Understanding management as performance
1. Identifying *reactive* aspects of one's management style.
2. Identifying *proactive* aspects.
3. Understanding how environmental antecedents and consequences influence performance.

II. *Developing a Strategic Plan for Human Service Management*
A. Defining or reviewing the program's mission
B. Assessing needs and resources
1. Identifying data sources for needs assessment.
2. Completing a resource inventory.
C. Specifying goals and objectives
1. Conducting "goal analysis."
2. Analyzing objectives.
D. Identifying operative or potentially operative contingencies in the human service settings
E. Selecting systems and/or procedural strategies
1. Identifying selection criteria.
2. Reviewing the available literature.
3. Selecting flexible, feasible, accountable, effective systems and/or procedures for implementation.
F. Preparing the environment (staff, facilities, and patients) for the implementation of a system or procedure
G. Implementing systems and/or procedures
1. Implementing organizational systems.
2. Implementing problem-specific strategies.
H. Evaluating effectiveness
1. Observing and recording performance.
2. Graphing and analyzing results.
3. Communicating results.

III. *Structuring the Human Service Organization*
A. Understanding the organizational problems characteristic of human service settings
B. Selecting an organizational strategy
1. Identifying selection criteria.
2. Understanding basic organizational design (pyramidal vs. matrix structure).
3. Understanding "adaptive" organizational structure.
C. Implementing "adaptive" organizational structure
1. Utilizing organizational charts.

        2. Developing policy and procedure manuals.
        3. Contracting with staff for a specific standard of work performance.
        4. Orienting and training staff in organizational structure.
        5. Utilizing committees and project teams.
        6. Conducting staff meetings and distributing written memoranda.
   D. Evaluating the effectiveness of organizational structure
        1. Obtaining feedback from staff.
        2. Evaluating staff performance.
        3. Obtaining evaluative feedback from external consultants and peer reviewers.

IV. *Getting Staff On-Task*
   A. Orienting staff to the task they are to perform
        1. Developing work performance standards for each position in the organization.
        2. Contracting with staff for performance consistent with standards.
        3. Evaluating staff members' understanding of the tasks they are to perform.
   B. Orienting staff to the work environment
        1. Developing and implementing an ''orientation checklist.''
        2. Evaluating the effectiveness of orientation procedures.
           a. Determining the extent to which staff members are familiar with the work environment (interviews, written quizzes).
           b. Obtaining satisfaction ratings from staff.
   C. Training staff for the work they are to perform
        1. Conducting a job analysis for each position.
        2. Developing and implementing an effective training program.
           a. Utilizing training procedures of demonstrated effectiveness in improving the performance of similar staff in similar settings.
           b. Programming for the similarity of training and work environments.
           c. Ensuring that trainees have a sufficient understanding of the basic principles underlying the procedures that they are being trained to employ.
           d. Providing feedback for appropriate staff performance in training sessions as well as in the work environment.
           e. Providing opportunities for trainees to practice new skills.
           f. Promoting maintenance and generalization of new skills through ongoing training and contingent feedback.
        3. Promoting trainee attendance and participation
           a. Using a training contract.
           b. Providing a written syllabus or agenda.
           c. Preparing a resource packet for trainees.
           d. Rehearsing training procedures prior to implementation.
           e. Providing access to the trainer outside of training sessions.

4. Evaluating the effectiveness of staff training
   a. Observing and recording trainee on-the-job performance.
   b. Evaluating the trainee's performance in response to specific situations.
   c. Giving written tests.
   d. Requiring the completion of assignments and specific projects.
   e. Rating trainee attendance and participation in training.
   f. Obtaining satisfaction ratings from trainees.
   g. Observing and recording patient progress.
5. Graphing and communicating results
6. Promoting maintenance and generalization by providing feedback contingent upon staff performance.
   a. Fading the density of feedback.
   b. Cueing or prompting.
   c. Providing ongoing training.

V. *Ensuring Job Completion*
   A. Scheduling personnel resources to areas of need
      1. Identifying specific tasks that must be performed in a particular department of the program and the skills needed to perform them effectively.
      2. Developing a master staffing schedule, matching personnel to tasks/skills needed.
      3. Negotiating time and location scheduling with each employee as part of his or her work performance standards, minimizing the amount of part-time scheduling.
      4. Posting the staffing schedule.
      5. Evaluating the effectiveness of policies and procedures for staff scheduling.
      6. Maintaining an effective staffing schedule.
         a. Employing a staff scheduling specialist.
         b. Orienting and training staff in schedule maintenance procedures.
         c. Engaging in proactive staff recruitment/hiring practices.
   B. Supervising program personnel
      1. Identifying criteria for effective supervisory performance.
      2. Implementing effective supervisory strategies.
         a. Recruiting competent supervisory personnel.
         b. Orienting and training supervisors.
         c. Developing a professional work force.
         d. Utilizing routines and checklists for tasks most frequently performed by staff.
         e. Establishing and maintaining an effective feedback loop.
         f. Obtaining professional consultation and peer review.
         g. Utilizing additional supervisory personnel.

C.   Evaluating staff performance
    1.   Identifying criteria for effective performance evaluation.
    2.   Determining representative sources of data for performance evaluation.
    3.   Observing, recording and analyzing change in performance.
    4.   Providing follow-up evaluation.
D.   Providing feedback contingent upon performance
    1.   Identifying criteria for effective feedback.
    2.   Sampling consequences for performance to see what could potentially function as positive and what could function as negative feedback for staff.
    3.   Informing the employee of evaluative results.
        a.   Following rules for giving and receiving feedback.
        b.   Promoting two-way performance feedback.
        c.   Utilizing standard evaluation forms.
    4.   Delivering consequences contingent upon performance.
        a.   Providing effective, equitable rewards for positive performance.
        b.   Conducting the corrective interview.
        c.   Taking formal corrective action.
    5.   Conducting a follow-up evaluation to determine effectiveness of consequences.

VI. *Solving Budget Management Problems*
A.   Increasing financial resources
    1.   Increasing fee collection.
        a.   Understanding problems associated with traditional fee-collection procedures.
        b.   Implementing "credit criterion" procedures for fee collection.
    2.   Obtaining funds from philanthropic sources.
    3.   Implementing a private contribution mailing system.
    4.   Conducting an annual fund raising project.
    5.   Obtaining community sponsorship of fund raising efforts.
B.   Managing financial resources
    1.   Utilizing traditional budgeting models.
        a.   Budgeting by line-items.
        b.   Budgeting by increment.
        c.   Utilizing a planning-programming-budgeting system.
        d.   Utilizing zero-base budgeting.
    2.   Utilizing the revenue-base planning budget.
        a.   Developing the revenue-base review committee.
        b.   Preparing budget policy papers.
        c.   Announcing revenue allocation.
        d.   Preparing department cost centers.

   e. Submitting budgets.

   f. Obtaining a final decision from the Governing Board.

VII. *Getting the Most Out of Program Evaluation Efforts*

  A. Understanding the importance of program evaluation

  B. Designing an effective program evaluation system

   1. Planning.

    a. Identifying types of results that evaluation should yield.

    b. Specifying sources of data.

    c. Determining levels of program evaluation (structure, system, outcome).

    d. Getting program structure, process, and outcome into measurable form.

    e. Identifying and researching systems and procedures for evaluation.

    f. Deciding how the task of evaluation will be performed (internal and external evaluation).

   2. Specifying goals and objectives for evaluation.

   3. Assessing the baseline status of the program.

   4. Providing on-going and follow-up evaluation of program operation.

   5. Analyzing and disseminating the results of program evaluation.

  C. Utilizing in-house evaluation strategies

   1. Establishing patient tracking systems.

   2. Obtaining feedback from in-house peer review.

    a. Conducting treatment team meetings.

    b. Conducting peer review of performance.

    c. Reviewing case record documentation.

  D. Obtaining feedback from external evaluation and review

   1. Obtaining evaluative feedback from consumers of the program's services.

   2. Contracting with outside consultants for evaluation and review.

    a. Managing the performance of the individual consultant.

    b. Developing a Professional Advisory Board.

    c. Obtaining professional peer review (case consultation, on-site program review).

  E. Establishing a framework for program evaluation

   1. Understanding the importance of a coordinated, product-oriented program evaluation system.

   2. Developing a format for a biannual progress report.

   3. Preparing and disseminating the report.

   4. Obtaining feedback concerning the report.

   5. Revising the format of the report, as necessary, in response to feedback.

      6.   Using the report in structuring program evaluation efforts and in promoting a positive image of the program.

VIII. *Safeguarding Patients' Rights*

    A.   Identifying the rights of the patient receiving human services and understanding the necessity to ensure that patients' rights are protected

    B.   Identifying criteria for legally safe human service programming

        1.   Identifying pertinent litigation.

        2.   Identifying ethical issues for human services.

        3.   Identifying pertinent professional codes of ethics.

        4.   Identifying standards and guidelines of pertinent national or state regulatory and licensing agencies.

        5.   Determining policies and procedures conducive to legally safe human service programming.

            a.   Defining the program's philosophy of service delivery and its commitment to protect the rights of its patients.

            b.   Identifying and utilizing treatment procedures that are consistent with patients' rights.

            c.   Obtaining ongoing peer review of program operation.

            d.   Obtaining the patient's informed consent prior to any service he or she receives.

            e.   Developing a Human Rights Committee.

    C.   Assessing the current status of the program relative to those criteria

    D.   Utilizing strategies designed to ensure that the program and its services are "legally safe"

        1.   Educating the patient about his or her rights and the services he or she is to receive.

            a.   Using standardized audiovisual presentations.

            b.   Using standardized forms (patients' rights form, brochure about the program and its services).

        2.   Obtaining the patient's informed consent.

            a.   Using standardized audiovisual presentations.

            b.   Using standardized forms (authorization for services form, contractual service plan).

        3.   Maintaining confidentiality.

            a.   Using standardized forms (authorization for service form).

            b.   Developing standards for case records.

            c.   Coding patient records and limiting access to them.

            d.   Conducting regular reviews of case records to determine their compliance with program standards.

        4.   Developing a Human Rights Committee.

            a.   Developing policy and procedure for committee function (case review, on-site program review).

            b.   Recruiting, orienting, and training committee members.

      c. Obtaining written documentation of committee activity (due process summary report, summary report of Human Rights Committee review of patient service plan).

    5. Training staff to identify and preserve patient rights.

IX. *Working Effectively with Boards*

  A. Understanding the types of boards (governing vs. advisory) and the needs of prospective board members

    1. Understanding the needs of board members as volunteers.

    2. Understanding the needs of board members as integral part of the program.

    3. Understanding what should be expected of individuals in their roles as board members.

  B. Specifying the roles of program manager and board chairperson

  C. Contracting with board members for an acceptable level of performance

  D. Developing a charter and set of bylaws for the board

  E. Organizing the board

    1. Establishing the executive committee.

    2. Forming standing committees.

    3. Developing subcommittees and special committees.

  F. Training board members for the tasks that they must perform

    1. Identifying objectives for training.

    2. Developing a training curriculum.

  G. Evaluating board performance

APPENDICES

Appendix A

Sample work performance standards for the administrative staff of a private non-profit human service institution providing residential, psychological, educational, and basic health-care services to developmentally disabled, emotionally disturbed, and mentally ill patients. Sample performance standards for the program manager are presented in Chapter 4.

Position Title: Director of Clinical Services

Description of Assignment

I. Training and supervision of staff assigned to the Department of
    Clinical Services (child development specialists; behavioral pro-
    gramming specialists; evaluation, research, and training special-
    ists), training and/or supervision of volunteers, interns, and
    practicum students assigned to residential units and to the commun-
    ity-based group home; health care services staff.

    A. Interview and select new employees with assistance of the
        Director of Administrative Services.
    B. Orientation for new employees completed within first two weeks
        of their employment.
    C. Staff training completed within first month of employment for
        new employees. Evaluation made of the effectiveness of staff
        training programs for report to supervisor (Executive Director)
        within one week of the completion of each training program.
    D. Written evaluation of each employee's performance made at
        six-month intervals from the individual's date of employment;
        evaluations submitted to supervisor for final approval.
    E. Weekly meetings with staff members from each ward or residential
        unit (including residential and educational staff, the Director
        of Education, Director of Transitional Services, and other
        pertinent staff) conducted, for communication, evaluation of
        each patient's progress, treatment planning, and training/con-
        sultation.
    F. Daily monitoring of staff performance in residential settings
        conducted.

II. Case records and program evaluation

    A. A current treatment plan for each patient developed within first
        two weeks of the patient's admission. Target behaviors, proce-
        dures to be employed, goals, criteria for success and method of
        evaluating success, and treatment authorization from patient
        and/or legal guardian specified.
    B. Review of progress being made with each patient completed at
        three-month intervals, with progress reviews addressing target
        behaviors as specified on treatment plan documented in writing
        in each patient's case record; written summary of progress of
        treatment for each patient sent to parents/legal guardians with
        assistance of the Director of Transitional Services at three-
        month intervals.
    C. Behavioral evaluation utilizing an appropriate standardized
        assessment instrument completed on each patient at twelve-month
        intervals. Written evaluative summary (including analysis of
        the improvement of skill gains made for each patient submitted
        to supervisor in June of each year (a date chosen to coincide
        with due date for biannual report to the program's Board of
        Trustees).

III. Applied research

    A. Applied research projects conducted with approval of supervisor.
        1. At least two proposals for the presentation of a paper at
            a professional conference or convention submitted annually.
        2. At least two manuscripts submitted for publication annually.

B. Grant support for applied research investigated.
   1. At least two preliminary proposals, including statement of the problem to be researched and possible funding source, submitted for grant support to the supervisor each year -- first due _____.
   2. At least one grant proposal as principal investigator for the support of an applied research or program development project submitted by _____.
   3. Assist supervisor and Director of Education in obtaining affiliation with universities for the purpose of arranging academic credit for staff completing training programs, and in developing research and training settings for interns and/or university practicum students.

IV. Special projects Assist supervisor, Director of Education, Director of Transitional Services, and Director of Administrative Services with special projects in areas of program development, public relations, and fund raising.

V. Additional responsibilities
   A. Cooperate with program policy and procedures.
   B. Cooperate with special requests (for example, special projects which may involve personnel from other departments) made by supervisor, as per request.
   C. Attend weekly meetings of the administrative staff; attend weekly individual meeting with supervisor for discussion/consultation concerning status of the clinical service program.
   D. Assist supervisor in public relations and fund raising activities, as per request.
   E. In absence of supervisor, administer the program in cooperation with the Directors of Education, Transitional Services, and Administrative Services, specifically with respect to clinical service programs and personnel.

Position Title: Director of Educational Services

Description of Assignment

I. Training and supervision of personnel assigned to educational programs (academic teachers, evaluation, research and training specialists, language development specialists, and physical education teacher); training and/or supervision of volunteers, interns, practicum students, and research assistants assigned to classroom programs.

(Similar to Assignments A - F on page 214.)

II. Case records and program evaluation

A. Develop a current educational plan for each student specifying target behaviors, procedures employed, goals, criteria for success and method of evaluating success, and treatment authorization from student and/or legal guardian.

B. Communicate with each student's home school district to ensure that approved individual educational plan is developed and followed (with assistance of the Director of Transitional Services); assist in preparing of public school teaching personnel for the student's discharge from the program.

C. Review of progress being made with each student completed at three-month intervals, with progress reviews addressing target behaviors as specified on treatment plan, documented in writing in each student's case record; written summary of progress of treatment for each student sent to parents/legal guardian with assistance of Director of Transitional Services at three-month intervals.

III. Applied research

(Similar to Assignments III(A) and III(B) on pages 214-215.)

IV. Special Projects

(Similar to Assignment IV on page 215.)

V. Additional Responsibilities

(Similar to Assignments A - E on page 215.)

Position Title: Director of Transitional Services

Description of Assignment

I. <u>Training and supervision of personnel assigned to the Department of Transitional Services</u> (parent training specialists, the Coordinator of Social Services, and interns/practicum students assigned to parent training and/or social service programs).

(Similar to Assignments A - F on page 214.)

II. <u>Transition planning</u> Admission and discharge planning for patients served by the program such that each patient receives the least restrictive program of educational, clinical and health care services effective in meeting his or her special needs.

A. Individual and/or group training for parents conducted utilizing parent training methodology of demonstrated effectiveness in increasing parents' understanding of their child's behavior and in enabling them to manage and work effectively with the child in the home environment. Training conducted at the program <u>and</u> at locations convenient to each parent's home community (to the extent possible); in-home observation and consultation conducted in conjunction with parent training sessions.

B. Evaluation of the effectiveness of parent training made using measures such as (1) attendance and participation; (2) observation of parent-child interactions at the program and in the home environment; (3) results of behavior change projects conducted by parents; (4) pre- and post-training quizzes designed to assess mastery of course content; and (5) consumer satisfaction ratings.

C. Documentation made of parent training and in-home observation/consultation activity with case notes in each patient's case record and in a written evaluative summary report submitted to supervisor within thirty days of the completion of a parent training program.

D. Communication maintained with parents, Parent Advisory Board, social service agencies, and school districts concerning patients served by the program and the services they receive (within the limits of patient privacy and confidentiality).

III. <u>Visitation</u> Visitation by parents and other concerned persons (representatives of referring agencies, and so on) coordinated in such a way that there is advance notice of a visit (whenever possible) and the visitors adhere to program policy and procedure concerning visitation, visitor sign-in, trips off ground, etcetera.

IV. <u>Vacation-planning</u> Vacation-planning coordinated in such a way that supervisor and other members of the administrative staff receive at least two weeks' advance notice of the vacation plans for each patient.

V. <u>Individual educational planning</u> Assist Director of Education, Director of Clinical Services and their personnel in individual educational planning (development and maintenance of a current individual educational plan for each student) for program clients. Plan for each student served by the program current as of _____ of each year.

VI. Case records and program evaluation Case record review coordinated as per program case record standards and policy and procedure concerning review of case records. Written report of quarterly review of at least 25 percent of program's active case records submitted to supervisor on _____ and at three-month intervals thereafter.

VII. Applied research

(Similar to Assignments A and B on pages 214-215.)

VIII. Special Projects

(Similar to Assignment IV on page 215.)

IX. Additional Responsibilities

(Similar to Assignments A - E on page 215.)

<u>Position Title</u>: Director of Administrative Services

<u>Description of Assignment</u>

I. <u>Training and Supervision of personnel assigned to the Department of Administrative Services</u> (account clerk, kitchen supervisor, kitchen aides, maintenance supervisor, maintenance assistants, housekeepers, groundskeeper, personnel clerk, clerical supervisor, receptionist, and secretaries).

(Similar to Assignments A - F on page 214.)

G. Food Services
   1. Work with Dietary Supervisor to ensure monitoring of the quality of food served; a written weekly menu submitted to supervisor (Executive Director) at least one week in advance.
   2. Changes in menu and serving practices suggested by program medical and nutrition consultants implemented as per requests by supervisor.
   3. Inventory of food services equipment (utensils, appliances, food supplies, etcetera) submitted to supervisor by _____.

H. Maintenance and Housekeeping
   1. Description of needed repairs and equipment, ongoing maintenance and repair projects, and ongoing construction/renovation projects submitted to supervisor during the first week of each month.
   2. Inventory of tools, equipment and building materials and their present condition, submitted to supervisor by _____.
   3. Standards and monitoring procedures (for example, daily checklist) developed to ensure that buildings are adequately cleaned each day and receive requested repairs. Report concerning needed maintenance and repairs submitted to supervisor for approval by _____, and implemented within two weeks of supervisor approval.

I. Clerical Services
   1. Routing and quality control procedures maintained to ensure efficiency of clerical services.
   2. Small library of program books developed. Books presently owned catalogued and labeled with system for checkout by _____.
   3. Inventory of office machines, equipment, and materials submitted to supervisor by _____.

II. <u>Budget Control</u>. Budgetary preparation, implementation and monitoring of bookkeeping, billing, and payment mechanisms for the program.

A. Report containing following information completed on a monthly basis and submitted to supervisor for approval and distribution to the Board of Trustees and/or supervising state officials.
   1. Budget control form.
   2. Statement showing changes in fixed assets.
   3. Running record of working capital, including current balances in the program checking and savings accounts.
   4. Statement of accounts receivable and accounts payable. Monthly statements submitted to supervisor by the _____ day of the following month.

B. Verbal report made to supervisor on a weekly basis concerning current financial condition, problems anticipated (for example, current balances of savings and checking accounts, plans for meeting payroll).

C. Payroll accounting (salaries, hours worked) conducted with co-operation of administrative staff; payroll checks to employees disbursed; withholding taxes, social security, and health insurance deductions for each employee monitored; monthly report made to supervisor concerning payroll operation.

D. Reports to the state rate-setting commission and rate negotiations with other states made.
   1. Completed draft of report for current fiscal year submitted to supervisor for approval at least ten days prior to deadline for receipt of the report by the rate-setting commission.
   2. Workshops and conferences relative to rate-setting procedures and guidelines attended as per request by supervisor.

III. Personnel Management. Recruitment, interviewing, hiring, and time-scheduling of non-administrative personnel subject to guidelines and requirements (for example, qualifications, special needs of a particular department) specified by supervisor and the Directors of Clinical Services, Educational Services and/or Transitional Services.

A. Interviewing and hiring of personnel coordinated in cooperation with supervisor and other members of the program's administrative staff.

B. Prospective employees informed concerning status of their applications for employment.

C. Work schedules for personnel developed and maintained with the assistance and subject to the approval of the Directors of Clinical Services and Education and consistent with state regulations concerning staff-to-patient ratios in classroom, residential, and health care areas.

D. A current, comprehensive manual of program policy and procedures maintained, as per requirements of supervisor.

IV. Special Projects.

(Similar to Assignment IV on page 215.)

V. Additional Responsibilities.

(Similar to Assignments A - E on page 215.)

Appendix B

Sample work performance standards for selected nonadministrative personnel of a private nonprofit human service institution providing residential, psychological, educational, and basic health-care services to developmentally disabled, emotionally disturbed, and mentally ill patients. Sample performance standards for the program manager and the program's administrative personnel are presented in Chapter 4 and Appendix A, respectively.

Position Title: Coordinator of Health Care Services (R.N.)

Department: Clinical Services

Description of Assignment

I. Training and supervision of health care services staff (registered
    nurses, licensed practical nurses, and medical consultants).

    (Similar to Assignments A - F on page 214.)

II. Operation of nurses' station; monitoring of medication, health
    services equipment, and in-office medical records.

    A. Current inventory of all materials and equipment located in
        health services office submitted to supervisor (Director of
        Clinical Services) by _____.

    B. Requisition for needed equipment and supplies, repairs and
        maintenance for health services office submitted to supervisor
        by _____.

    C. Security of medications and equipment located in health services
        office maintained.
        1. Daily inventory of barbiturate and other prescription medica-
            tions maintained and report made to supervisor of medication
            unaccounted for at daily check.
        2. Security of the health services office maintained. Security
            problems reported to supervisor.

III. Provision of basic health care for patients and program staff in
     cooperation with the program's medical consultants.

    A. Review of developmental history and previous medical treatment
        for each patient made at the time of admission; Coordinator of
        Social Services assisted in ensuring that all necessary medical/
        developmental history information is obtained for inclusion in
        the patient's case record.

    B. Physical examination of each patient performed within one week of
        his or her admission and at least once a year thereafter. Docu-
        mentation of physical exam included in patient's case record.
        Physical examinations to be current for all patients by _____.

    C. Special health problems for each patient (for example, allergies
        to foods or medications) monitored and staff educated concerning
        such problems. Notice placed in medical log of each residential
        unit.

    D. Necessary immunization current for each patient by _____.
        Timely reports made to county health department.

    E. Preventive health care, medication (as prescribed), first aid,
        and emergency care procedures administered as necessary for
        patients and staff.
        1. Patients and staff with communicable disease isolated to
            extent possible, in cooperation with program administrative
            staff.
        2. Medical/dental appointments for patients scheduled and
            results documented in each patient's case record.
        3. In-service training for program staff in basic health care,
            disease prevention, and emergency care procedures educated.
        4. Supervisor and Executive Director notified when staff are
            too ill to work and sick leave is recommended.

F. Patients and staff scheduled for weekly visits by medical consultants; medical consultants informed concerning health care services for staff and patients; monthly report of activity submitted to supervisor.

G. Patients receiving medication reviewed monthly with medical consultants and program administrative staff; recommended changes in type and/or dosage of medication implemented promptly.

IV. Clinical records.

A. Current Medication Treatment Plans maintained for all patients receiving psychotropic medication.

B. Problem-oriented medical records maintained for each patient.

C. Monthly medication review documented in each patient's case record within one week of review date.

D. Case records reviewed quarterly to ensure that medical forms (for example, emergency medical form, medication treatment plan, if applicable) and frequency of documentation are as per case record standards. Biannual report submitted to supervisor with next report due on _____.

V. Attendance at conferences and workshops. Attend as necessary to remain informed concerning advances in medical treatment and technology of importance to health services and to comply with the laws and regulations pertaining to continuing education and renewal of nursing registration.

VI. Special projects.

VII. Additional responsiblities.

(Similar to Assignments A - E on page 215.)

Position Title: Language Development Specialist

Department: Educational Services

Description of Assignment

  I. Assessment and observation to determine the needs of patients served
      by the program in the area of speech/language development and com-
      munication skills. Written summary of needs assessment documented in
      each patient's case record.

 II. Individual language acquisition training for selected patients.

      A. Schedule for individual training sessions submitted to supervisor
          (Director of Education) for review at three-month intervals
          beginning _____.

      B. Ongoing evaluation of each patient's progress made as per the
          research design and intervention strategy being employed; data
          obtained from training sessions plotted and graphed and entered
          in patient's case record whenever possible.

      C. Weekly progress note written for each patient in individual
          training. Progress note entered in each patient's case record
          and initialed by the language development specialist within one
          week of its entry.

      D. Brief quarterly progress reports on patients in individual train-
          ing prepared for dissemination to parents and/or referring
          agencies as part of the program's quarterly progress reporting
          procedure.

      E. Case manager duties completed with respect to communication of
          short- and long-term objectives for each patient in individual
          training (for example, specification of objectives and target
          behaviors; development, completion, and evaluation of behavior
          change projects based on speech/language objectives; progress
          reporting).

      F. Consultation held with other program staff concerning progress of
          individual training, their possible roles, etcetera.

III. Consultation with other educational and clinical services staff con-
      cerning ongoing behavior change projects in the area of communication
      for those patients not receiving individual training.

      A. Meetings of clinical and educational staff attended when
          possible.

      B. When appropriate, materials prepared for educational and/or
          clinical staff to assist in their work with patients in promoting
          increased communication skills.

      C. Program staff assisted in developing treatment objectives, be-
          havior change projects, and procedures for assessing progress
          being made by patients not involved in individual training
          sessions; program staff and administration assisted in speech
          and language considerations as per individual educational plans
          for all patients.

 IV. Evaluation and needs assessment made of newly admitted patients as
      necessary.

  V. Training and supervision of volunteers, interns, and/or practicum
      students assigned to the speech services program, as per request by
      supervisor; in-service training for program staff in language
      training conducted as per request by supervisor.

 VI. Current inventory of equipment and materials used in speech services
      program submitted to supervisor by _____.

VII. Pertinent state regulations concerning language acquisition training and speech therapy for patients receiving human services in residential settings and/or for a given patient as per his or her most current treatment plan reviewed and monitored. Supervisor informed concerning deficiencies when they are found to exist.

VIII. Affiliation(s) developed and maintained with universities or colleges with training programs in language development, concerning placement or undergraduate interns at the program, as per request by supervisor.

IX. Literature in language acquisition training reviewed to ensure continued knowledge and expertise in area of specialty; such knowledge and expertise evaluated in regular meetings with supervisor.

X. Special Projects.

XI. Additional Responsibilities.

(Similar to Assignments A - E on page 215.)

Position Title: Coordinator of Social Services

Department: Transitional Services

Description of Assignment

I. Communication with parents/legal guardians, referring agencies, and other persons and agencies concerned with the patient and his or her program of treatment.

   A. Telephone and written contact scheduled with concerned agencies and individuals; documentation of the date of each contact included in each patient's case record. Log submitted to supervisor (Director of Transitional Services) for review at three-month intervals beginning _____.

   B. Samples of each student's school work sent to parents at least once each quarter in cooperation with educational staff and the Director of Education. Documentation provided in case record within one week of time that sample is sent to parents.

   C. Vacation-planning for patients coordinated. Parents/legal guardians and concerned persons contacted regarding patients' behavior during vacation visits -- in cooperation with the Director of Clinical Services, Director of Education, and the parent training specialist.
      1. Assessment instruments (checklist forms, and so on) distributed to the patient's parent/legal guardians, relatives, and so on prior to vacation visits.
      2. Assessment data and summary of information collected at the conclusion of each visit for inclusion in each patient's case record. Entry made in case record within one week after each vacation visit.
      3. Phone contact made with parents/legal guardians, relatives, and concerned persons, at least once during each vacation visit of more than five days. Documentation of each contact placed in patient's case record.

   D. Personal contact with parents/legal guardians, concerned persons, and/or representatives of referral agencies made during their visits to the program. Progress note documenting nature of visit entered in case record within one week of visit.

   E. Individual educational planning conducted in cooperation with the Director of Education, Director of Clinical Services, and educational staff; parents, program staff, social service agencies, and school districts contacted as necessary to ensure timely case evaluations and individual educational plan preparation. Plan for each patient served by the program current as of _____ of each year.

   F. Current information maintained on aspects of each patient's home situation (for example, parents' employment, prospects for patient's returning home) through regular contact with parents and referring agencies. Regular update of information included in social history section of patient's case record.

   G. Parent training and home observation/consultation conducted in association with other program staff as per requests by supervisor.

   H. Assist Coordinator of Health Care Services in making phone contact with parents/legal guardians and other concerned persons if patient becomes seriously ill and is confined to bed for two or more days. Documentation of contact entered in case record.

II.   Patient advocacy.

    A.   Notify supervisor when progress reports are due for each patient. Written list submitted to supervisor for submission to program administrative staff one month in advance of due date.

    B.   Case records (for example, progress notes, authorization forms) reviewed quarterly to ensure that each patient's rights are being protected in receiving services from the program and that program case record standards are being adhered to. A record review form completed on each case. A quarterly report made to supervisor concerning suspected rights violations, with first report due on _____ .

III. Admission screening and discharge planning.

    A.   Admission screening coordinated from initial contact through various stages of the admission interview; pre-admission interview and post-interview briefing conducted with program administrative staff for each potential admission. Biannual report of admission activity submitted to supervisor with the next report due on _____ .

    B.   Follow-up contact with patients, families, and/or referring agencies maintained after completing admission interview. Continuing contact maintained with patients accepted and waiting for admission. Biannual report of activities submitted to supervisor with next report due _____ .

    C.   Admission planning conducted to ensure that the program's patient population is appropriate in terms of presenting problems and the program is as near to operating capacity as possible.

    D.   Information provided, in cooperation with other program staff, as requested in discharge planning with other agencies (for example, evaluations, social histories, recommendations). Evaluations submitted to supervisor for final approval.

    E.   Comprehensive discharge summary (as per case record standards) completed for inclusion in case record within two weeks of a patient's discharge.

    F.   Follow-up contact concerning patients discharged from the program made at three-month intervals for the first year and at six-month intervals thereafter. Documentation of this activity entered as case note in patient's case record.

IV.   Special projects.

V.   Additional responsibilities.

(Similar to Assignments A - E on page 215.)

Position Title: Account Clerk

Department: Administrative Services

Description of Assignment

I. Maintenance of program financial accounts.

    A. Current, accurate accounts maintained in accordance with gener-
        ally accepted accounting principles as evaluated by an indepen-
        dent audit of the program's accounting practices conducted each
        year.
        1. Accounts receivable.
        2. Accounts payable.
        3. Grant accounts.
        4. Internal expense accounts (for example, maintenance supplies).
        5. Special project accounts.
        6. Tax deferred annuity accounts/pension plans.

    B. Advise supervisor (Director of Administrative Services) of status
        of specified accounts on weekly basis.
        1. Accounts payable forty-five days or older.
        2. Accounts receivable sixty days or older.

    C. Current receipts/disbursement records available for review by
        supervisor.
        1. Maintain petty cash account.
        2. Maintain cash receipts journal.
        3. Prepare and record all bank deposits.
        4. Reconcile monthly bank statements.

II. Preparation of financial reports.

    A. Assist supervisor in preparation of monthly financial reports.
        1. Necessary financial data, supporting documentation, and
            new or corrected information directed to the program's
            accountant by the twelfth of the month following the report
            month.
        2. Upon receipt of financial statements from the program's
            accountant, the monthly budget control form and ancillary
            reports prepared for submission to supervisor by the
            twentieth of the month.
        3. Double-check made of all figures. Calculator tape of figures
            attached to each financial report.
        4. Assist supervisor in modification of reporting formats as
            requested.
        5. Prepare forms and reports to funding agencies as per request
            from supervisor.

    B. Prepare monthly Bureau of Nutrition report/reimbursement.
        1. Receive inventory information and food consumption figures
            from Dietary Supervisor.
        2. Finalize report as per instructions from Bureau of Nutrition.
        3. Advise supervisor if receipt of above information is delayed.

III. Employee benefits/personnel.

    A. Provide employees with information and assistance concerning
        insurance and benefit enrollment forms.

    B. Submit monthly statements to insurance companies, etcetera, as
        required.

    C. Assist supervisor in establishment of individualized employee
        payroll record cards by _____.

228

IV. Payroll accounting.

    A. Bi-weekly payroll prepared from employee time records.

    B. Payroll submitted to supervisor for approval prior to bank processing.

    C. Payroll checks disbursed.

    D. Assist supervisor in payroll corrections as necessary.

V. Purchasing/receiving.

    A. Purchase requests which are approved by the supervisor of the employee making the request received.

    B. Purchase order number assigned, purchase order prepared and submitted to supervisor for approval.

    C. Purchase orders maintained in pending file in accordance with internal bookkeeping procedures.

    D. Merchandise received, packing-slip checked with contents and original purchase order, and material disbursed to staff after approval of supervisor.

VI. Special projects.

VII. Additional responsibilities.

(Similar to Assignments A - E on page 215.)

Appendix C

FORMS

Staff Monitoring Checklist*

TASK 1: BATHING

Staff member observed: _____

Supervisor: _____

Date: _____

TRAINING: Watch new staff member conduct one complete bath.

MONITORING: Observe a different staff member each week, watching each staff member once a month.

SCORING: Criterion = 100 percent "yes" (or Not Applicable). Procedures must be completed in the listed sequence to be scored "yes".

ROUTINE:
1. Supervisor immediately gives completed checklist to staff member for initialing.
2. Staff member initials and returns to supervisor.
3. Supervisor gives completed checklists to program manager each week.

Circle One

1. Did the staff member wash his or her own hands before touching the patient?	Yes	No
2. Were all of the materials assembled within reach of the bath tub before the patient was brought to the area?	Yes	No
3. Did the staff member explain to the patient that he or she was going to take a bath?	Yes	No
4. Were the patient's dirty clothes and diaper placed in the proper receptacles?	Yes	No
5. Did the staff member brush the patient's teeth and rinse his or her mouth with the mouthwash?	Yes	No
6. Was patient's hair washed (if indicated on the bathing chart)?	Yes	No
7. Did the staff member clean the patient's hair, face, and body in that order?	Yes	No
8. Was special soap or lotion used (if indicated on bathing chart)?	Yes	No
9. Did the staff member dry the patient and place him or her on the towel?	Yes	No
10. Was deodorant applied?	Yes	No
11. Did the staff member conduct and record a health check?	Yes	No
12. Was the patient's hair brushed?	Yes	No
13. Was the patient taken to the appropriate activity, play or feeding?	Yes	No
14. Did the staff member record appropriately on the master schedule board, bathing charts, and health chart?	Yes	No
15. Check the patient to see how clean he or she is. Look at the following body areas to see if there is any obvious dirt: eyes, ears, nose, fingernails, hands, and between toes. Was each clean?	Yes	No
16. Were patient's fingernails short enough?	Yes	No

*Adapted from checklist in Risley, T.R., and Favell, J.E. Constructing a living environment in an institution. In L.A. Hamerlynck (Ed.), Behavioral systems for the developmentally disabled: II: Institutional, clinic, and community environments. New York: Brunner/Mazel, 1979, pp. 3-24. Copyright Brunner/Mazel Publishers, used with permission.

Shift Communication Checklist

Unit/Ward _____

Date: _____

Patient

Shift Present				
Toileting				
1. Toilet accidents (#)				
2. Bowel movements (#)				
Night-Time Behaviors				
1. Bedwetting incidents (#)				
2. Out of bed incidents (#)				
Health				
1. Health incidents				
2. Meals missed (BLD)				
Disruptive Behaviors				
1. Aggressions				
2. Tantrums				
3. Destruction of property				
4. Restraint required				
Activities				
1. Home				
2. Overnights out				
3. Visits				
4. Visitors				
5. Van ride				
6. Walk				
7. Picnic				
8. Party				
9. Workshop				
10. Other: _____				
Additional Comments:				

Reviewed by: (Initial/shift) _____

Incentive Survey

Employee's name _____

Date _____

Date of previous survey _____

DIRECTIONS: In order to assist program management in providing the most appropriate, effective incentives for your performance, we would appreciate your providing us with information concerning your preferences. Please rate the following items from most desirable (rating of 1) to least desirable (rating of 23). Please note that a number of negative consequences for performance are included (for example, suspension from work without pay). Nevertheless, each item should be given a rating.

_____ Increased benefits.

_____ Positive feedback (verbal) from supervisor.

_____ Promotion to higher status job.

_____ Type of work (for example, opportunity for job rotation).

_____ Positive work evaluation with copy to personnel file.

_____ Job security (for example, being promoted from probationary to permanent status).

_____ Opportunity for advancement.

_____ Improved social relationships (for example, transfer within the organization).

_____ Demotion to lower status job.

_____ Increased pay.

_____ Travel to professional conferences.

_____ Disciplinary (negative) letter from supervisor.

_____ Letter of commendation (positive) from supervisor.

_____ Disciplinary (negative) verbal feedback from supervisor.

_____ Suspension from work without pay.

_____ Termination.

_____ Negative work performance evaluation (written).

_____ Decreased pay.

_____ Opportunity to have greater voice in deciding program policy and procedure (for example, opportunity to serve on program policy committee).

_____ Leave without pay.

_____ Improved working conditions (specify).

_____ Increased leave.

_____ Letter of commendation (positive feedback) from program's chief administrative officer.

Are there additional incentives that you prefer? If so, list and assign each a rating:

_____ _____

_____ _____

_____ _____

_____ _____

Please indicate your most preferred and least preferred incentive:

      Most preferred: _____

      Least preferred: _____

Additional comments:

Received by: _____ _____
                       (supervisor)   (date)

Human Service Project Form

Name of Patient _____

Date _____

1. Specific behavior: _____

2. Definition: _____

_____

3. Skill area (Circle One); Social   Self-care   Health Care   Motor

Language   Academic

4. Objective/criteria for success: _____

_____

5. Procedures:

Phase	Procedure	Method of Measurement
Baseline		
Treatment		
Maintenance		

6. Potential risks of the program or procedure: _____

_____

7. Potential benefits: _____

_____

8. Staff involved: _____

_____

9. Results: A. The objective was met/not met (circle one)

B. The staff was satisfied/dissatisfied with the results (circle one)

10. Results documented in patient's case record: Date: _____

Staff Initials: _____

11. Reviewed by supervisor: Date: _____ Supervisor Initials: _____

Employee Feedback Form

Employee _____   Month _____

Name of supervisor completing review _____

1. From your interactions with this person this month, indicate some-
   thing(s) you were particularly pleased about.

2. Consider the following areas in reviewing the employee's performance.
   Provide specific feedback, with suggestions for how to make improvement. If no comment is made, the employee may assume that no improvement is needed.

   AVAILABILITY AND APPROACHABILITY

   TAKING INITIATIVE

   TAKING RESPONSIBILITY FOR SOLVING PROBLEMS

   MEETING PERFORMANCE STANDARDS

   COOPERATION/TEAMWORK

   CONCERN FOR PATIENTS

3. Overall, how satisfied were you with this person's performance this
   month?

   ( ) Completely dissatisfied
   ( ) Dissatisfied
   ( ) Slightly dissatisfied
   ( ) Neither satisfied nor dissatisfied
   ( ) Slightly satisfied
   ( ) Satisfied
   ( ) Completely satisfied

Feedback received: _____
                        (employee's initials)

                                        _____
                                             (date)

Supervisor Feedback Form

Supervisor: _____   Month _____

Name of employee completing review: _____

1. From your interactions with this person this month, indicate some-
    thing(s) you were particularly pleased about.

2. Consider the areas below in reviewing the supervisor's performance.
    Provide specific examples of situations needing improvement, and give
    suggestions for alternative actions. If no comment is made, the super-
    visor may assume that no improvement is needed.

    AVAILABILITY, APPROACHABILITY (listens; is concerned; is open-minded)

    ALLOCATION OF RESOURCES (fairness)

    LEADERSHIP/ORGANIZATION/MANAGEMENT (communicates clearly; provides
    direction; makes informed decisions; provides rationales; follows
    through)

3. Overall, how satisfied were your with your supervision this month?

    ( ) Completely dissatisfied   ( ) Somewhat satisfied
    ( ) Dissatisfied   ( ) Satisfied
    ( ) Somewhat dissatisfied   ( ) Completely satisfied
    ( ) Neither dissatisfied nor satisfied

4. Overall how satisfied were you with your job this month?

    ( ) Completely dissatisfied   ( ) Somewhat satisfied
    ( ) Dissatisfied   ( ) Satisfied
    ( ) Somewhat dissatisfied   ( ) Completely satisfied
    ( ) Neither dissatisfied nor satisfied

    Comments:

Feedback received: _____
                          (supervisor's initials)

                                              _____
                                                (date)

Narrative Format for Performance Evaluation

Employee _____ SS# _____

Position _____ Supervisor _____

Date of employment _____ Date of review _____

A. Evaluation of Performance: Relative to established performance
   standards (attach documentation if necessary).

   _____
   _____
   _____
   _____
   _____
   _____
   _____

B. Recommendations for Future Performance.

   _____
   _____
   _____
   _____
   _____
   _____
   _____

C. Evaluation Summary:

   _____ Unacceptable   _____ Above-standard

   _____ Must improve   _____ Outstanding

   _____ Standard

D. Consequences:

   _____
   _____
   _____

   Supervisor: _____ Date _____

E. Employee Comments: Employee must comment if evaluation is below-
   standard.

   _____ Agree   _____ Disagree

   _____ Request review

   Employee's signature: _____ Date _____

F. Program Supervisory Review:

   _____ Agree   _____ Disagree (comments):

   _____

   Name and title: _____ Date _____

238

Checklist/Narrative Format

for Performance Evaluation

Position: Child Development Specialist   Employee _____

Date of Employment _____

Supervisor _____

Date of Evaluation _____

PERFORMANCE STANDARD   RATING

1. Provides for the health and well-being   ____ Outstanding
    of the patients in his or her care by
    assisting health care staff in dispensing   ____ Above-standard
    medication, assisting patients in daily   ____ Satisfactory
    personal hygiene tasks, providing
    necessary supervision, assisting in   ____ Needs improvement
    emergency treatment and keeping informed   ____ Unacceptable
    of social and medical information concerning
    each patient.

    Supervisor's comments:

2. Implements treatment procedures as   ____ Outstanding
    specified in each patient's treatment
    plan including assessing and drawing   ____ Above-standard
    up objectives as well as developing,   ____ Satisfactory
    implementing and evaluating procedures
    to meet the objectives.   ____ Needs improvement
                                                   ____ Unacceptable

    Supervisor's comments:

3. Provides parents, legal guardians and   ____ Outstanding
    approved agency representatives with
    pertinent information about patient's   ____ Above-standard
    progress.   ____ Satisfactory
                                                   ____ Needs improvement
    Supervisor's comments: ____ Unacceptable

4. Provides patients with a favorable   ____ Outstanding
    living environment by assisting in the
    day to day maintenance of their living   ____ Above-standard
    area and their personal belongings as   ____ Satisfactory
    well as by cooperating with special
    projects designed to improve the living   ____ Needs improvement
    environment.   ____ Unacceptable

    Supervisor's comments:

5. Demonstrates an understanding of the program's philosophy of treatment, policies and procedures; demonstrates proficiency in using procedures required to meet the needs of the program's patients.

   Supervisor's comments:

   ____ Outstanding
   ____ Above-standard
   ____ Satisfactory
   ____ Needs improvement
   ____ Unacceptable

6. Maintains open lines of communication with co-workers, administrative and support services personnel by attending meetings, informing appropriate administrative staff of needs and cooperating with special requests made by supervisor.

   Supervisor's comments:

   ____ Outstanding
   ____ Above-standard
   ____ Satisfactory
   ____ Needs improvement
   ____ Unacceptable

7. Preserves the rights of patients, their families, and so on by maintaining confidentiality, employing restrictive procedures only when specified in patient's treatment plan, and following the program's ethical standards.

   Supervisor's comments:

   ____ Outstanding
   ____ Above-standard
   ____ Satisfactory
   ____ Needs improvement
   ____ Unacceptable

8. Assists in promoting a good public image of the program, its patients, staff, and services.

   Supervisor's comments:

   ____ Outstanding
   ____ Above-standard
   ____ Satisfactory
   ____ Needs improvement
   ____ Unacceptable

9. Complies with program policies concerning personnel practices (for example, hours of employment, approved leave, etcetera).

   Supervisor's comments:

   ____ Outstanding
   ____ Above-standard
   ____ Satisfactory
   ____ Needs improvement
   ____ Unacceptable

10. Overall job performance.

    Supervisor's comments and recommendations for future performance:

    ____ Outstanding
    ____ Above-standard
    ____ Satisfactory
    ____ Needs improvement
    ____ Unacceptable

    _____
    (supervisor)

Employee's comments: (employee must comment if overall job performance is rated as "needs improvement" or "unacceptable")

_____

_____

_____

_____

Consequences:

_____

_____

_____

Employee's signature: _____ Date_____

Reviewed by (if applicable);

_____ Date_____
                        Program Director

Appendix D
Patient Problem Behaviors:
The Comprehensive Problem Behavior Survey

Patient Problem Behaviors:

The Comprehensive Problem Behavior Survey*

INSTRUCTIONS:

This survey can be used as a behavior checklist or a behavior rating scale. As a behavior checklist, the frequency of occurrence of behavior can be recorded for an individual patient or for groups of patients. When used as a behavior rating scale it is possible to rate the extent to which a behavior typifies a patient over a specified amount of time. The numbers preceding each item are listed strictly for use in computer storage and retrieval (** indicates items specific to the child patient).

Instruction A: For use as a behavior checklist:

1. Assign each patient an identifying code (for example, initials).

2. When several patients are involved, record their identifying codes on the lines preceding the behaviors they exhibited. Spaces are provided for recording the total number of patients listed in each major category and for the instrument as a whole.

3. When one patient is involved, place his or her identifying code at the top of the page and place tally or checkmarks on the lines preceding each behavior he or she exhibited. Behavior may be further specified by underlining items listed as examples. Record the frequency totals for each major category and the instrument as a whole in the spaces provided.

Instruction B: For use as a behavior rating instrument:

1. Record the patient's name or identifying code at the top of the page.

2. Rate each behavior according to how frequently it has been observed (displayed by the patient) during the past two months, by assigning one of the following numerical values in the space provided next to each item on the list: 0 = never observed; 1 = rarely observed (less than once monthly); 2 = occasionally observed (at least once a week); 3 = often observed (at least once a day); 4 = frequently observed (more than once a day). Record the total rating scores for each category and the instrument as a whole in the spaces provided.

PATIENT NAME _____ Observer's Name _____

Date_____ Total number of behaviors or individuals recorded _____

BEHAVIORS RELATED TO HEALTH   TOTAL _____

111 _____ Missed appointment treatment, therapy or medication, etc.

112 _____ Was late for appointment, or in receiving treatment, therapy, or medications.

113 _____ Failed to cooperate with treatment (lost or refused medication; refused therapy; had to be coaxed or forced to take treatment; over-used or under-used medications; etc.).

114 _____ Used abusive language toward anyone providing treatment (name-calling, ridiculing, etc.).

115 _____ Fought or was physically aggressive toward anyone providing treatment (hit, pushed, etc.).

116 _____ Complained about treatment or the person or institution providing treatment.

117 _____ Reported physical symptoms (headache, toothache, breathing
difficulty, etc.).

118 _____ Experienced physical reactions (coughed, wheezed, had seizure,
fainted, etc.).

BEHAVIORS RELATED TO HOUSEHOLD AND PERSONAL RESPONSIBILITY   TOTAL _____

211 _____ Failed to take care of bedroom, sleeping or play area (bed not
made, litter not picked up, etc.).

212 _____ Discharged other assigned work poorly (needed reminders; was
sloppy, incomplete, slow, etc.).

213 _____ Discharged personal hygiene responsibilities poorly (did not
brush teeth, comb hair, etc.).

214 _____ Was openly defiant, sassy, physically or verbally abusive or
resistive, talked back, etc., regarding household or hygiene
responsibilities.

BEHAVIORS RELATED TO SOCIAL INTERACTIONS AND CONDUCT   TOTAL _____

310 _____ Destroyed his or her own, another person's or public property,
either by being careless or by intentionally breaking, burning,
marring, etc.

311 _____ Broke ordinary rules or exceeded limits regulating behavior
(traveled too far from home, stayed outdoors past curfew time,
visited places off-limits, etc.).

312 _____ Failed to comply with or resisted instructions, requests or
commands (was negative, defiant, sassy, talked back, needed
reminders, etc.) other than those pertaining to household
duties (214) or health (115).

313 _____ Was dishonest (stole, cheated, lied, etc.).

314 _____ Used tobacco, alcohol, illicit drugs (circle those that apply).

315 _____ Engaged in inappropriate sex behavior (masturbated openly;
approached others for homosexual acts; used seductive behavior
or dress; exposed genitals, etc.).

316 _____ Set fire or played with matches, fireworks, or other flammable
materials.

317 _____ Was inconsiderate (interrupted conversations, was impolite,
borrowed without asking, made constant or unreasonable demands
on others, etc.).

318 _____ Was verbally abusive toward other patients (argued, teased,
called names, criticized, etc.).

319 _____ Was physically aggressive toward other patients (hit, pushed,
tripped, picked on, pulled at hair or clothing, threw things,
etc.).

320 _____ Was uncooperative with other patients in work or play activities (did not share, showed no give-and-take, was a poor loser,
quit when losing, etc.).

321 _____ Was picked on, or teased, by other patients.

322 _____ Reported mistreatment by other patients.

323 _____ Did not take advantage of opportunity to participate in group activities with others (recreation, discussion, scouts, etc.).

324 _____ Was avoided, and/or ignored, by other patients.

325 _____ Stayed to self and avoided social interactions.

326 _____ Spent considerable time with individuals younger than him or herself.

327 _____ Spent considerable time with individuals older than him or herself.

328 _____ **Spent considerable time with adults.

329 _____ **Avoided the company or presence of adults (left peer group when adult entered, etc.).

330 _____ **Had difficulty in talking with parents or other adults (exhibited stiffening, stammering, long pauses or periods of silence, stuttering, etc.).

331 _____ Complained about anything other than homesickness, mistreatment by peers or siblings, physical well-being, and meals.

332 _____ Was not assertive (refused to defend self, did not initiate action, etc.).

BEHAVIORS RELATED TO AFFECT AND HABITS   TOTAL _____

411 _____ Cried.

412 _____ Complained of homesickness or of being away from home, parents, spouse, etc.

413 _____ Was fearful; complained of being afraid (other than night fears); avoided persons or situations out of fear, etc.

414 _____ Was frequently silly, giggling, laughing, clowning, etc.

415 _____ Was sad, solemn, etc.

416 _____ Did not express feelings openly (did not cry, laugh, smile when the situation or occasion called for such expression).

417 _____ Was tense (exhibited tight or stiff muscles, tremor, shaking, twitching, nail- or lip-biting, etc.).

418 _____ Was overactive (did not sit still or finish activities, was restless, etc.).

419 _____ Showed poor physical coordination (tripped, fell, was clumsy in sports or other activities, etc.).

420 _____ Was verbally or physically self-abusive (criticized self, threatened or attempted to harm self, expressed wish to die, etc.).

421 _____ Exhibited behavior which reflected a superior attitude (boasted, bragged, etc.).

422 _____ Had temper tantrum.

423 _____ Wet or soiled clothing during waking hours.

424 _____ Expressed displeasure, disgruntlement, hostility or indirect anger (sulked, griped, grumbled, kicked, hit or threw things, slammed doors, etc.).

BEHAVIORS RELATED TO EATING AND MEALTIME ROUTINE   TOTAL _____

511 _____   Exhibited poor eating or dining habits (was picky, slow or
             finicky; overate; ate too fast; used utensils or napkin im-
             properly; ate with hands, etc.).

512 _____   Complained about food, dining facilities, meal scheduling,
             service, etc.

513 _____   Was late for meal or missed meal.

514 _____   Was disruptive at mealtime (was noisy, impolite, physically
             or verbally disturbing to others; threw things; argued, fought,
             stole food, grabbed from others, etc.).

515 _____   Discharged kitchen duties poorly (did not clear table properly;
             did not scrape plate; was verbally resistive; complained,
             delayed).

BEHAVIORS RELATED TO BEDTIME ROUTINE AND SLEEP   TOTAL _____

611 _____   Had difficulty going to bed (was slow doing pre-bedtime chores,
             made excuses to stay up longer, etc.).

612 _____   Sobbed, cried, or moaned while asleep.

613 _____   Slept restlessly (turned, tossed, etc.).

614 _____   Walked or talked while asleep.

615 _____   Rocked body or banged head prior to or during sleep, or upon
             awakening.

616 _____   Was fearful (reported fear of the dark, bad dreams, nightmares,
             etc.).

617 _____   Slept at times other than usual bed- or nap-time.

618 _____   Had difficulty going to sleep (would not quiet down, called out
             for someone, etc.).

619 _____   Had difficulty awaking or arising in morning.

620 _____   Wet or soiled the bed.

BEHAVIORS RELATED TO SCHOOL AND STUDY   TOTAL _____

711 _____   Was late to school or tutoring (check whenever brought to your
             attention).

712 _____   Had unexcused absence from school or tutoring (check whenever
             brought to your attention).

713 _____   Misbehaved at, or on the way to and from, school (check
             whenever brought to your attention).

714 _____   Studied poorly (needed reminders, did not apply self, refused,
             etc.).

715 _____   Turned in incomplete or late homework (check whenever brought
             to your attention).

OTHER BEHAVIOR   TOTAL _____

716 _____   Other significant behavior (specify, for example, work-related):

EVENTS

811 _____   Communicated with others by letter; 812 _____   phone;
813 _____   visit.
814 _____   Appointment with medical; 815 _____   psychological;
816 _____   lab.
817 _____   Other.

*Adapted from Renne, C.M., and Christian, W.P. Comprehensive Problem
Behavior Survey. Unpublished manuscript, 1975. Available from the May
Institute, Inc., P.O. Box 703, Chatham, MA 02633.

Appendix E
Example
of an Employee
Incentive System

An Employee Incentive System*

PURPOSE: To reinforce the behavior of staff who repeatedly
exceed the work performance standards for their
positions.

ELIGIBILITY: All members of the program staff.

BONUS PERFORMANCE: Bonus performance has been specified in three general
categories: (1) special projects; (2) work perfor-
mance standards; (3) research and professional development. Sample bonus performances in each of these
categories are listed below.

Category 1: Special Projects

Sample Bonus Performance	Documentation
1. Development and implementation of a "regularly scheduled event" for an entire ward or unit -- for example, vocational, social, educational or other functional and socially valid activity.	Written description of event with a copy of the classroom or cottage schedule.
2. Successful application of a new program or behavior change procedure.	Written description of procedure with data indicating its effective- ness.
3. Participation in the writing of a grant.	Written description of the grant with a copy of the proposal.
4. Development and implementation of methods to improve staff communication.	Written description of the communication system.
5. Work (with prior approval) that results in significant improvement of one's work environment -- for example, grounds, living areas, classrooms.	Written description of improvements; examin- ation of improvement by supervisor.

Category 2: Work Performance Standards

Sample Bonus Performance	Documentation
1. Exceeding three points of reliability per phase on a human service project designed to meet an objective listed on a patient's treatment plan.	Pertinent data.
2. Exceptionally competent performance of a supervisor-requested patient-relevant task beyond standard work performance expectations.	Written description of the performance; name of the supervisor request- ing the performance; the products that resulted from the performance.

*Adapted from Christian, W.P., Luce, S.C., Newsom, C.D., and Troy, P.J.
Teaching human service staff to prompt management for reinforcement.
Paper presented at the Annual Convention of the Association for Behavior
Analysis, Milwaukee, May 1982.

3. Competent performance of a self-initiated patient-relevant task beyond standard work performance expectations.	Written description of the performance; the products that resulted from the performance.
4. Perfect attendance at treatment team meetings.	Written log of meetings attended with verification.
5. Finishing work on an assignment or project 24 hours in advance of the deadline set for the assignment.	Written description of assignment and the time submitted (verified by person receiving the assignment).
6. Adhering perfectly to the posted work schedule without initiating unauthorized switches or taking unauthorized annual leave.	Statement from director supervisor.

Category 3: Research and Professional Development

Sample Bonus Performance	Documentation
1. Development, implementation and empirical validation of a novel or improved treatment procedure.	Written description of procedure with data showing effectiveness.
2. Presentation of new material at a national or regional conference.	Scheduling of the title of the presentation or poster in the conference program.
3. Authorship of a professional publication.	Copy of the manuscript as accepted for publication.
4. Successfully recruiting a new staff member.	Name of applicant and position for which he or she was hired.
5. Coordination of and/or participation in an activity promoting community awareness of the program.	Written description of the activity and its community participants.
6. Demonstrating knowledge of a recommended reading assignment.	Exceeding 80 percent on written or oral quiz based on the reading.

Bonus Rewards

Bonus rewards are contingent upon outstanding work performance, that is, performance above and beyond the standards specified for one's position. Successful documentation and approval by one's supervisor and/or the Employee Incentive Committee will result in an employee's earning bonus rewards independent of his or her other salary adjustments -- for example, (a) the cost-of-living increases typically available each year, and (b) step promotions and merit increases contingent upon satisfactory performance relative to the work performance standards for one's position.

Bonus rewards may include, but are not limited to, the following:
1. Money.
2. Increased annual leave.
3. An approved leave of absence.
4. A trip to an approved professional workshop or conference.
5. A letter of commendation.

Reward Selection:

1. Rewards (type and amount) are selected by the Employee Incentive Committee (EIC) which is made up of direct service as well as management-level employees. The EIC will attempt to follow the employee's preference concerning rewards to the extent possible.

2. The selection of rewards or incentives will be made after the employee has provided his or her supervisor with adequate appropriate documentation (see attached form).

Scheduling:

1. Documentation should be submitted by staff monthly (between the first and tenth of each month for the preceding month).

2. Rewards will be determined and distributed biannually (for example, in January and June of each year). If bonus rewards are in the form of money, they will be provided through regular payroll procedures.

Reliability and Validation:

A completed documentation form (see attached) must be initialed by one's direct supervisor. Note: In some cases, additional verification may be necessary, as indicated above.

Evaluation:

The Employee Incentive System will be evaluated along at least three important dimensions: (1) staff performance; (2) staff satisfaction; and (3) program improvement.

Additional Information:

More information regarding the Employee Incentive System can be obtained by consulting one's supervisor.

BONUS PERFORMANCE DOCUMENTATION FORM

NAME: _____   POSITION: _____

DATE: _____

Bonus Performance Category: (Check one)

_____ Special project

_____ Work performance standards

_____ Research and professional development

Behavioral Description:

In the space below indicate what you did, how it benefitted the program or its patient(s), and why it would be considered "above-standard"
job performance.

What:_____

_____

_____

How:_____

_____

_____

Why:_____

_____

_____

Documentation: Describe the exemplary performance and attach any additional permanent product documentation available in support of your perfor-
mance._____

_____

_____

Incentive Preferred: (number in order of your preference)

_____ Cash

_____ Additional annual leave

_____ Trip to _____ (specify a conference or workshop)

_____ A letter of commendation

_____ Other (specify) _____

Additional Comments:_____

_____

_____

Employee Signature:

_____ Date: _____

Approval:

_____ Not approved

_____ Additional documentation needed: _____

_____

_____ Approved. Recommended incentive: _____

_____

Supervisor Signature: _____

Date: _____

Executive Director Approval:

_____ Date: _____
Signature

Appendix F

FORMS

Patient Tracking Overview*

Therapist _____

Week (Month) beginning _____

	Case number	Patient name	Progress review due date	Title XX applic. date	Title XX expir. date	Face sheet current	Comments
Individual counseling							
Group therapy							
Follow-up							

*This information is stored in memory (memory typewriter, word processing unit) and is distributed to each service provider on a weekly or monthly basis.

Patient Tracking Worksheet*

Therapist_____

Week (Month) Beginning_____

	Case number	Patient name	Service contact this week/month	Case note done	Serv. term.	Case record review	Title XX plan and goal	Serv. deliv. form	Comments
		Memory		Service provider			Business office		
Individual counseling									
Group therapy									
Follow-up									

*This information is filled in and submitted by the service provider and the business office at the end of each week or month.

INTERDEPARTMENTAL PEER REVIEW FORM

TO: _____   _____
    Department Supervisor   Period under review

<u>Areas to consider in preparing review</u>: availability and approachability,
cooperation, compliance with established procedures and lines of authority,
promptness in providing assistance, practicality of suggestions, helpful-
ness, reasonableness of requests.

1. In reviewing my interactions with your department, I was particularly
    pleased with:

2. However, some concerns did arise. These areas and my suggestions for
    how your might remedy them are listed below.

Peer review provided by_____

Date_____

Record Review Form

Case number _____ Patient's initials _____ Reviewer's initials _____

Therapist's (case manager's) initials _____ Date of review _____

Type of Service _____

The following information is obtained from the <u>left side</u> of the case record. Describe any departure from case record standards in comments section.

LEFT SIDE

_____1. <u>Screening application</u> complete (consult standards).

_____ Includes summary of presenting problems.

_____ Signed by patient (guardian).

_____2. Welfare eligibility date.

_____ Financial information form signed by patient (guardian).

_____ Records of insurance billings.

_____3. <u>Authorization for services</u> signed by patient (guardian) and program representative.

_____ Applicable sections initialed by patient (guardian).

_____4. <u>Patients' rights notification form</u> signed by patient (guardian) and program representative.

_____5. Additional Forms

_____ <u>Audiovisual consent form</u> signed by patient (guardian) and program representative.

_____ <u>Authorization for medical and dental services</u> signed by patient (guardian) and program representative.

_____ <u>Emergency medical authorization</u> signed by patient (guardian) and program representative.

_____ <u>Field trip permit</u> signed by patient (guardian) and program representative.

_____ Other (list)

_____

_____

_____

Section B

_____6. Medical data complete (medical form present and filled out by physician).

_____ Signed by physician <u>and</u> therapist (nurse, etc.) <u>currently active with case.</u>

_____ Regular reviews conducted of medication (if applicable).

_____ Date of last review.

_____ Evidence of regular examination by physician.

_____ Date of last examination.

_____ Current graphs of daily temperature and blood pressure readings present in record (if applicable).

_____ How many readings were not recorded during last 30 days?

_____ Date of last recorded reading.

_____ Do nurses' notes meet standards for content?

_____ Do nurses' notes meet standards for frequency of entry?

Section C

_____7. Social Services (Title XX) Patients.

_____ Service face sheet present.

_____ Service plan and goal present.

_____ Service delivered forms completed on monthly basis.

_____ Results of planned services.

The following information is obtained from the <u>right side</u> of the case record. Describe any departure from case record standards in comments section.

Section A. Case Notes

1. <u>Frequency</u>

_____ 1 per week clinical and counseling services (nonresidential).

_____ 2 per week educational services.

_____ 3 per week residential services.

_____ 1 per month follow-up

2. <u>Quality</u>: Assign rating as per standards outlined in manual of case record standards.

Are the case notes clear and complete? (circle one)

Unacceptable	Need improvement	Satisfactory	Good	Outstanding
1	2	3	4	5

Are the case notes consistent with the patient's service agreement and individualized treatment plan (reflecting treatment plans and goals)? (circle one)

Unacceptable	Need improvement	Satisfactory	Good	Outstanding
1	2	3	4	5

_____3. Case notes signed by case manager, therapist, etc. responsible for them.

_____4. Date of last case note.

_____ Within one week of today's date?

_____5. Screening summary adequate (presenting problems listed)?

_____6. Date of first service contact (first session with patient).

_____7. Case notes documenting a review of progress at 3-month intervals from date of first contact.

_____ Is progress regularly documented in case notes, for example, data summaries, goal attainment, etc.?

_____ 8. Adequate termination summary (as per standards).

Section B: Treatment Plan

_____ 9. Treatment plan present, all sections completed, signed by patient and case manager or therapist.

_____ 10. Description of risks and benefits included for each program of service or treatment procedure with which patient is involved.

_____ 11. Treatment plan revision present (if applicable). Treatment plan revision must reflect each change in program of service.

_____ All sections completed, signed by patient and case manager or therapist.

_____ 12. Target behaviors on treatment plan and treatment plan revision clear and specific.

_____ 13. Treatment goals specified.

_____ Treatment goals realistic.

_____ 14. Treatment procedures clear and specific.

_____ Is there documentation to support the choice of treatment procedures? (Do they represent the most effective, least restrictive alternatives?)

_____ 15. Is case consultation with Medical Director and/or other program staff documented in case notes?

_____ 16. What criterion is used to determine effectiveness as success of treatment?

_____ Is there a criterion for success specified for each target behavior?

17. How is the effectiveness of treatment measured, documented and evaluated? _____

_____

_____

18. What is the major strength of this case record? _____

_____

_____

What is its major weakness? _____

_____

_____

19. General Impression:

Unacceptable	Needs improvement	Satisfactory	Good	Outstanding
1	2	3	4	5

20. How would you improve this case record?_____

_____

_____

_____

Additional comments:

Patient Satisfaction Survey

Date: _____

Type of Service Received_____

Please answer the following questions to the best of your ability. Your responses will greatly assist us in our efforts to improve (program) and the services it provides.

1. Were the goals for the services you received specific? (In other words, did you have a clear understanding of what the therapist intended to do for you?)

       _____ Yes   _____ No

2. Were you given a written plan of the service(s) you were to receive?

       _____ Yes   _____ No

3. Did you feel that you received the services as planned? If no, please explain.

       _____ Yes   _____No

4. Did you receive the services you expected? If not, please explain.

       _____ Yes   _____ No

5. Did the services you received solve the problems that brought you to (program)? If not, please explain.

       _____ Yes   _____ No

6. Would you return to (program) for service if the need should arise in the future? If not, please explain.

       _____ Yes   _____ No

7. Would you recommend (program) to a friend with a similar problem?

       _____ Yes   _____ No

Please indicate (circle) how useful these items were in helping you to benefit from the services you received.

8. Assigned readings.   very useful   useful   not useful

9. Discussing readings with your therapist.   very useful   useful   not useful

10. Written handouts.   very useful   useful   not useful

11. Therapist's explanations of techniques and concepts   very useful   useful   not useful

12. Practicing techniques during the therapy session.   very useful   useful   not useful

13. Practicing techniques at home.   very useful   useful   not useful

14. Comments and suggestions from other patients (for group therapy participants).   very useful   useful   not useful

15. Overall evaluation of the whole service experience.   very useful   useful   not useful

Please indicate your satisfaction with the performance of your therapist.

16. Were you satisfied that the therapist had sufficient knowledge to help you with your problem?
_____ Satisfied
_____ Neither satisfied nor dissatisfied
_____ Dissatisfied

17. Were you satisfied with your participation in therapy? For example, were you satisfied with the opportunities you were provided to discuss problems or ask questions?
_____ Satisfied
_____ Neither satisfied nor dissatisfied
_____ Dissatisfied

18. Were you satisfied with the therapist's ability to:
a. Answer impromptu questions?
_____ Satisfied
_____ Neither satisfied nor dissatisfied
_____ Dissatisfied
b. Apply information to life situations?
_____ Satisfied
_____ Neither satisfied nor dissatisfied
_____ Dissatisfied

19. Were you satisfied with the therapist's willingness to help outside of scheduled sessions?
_____ Satisfied
_____ Neither satisfied nor dissatisfied
_____ Dissatisfied

20. Were you satisfied that the therapist was attentive to the point that you were trying to get across?
_____ Satisfied
_____ Neither satisfied nor dissatisfied
_____ Dissatisfied

21. Was your therapist negative or critical toward you?

all the time   sometimes   never

22. Was your therapist friendly and warm toward you?

all the time   sometimes   never

23. Did your therapist seem to understand about your feelings and thoughts?

all the time   sometimes   never

24. Do you feel your therapist helped you?

all the time   sometimes   never

25. Did you enjoy your experience at (program)?

all the time   sometimes   never

Please answer the following questions to the best of your ability.

26. a. List below any suggestions you have for improving (program) services:

b. List below any suggestions you have for additional services and/or information not provided:

c. General Comments:

Consumer Evaluation Form
Social Service Agency

Name of agency_____

Name of program _____

Evaluation period _____

1. Are you satisfied that program staff understand patients' needs and
    set reasonable goals for treatment?

    _____ Completely satisfied
    _____ Satisfied
    _____ Slightly satisfied
    _____ Neither satisfied nor dissatisfied
    _____ Slightly dissatisfied
    _____ Dissatisfied
    _____ Completely dissatisfied

    Comments: _____
    _____
    _____

2. Are you satisfied that program staff understand the patients' legal
    rights and make a conscientious effort to protect them in providing
    services?

    _____ Completely satisfied
    _____ Satisfied
    _____ Slightly satisfied
    _____ Neither satisfied nor dissatisfied
    _____ Slightly dissatisfied
    _____ Dissatisfied
    _____ Completely dissatisfied

    Comments: _____
    _____
    _____

3. Are you satisfied with the services patients received?

    _____ Completely satisfied
    _____ Satisfied
    _____ Slightly satisfied
    _____ Neither satisfied nor dissatisfied
    _____ Slightly dissatisfied
    _____ Dissatisfied
    _____ Completely dissatisfied

4. Are you satisfied that the program is effective in meeting the needs
    of the patients it serves?

    _____ Completely satisfied
    _____ Satisfied
    _____ Slightly satisfied
    _____ Neither satisfied nor dissatisfied
    _____ Slightly dissatisfied
    _____ Dissatisfied
    _____ Completely dissatisfied

5. Are you satisfied that the program operates in compliance with applicable regulations and guidelines specified by your agency?

_____ Completely satisfied
_____ Satisfied
_____ Slightly satisfied
_____ Neither satisfied nor dissatisfied
_____ Slightly dissatisfied
_____ Dissatisfied
_____ Completely dissatisfied

6. Are you satisfied with the amount of cooperation you have received from program staff in their interactions with your agency?

_____ Completely satisfied
_____ Satisfied
_____ Slightly satisfied
_____ Neither satisfied nor dissatisfied
_____ Slightly dissatisfied
_____ Dissatisfied
_____ Completely dissatisfied

7. Are you satisfied that the costs of services are reasonable?

_____ Completely satisfied
_____ Satisfied
_____ Slightly satisfied
_____ Neither satisfied nor dissatisfied
_____ Slightly dissatisfied
_____ Dissatisfied
_____ Completely dissatisfied

8. Are you satisfied with the program's facilities?

_____ Completely satisfied
_____ Satisfied
_____ Slightly satisfied
_____ Neither satisfied nor dissatisfied
_____ Slightly dissatisfied
_____ Dissatisfied
_____ Completely dissatisfied

9. Are you satisfied that the program provides a useful service to the community?

_____ Completely satisfied
_____ Satisfied
_____ Slightly satisfied
_____ Neither satisfied nor dissatisfied
_____ Dlightly dissatisfied
_____ Dissatisfied
_____ Completely dissatisfied

Any additional comments, opinions, or suggestions concerning the program or its staff would be most appreciated.

Agency representative:_____

Date: _____

Peer Reviewer's Evaluation Form

Program reviewed: _____

Program area: _____

Program personnel interviewed (name and title): _____
_____
_____
_____

1. What are the program's strengths in this area? _____
    _____
    _____
    _____

2. What are the program's weaknesses in this area? _____
    _____
    _____
    _____

3. What improvements/program changes in this area might be recommended?
    _____
    _____
    _____
    _____

4. Additional comments (use back of form if necessary) _____
    _____
    _____
    _____

    Reviewer's name _____ Date _____

Appendix G

FORMS

Patients' Rights Form

Every patient of (program) has the following rights:*

1. To receive medical, psychosocial and rehabilitative care and treatment, including a written plan for services.

2. To be advised of or have his or her guardian advised of the nature and possible outcomes of treatment and alternative methods of treatment.

3. To refuse to have his or her guardian refuse treatment.

4. To inspect his or her case record and to be informed of his or her status at reasonable intervals of no longer than three months in length.

5. To receive the government-regulated minimum wage when working for the maintenance of the program facility.

6. To wear his or her own clothing and use personal articles such as toiletries, unless these items are dangerous to self or others.

7. To have access to personal storage space.

8. To have visitors every day.

9. To have reasonable access to telephone.

10. To keep and spend money.

11. To have access to letter-writing material and to receive unopened correspondence.

12. To be free of mechanical restraints unless the existing conditions justify their use.

13. To know his or her rights under the pertinent state laws, the release procedures, legal process for judging mental incompetence, and the legal process for appointing a guardian.

14. (Program) will NOT, on the ground of race, color, sex, religion or national origin:

    a. Deny an individual any services or other benefits provided under the program.
    b. Provide any service(s) or other benefits to an individual which are different, or are provided in a different manner, from those provided to others served by the program.
    c. Subject an individual to segregation or separate treatment in any matter related to his or her receipt of any service(s) or other benefits provided under the program.
    d. Restrict an individual in any way in the enjoyment of any advantage or privilege enjoyed by others receiving any service(s) or other benefits provided under the program.
    e. Treat an individual differently from others in determining whether he or she satisfies any eligibility or other requirement or condition which individuals must meet in order to receive any aid, care, service(s) or other benefits provided under the program.
    f. Deny any individual an opportunity to participate in the program through the provision of services or otherwise, or afford him or her an opportunity to do so which is different from that afforded others under the program.

---

*The "bill of rights" previously described (see page 180) can also be used as a form for notifying patients (guardians) of their rights.

15. The patient's signed authorization must be obtained prior to the release of information pertaining to any patient or former patient of (program), to any other person or institution.

16. In any treatment or training program in which recording devices or any other observational techniques are used, the patient must be informed of their use. If any of these materials are to be used for purposes other than the individual's treatment and training program, a signed authorization must be obtained from the patient for such use.

None of the above rights can be denied in receiving services from (program). In the event that rights are denied, denials must be reported to the program manager who in turn files a report with (program's ultimate supervising authority).

Unless a patient is judged by a court of law as incompetent to exercise the following rights or is under the legal age of majority, he or she retains the right to:

1. Marry
2. Dispose of property.
3. Make purchases.

4. Execute legal instruments.
5. Vote.
6. Hold a driver's license.

I have read and understand the above statement of patients' rights and I understand (program)'s commitment to protect them. I have also received a copy of this statement for my personal use.

_____
Patient or Legal guardian

_____   Date:_____
Program staff

Authorization for Services Form

Authorization for services regarding _____ (patient name) _____

I hereby authorize (program) and its staff to conduct the services initialed below:

Initials

Disagree Agree

_____ _____   I authorize the program to conduct whatever interviews,
                observations, medical exams, and intelligence and/or
                psycho-educational evaluations necessary for assessment
                related to my receiving services.

_____ _____   I authorize the program to make necessary information
                regarding my treatment available to its staff.

_____ _____   I understand that the program's function is to provide
                both clinical and training services for the community.
                I authorize whatever observation, information sharing,
                and trainee participation the program deems necessary
                for training interns and practicum students, staff, and
                volunteers and I understand that the program will use
                discretion both in selecting trainees and sharing in-
                formation related to my involvement with the program.

_____ _____   I authorize an exchange of information related to my
                treatment between (program) and (school district) (this
                authorization is required when patient's services are
                funded by a school district).

_____ _____   I authorize an exchange of information related to my
                treatment between (program) and (social service agency)
                (this authorization is required for patients receiving
                services that are funded by a social service agency).

_____ _____   I authorize (program) to contact the below-named in-
                dividuals and/or agencies for release of any or all
                academic, social, medical, and psychological informa-
                tion concerning:

                _____
                              (patient's name)

and for exchange of information that might be pertinent
to the progress of my treatment. I request that this
information be kept confidential and be used for professional reasons only.

Physician: _____

Other human service or social service agencies:
_____

Probation/law enforcement Agencies: _____
_____

Other: _____
_____

The nature and purpose of the above have been explained to me and I understand that if I have further questions, I may discuss them with a member
of the program staff. I understand that I may revoke this authorization
at any time, providing that I submit notification of such revocation in
writing.

_____   _____

Patient (Legal guardian)   Phone Number

_____

Address

I have explained the nature and purpose of the above to the patient (legal
guardian) who has signed this form.

_____

Program staff

_____

Date

Contractual Service Plan

Name of patient _____ Date of birth _____

Address _____

Name of service provider (therapist) _____

This agreement is:

    A. Original agreement: Date _____
    B. Revised agreement: 1 _____ 2 _____ 3 _____ 4 _____
                            5 _____ 6 _____ 7 _____ 8 _____

    Note: Terms of original agreement remain in effect until revised in writing.

To the Patient: Please consider the terms of this agreement carefully, discussing each provision with the therapist. This is an aid to your receiving the service that you desire in addition to being your assurance that the therapist is aware of your basic rights in requesting and receiving service. While this agreement offers no guarantee that the procedures herein described will be effective, it is the first step in establishing the cooperation between patient and therapist essential to any successful program of treatment.

I. Therapist's Agreement

    A. I agree to keep appointments as scheduled unless illness or emergency prohibits.
    B. I agree to inform the patient if an appointment has been cancelled.
    C. I agree to respect the confidentiality of the patient's communication and to give information to outside parties only with the patient's written consent except as required by law.
    D. After assessing the patient's presenting problem(s) and the patient's objective(s) upon entering this agreement, I have identified the following target behaviors and goals for treatment:
    E. Problem 1 _____
         _____

        Treatment goal 1 _____
        _____
        _____

        In order to attain the above stated goal, the following procedure(s) will be employeed _____
        _____
        _____

        The criteria by which progress to the goal will be measured are:
        _____
        _____

        Progress toward achieving this goal will be monitored as follows:
        Prior to initiating program procedures _____
        _____

        During treatment _____
        _____

        Follow-up _____
        _____

F. Problem 2 _____
    _____

    Treatment goal 2 _____
    _____

    In order to attain the above stated goal, the following proce-
    dure(s) will be employed: _____
    _____

    The criteria by which progress to the goal will be measured are:
    _____

    Progress toward achieving this goal will be monitored as follows:
    Prior to initiating program procedures _____
    _____

    During treatment _____
    _____

    Follow-up _____
    _____

G. Problem 3 _____
    _____

    Treatment goal 3 _____
    _____

    In order to attain the above stated goal, the following proce-
    dure(s) will be employed: _____
    _____

    The criteria by which progress to the goal will be measured are:
    _____

    Progress toward achieving this goal will be monitored as follows:
    Prior to initiating program procedures _____
    _____

    During treatment _____
    _____

    Follow-up _____
    _____

H. I propose to use the following services in assisting the patient
    to achieve the goal(s) specified above.

    _____ Individual counseling   _____ Educational services
    _____ Parent/family counseling   _____ Residential services
    _____ Group therapy   _____ Medication
    _____ Social skills training   _____ Assessment and evaluation
    _____ Preschool program   _____ Baseline assessment
    _____ Basic skills/language   _____ Other (specify)
            acquisition

II. Service Description*: _____ (service) _____

   A. Description of Program Procedures

   _____
   _____
   _____
   _____
   _____

   B. Additional Procedures
   In addition to procedures outlined above, the following proce-
   dure(s) is(are) to be used with _____ under the
   following circumstances. (These procedures are described on
   separate handouts.)

   Circumstances   Procedures

   _____   _____
   _____   _____
   _____   _____
   _____   _____
   _____   _____

   C. Possible Support Services Available at (program):

   _____
   _____
   _____
   _____
   _____

   D. Benefits and Reasonable Risks

   _____
   _____
   _____
   _____
   _____

   E. Supporting Research
   (service) has been described in the following professional references available in our agency library.

   _____
   _____
   _____
   _____

   * This information should be provided for each type of service that the
   patient is to receive.

273

F.   Possible Alternative Approaches

Alternative approaches to the treatment procedures outlined above
include:

_____

_____

_____

_____

_____

III.   Patient's (Legal Guardian's) Agreement

A.   I have discussed the presenting problem(s) and goal(s) for treatment as outlined above and I consent to work toward the achievement of this(these) goal(s).

B.   I have discussed the proposed program(s) of service and treatment procedure(s) as well as the alternative programs and procedures outlined in Section II of this agreement and I consent to
apply or to assist in the application of the specified treatment
procedure(s).

C.   I have entered into this agreement knowing the objectives of
treatment, the potential benefits and the reasonable risks
associated with the treatment procedure(s).

D.   I shall provide data as specified above, during treatment and
follow-up, in order to determine the effectiveness of the treatment.

E.   I shall provide (program) with the following compensation for
efforts in my behalf: _____ in accordance with the
following schedule: _____

F.   I shall keep all scheduled appointments and shall give at least
48 hours notice of my intention to cancel any appointment. If
I am unable to attend because of illness or emergency, I will
notify the therapist as soon as possible.

G.   I have been informed of my rights as a patient and understand
that I may stop participation in treatment at any time, for any
reason, without the need to offer an explanation, and without
penalty.

H.   I understand my obligations under the terms of this agreement and
I realize that failure to honor such obligations may be considered grounds for termination of service.

Additional agreements: _____

_____

_____

Date: _____

Patient (Legal guardian) _____

Therapist _____

Human Rights Committee Due Process Report*

Persons attending meeting: _____   Date:_____

_____

_____

_____

1. Instances where the Human Rights Committee has refused or delayed
    consent for the initiation of a treatment procedure and has requested
    additional information, opinions, or the use of less intrusive pro-
    cedures.

2. Instances of the committee seeking outside opinion and advice. (Note
    who, when, and topic of concern. Note whether the advice sought was
    from the Professional Advisory Board, professional peer reviewers,
    and so on; from outside, independent professionals; from the pro-
    fessional literature; or from a patient advocacy group.)

3. Instances of the committee deliberating in the absence of program
    personnel -- that is, executive sessions. (Note dates and who was
    in attendance.)

4. Instances of independence in selecting new members of the committee,
    such as the committee providing a list of potential new members and
    the program manager choosing from that list. (Characterize how the
    selection was done.)

5. Instances of public display and public awareness of the committee,
    its members, and its activities. (Note displays and any approaches
    to committee members by staff, outside persons, or agencies.)

6. Instances of the appointment of a committee as an advocate for a
    patient or case considered, and of the presentation subsequently made
    by that committee member. (Note the member's name and patient's
    initials or identifying number; note also the date when the appoint-
    ment was made and the date when the presentation was made.)

7. Instances of on-site visits made by committee members to observe
    program operation. (Note the names and dates.)

8. Instances of any revisions of a statement of approval for generally
    used procedures. Instances of any corollary statements of the con-
    ditions of use, monitoring, and reporting that were approved.

9. Instances of any revisions of a statement of approval for procedures
    that can be implemented on an interim basis but which require the
    committee's review and approval for continuation. Instances of
    subsequent review and approval/disapproval of procedures in this
    category.

10. Instances of the committee's prior review and approval/disapproval of
    other procedures.

Signatures of Human Rights Committee members participating:

_____   _____

_____   _____

*Adapted from Sheldon-Wildgen, J., and Risley, T.R. Balancing clients'
rights: The establishment of human rights and peer review committees.
In A. Bellack, M. Hersen, and A. Kazdin (Eds.), International handbook of
behavior modification. New York: Plenum Press, 1982.

Summary of the Human Rights Committee Review
of Patient Service Plan*

Patient's initials or identification code: _____ Admission date: _____

Name of designated client advocate: _____

Date of this review: _____

Long-range habilitative goal(s) with target date for each: _____

_____

_____

Current program goals (one year or less): _____

_____

Current treatment procedures in effect: _____

_____

    In reviewing this patient's service plan, the Human Rights Committee
has addressed each of the following questions and indicated by an "OK"
those questions that have been answered to the committee's satisfaction.
(Please note that wherever the term "patient" is used with an asterisk --
"patient*" -- each of the following should be considered as a patient:
the person in the program; the person's parent or guardian; the person or
agency providing funds for the treatment.)

A. Have the goals of treatment been adequately considered?   _____

    1. To ensure that the goals are explicit, are they written? _____
    2. Has the patient's* understanding of the goals been
        assured by having the patient* restate them orally or
        in writing?
    3. Have the therapist and patient* agreed on the goals _____
        of therapy?
    4. Will serving the patient's* interests be contrary
        to the interests of other persons? _____
    5. Will serving the patient's* interests be contrary
        to the patient's* long-term interest? _____

B. Has the choice of treatment methods been adequately
    considered? _____

    1. Does the published literature show the procedure
        to be the best one available for that problem? _____
    2. If no literature exists regarding the treatment
        method, is the method consistent with federally
        accepted practice? _____

*Adapted from the following sources: Association for Advancement of
Behavior Therapy. Ethical Issues for Human Services. New York: Association for Advancement of Behavior Therapy, 1978; and Sheldon-Wildgen, J.,
and Risley, T.R., Balancing clients' rights: The establishment of human
rights and peer review committees. In A. Bellack, M. Hersen, and
A. Kazdin (Eds.), International handbook of behavior modification. New
York: Plenum Press, 1982.

3. Has the patient* been told of alternative procedures that might be preferred by the patient*
   on the basis of significant differences in dis-
   comfort, treatment time, cost, or degree of
   demonstrated effectiveness?
4. If a treatment procedure is publicly, legally, or
   professionally controversial, has formal professional consultation been obtained, has the reaction of the affected segment of the public been
   adequately considered, and have the alternative
   treatment methods been more closely reexamined
   and reconsidered? _____

C. Is the patient's* participation voluntary? _____

1. Have possible sources of coercion on the
   patient's participation been considered?
2. If treatment is legally mandated, has the
   available range of treatments and therapists
   been offered? _____
3. Can the patient* withdraw from treatment without
   a penalty or financial loss that exceeds actual
   clinical costs? _____

D. When another person or a program is empowered to
   arrange for therapy, have the interests of the subordinated patient been sufficiently considered? _____

1. Has the subordinated patient been informed of
   the treatment objectives and did he or she
   participate in the choice of treatment
   procedures? _____
2. Where the subordinated patient's competence to
   decide is limited, have the patient and the
   guardian participated in the treatment decisions
   (and discussions) to the extent that the patient's
   abilities permit? _____
3. If the interests of the subordinated person and
   the superordinate persons or program conflict by
   dealing with both interests? _____

E. Has the adequacy of treatment been evaluated? _____

1. Have quantitative measures of the problem and its
   progress been obtained? _____
2. Have the measures of the problem and its progress
   been made available to the patient* during
   treatment? _____

F. Has the confidentiality of the treatment relationship
   been protected? _____

1. Has the patient* been told who has access to his
   or her case records? _____
2. Are records available only to authorized persons? _____

G. Does the therapist refer the patient* to other therapists
   when necessary? _____

1. If treatment is unsuccessful, is the patient*
   referred to other therapists? _____
2. Has the patient* been told that, if dissatisfied
   with the treatment, referral will be made? _____

H. Is the therapist qualified to provide treatment? _____

1. Has the therapist had training or experience in
   treating problems like the patient's?   _____
2. If deficits exist in the therapist's qualifications, has the patient* been informed?   _____
3. If the therapist is not adequately qualified, is
   the patient* referred to other therapists, or has
   supervision by a qualified therapist been provided? Is the patient* informed of the supervisory relation?   _____
4. If the treatment is administered by mediators,
   have the mediators been adequately supervised by
   a qualified therapists?   _____

Comments on the above questions?

Outside persons who have been consulted by staff or the Human Rights
Committee in determining recommended treatment (names and dates).

_____   _____
_____   _____
_____   _____

Based on this review, are any changes indicated in long- or short-term
goals or treatment procedures? (Characterize.)

_____   _____
_____   _____
_____   _____
_____   _____

Signatures of participating Human Rights Committee members:

_____   _____
_____   _____
_____   _____
_____   _____

Notes

CHAPTER 2

[1] See, for example, *Gary W.* v. *State of Louisiana,* 437 F. Supp. 1209 (1979); *Wyatt* v. *Stickney,* 325 F. Supp. 781, *aff'd on rehearing,* 344 F. Supp. 1341 (M.D. Ala. 1971), *aff'd on rehearing,* 344 F. Supp. 373, *aff'd in separate decision,* 344 F. Supp. 387 (M.D. Ala. 1972), *aff'd sub nom. Wyatt* v. *Aderholt,* 503 F. 2d 1305 (5th Cir. 1974). See also Title XIX of the Social Security Act.

CHAPTER 3

[1] For additional information concerning organizational theory, the reader should consult the following references: Dessler, G. *Organization theory: Integrating structure and behavior.* Englewood Cliffs, New Jersey: Prentice-Hall, 1980; Jackson, J., & Morgan, C. *Organization theory: A macro perspective for management* (2nd ed.). Englewood Cliffs, New Jersey: Prentice-Hall, 1982; Katz, D., & Kahn, R. L. *The social psychology of organizations* (2nd ed.). New York: John Wiley & Sons, 1978; Korman, A. *Organizational behavior.* Englewood Cliffs, New Jersey: Prentice-Hall, 1977; Mintzberg, H. Structuring of organizations. Englewood Cliffs, New Jersey: Prentice-Hall, 1979; Porter, L., Lawler, E., & Hackman, R. *Behavior in organizations.* New York: McGraw-Hill, 1975; Schein, E. *Organizational psychology.* Englewood Cliffs, New Jersey: Prentice-Hall, 1970; Thompson, J. D. *Organizations in action.* New York: McGraw-Hill, 1967; Woodward, J. *Industrial organization: Theory and practice.* New York: Oxford University Press, 1965.

[2] For additional information concerning organizational design, the reader should consult the following references: Lawrence, P., & Lorsch, J. *Organization and environment: Managing differentiation and integration.* Homewood, Illinois: Irwin, 1969.

[3] This section was adapted from information provided the authors by Dr. Emily Herbert.

CHAPTER 4

[1] Adapted from Christian, W. P. Programming quality assurance in the residential rehabilitation setting: A model for administrative work performance standards. *Journal of Rehabilitation Administration*, 1981, 5, 26–33. Used with the permission of *Journal of Rehabilitation Administration, Inc.*

CHAPTER 5

[1] Leidholt, P. A., Lipsker, L. E., Luce, S. C., & Christian, W. P. *A middle management strategy for increasing staff-to-client interaction in residential human service programs.* Paper presented at the Annual Convention of the Association for Behavior Analysis, Milwaukee, May 1981.

[2] Dyer, K., Schwartz, I. S., & Luce, S. C. *Improving the quality of planned activities through staff feedback.* Paper presented at the Annual Convention of the Association for Behavior Analysis, Milwaukee, May 1982.

[3] Adapted from guidelines appearing in the following: (a) Cort, R. P. How to get an idea across. *Personnel,* American Management Association, July 1951, 46–51; and (b) Phillips, E. L., Phillips, E. A., Fixsen, D. L., and Wolf, M. M. *The teaching family handbook.* Lawrence, Kansas: Bureau of Child Research, 1972.

[4] This section was adapted from information provided the authors by Dr. Emily Herbert.

[5] Adapted from information provided by Dr. Emily Herbert.

CHAPTER 6

[1] Adapted from Christian, W. P. How to obtain foundation grants for applied research and human service programming. *The Behavior Therapist*, 1982, 5, 129–133.

[2] *Ibid.*

[3] All private foundations are subject to special regulations imposed by the Internal Revenue Code of 1969. All must submit a 990-AR report to the Internal Revenue Service (IRS) each year and make the report available for public inspection in their offices for 180 days after filing. This form includes information about a foundation's granting activity such as a list of grants or contributions made during the year and the names and addresses of foundation managers or trustees. Another form, 990-PF, must also be filed with the IRS. It includes more detailed information on the foundation's assets and income than the 990-AR. Complete sets of IRS records for all foundations in the country are available for free public use in The Foundation Center's libraries in New York and Washington, D.C. The Center's field offices in San Francisco and Cleveland contain IRS records for foundations in the western and midwestern states respectively. The Foundation Center also has a nationwide network of foundation reference collections for free public use. Information concerning these libraries and reference collections can be obtained by calling The Foundation Center, toll free, at 800-424-9836.

CHAPTER 7

[1] The reader is encouraged to consult the following references for additional information concerning traditional rationales and strategies for program evaluation: Attkisson, Hargreaves, Horowitz, & Sorensen (1978); Broskowski & Atkisson (1981); Schulberg, Sheldon, & Baker (1969); Weiss (1972); and Zusman & Wurster (1975).

[2] From Christian, W. P. The biannual report: A model for structuring human service program evaluation and dissemination. *Journal of Rehabilitation Administration*, 1981, 5, 108–114. Used with the permission of *Journal of Rehabilitation Administration, Inc.*

CHAPTER 8

[1] Adapted from Liss-Levinson, N., & Nowinski, J. Client rights in sex therapy. In G. T. Hannah, W. P. Christian & H. B. Clark (Eds.), *Preservation of client rights: A handbook for practitioners providing therapeutic, educational, and rehabilitative services.* New York: The Free Press, 1981, p. 122–135.

[2] Adapted from Czyzewski, M. J., Hannah, G. T., Risley, T. R., & Sheldon-Wildgen, J. A sample policy for the human rights committee. Unpublished manuscript, 1981.

CHAPTER 9

[1] Adapted from Lindsay, M. C., & Stoessel, O. B. *Your advisory board and you: Some guides for administrators and board members.* Unpublished manuscript available from the Center for Public Service, Brandeis University, Waltham, Massachusetts, 02254.

[2] Adapted from National Institute of Mental Health. *Orientation manual for citizen boards of federally funded community mental health centers.* **U.S.D.H.H.S.,** 1980.

[3] *Ibid.*

References

CHAPTER 1

Argyris, C. *Increasing leadership effectiveness.* New York: John Wiley & Sons, 1976.

Binner, P. R., & Nassimbene, R. Mental hospital costs since the 1960s. *Administration in Mental Health,* 1980, *8,* 83–102.

Drucker, P. F. *Management: Tasks, responsibilities, and practice.* New York: Harper & Row, 1974.

Ghiselli, E. *Explorations in managerial talent.* Pacific Palisades, California: Goodyear Publications, 1971.

Levey, S., & Loomba, N. P. (Eds.). *Health care administration: A management perspective.* Philadelphia: Lippincott, 1973.

Martin, R. *Legal challenges to behavior modification: Trends in schools, corrections and mental health.* Champaign, Illinois: Research Press, 1975.

McClelland, D. Toward a theory of motive acquisition. *American Psychologist,* 1965, *20,* 321–333.

Meyer, N. G. *Provisional patient movement and administrative data, state and county psychiatric inpatient services.* Department of Health, Education, and Welfare, Public Health Service, National Institute of Mental Health Division of Biometry, Survey and Reports Branch. Washington, D.C.: U.S. Government Printing Office, April, 1975.

Parsons, H. M. What happened at Hawthorne. *Science,* 1974, *183,* 922–930.

Roemer, M. I. Evaluation of health service programs and levels of management. *Public Health Reports,* 1968, *82.* In S. Levey & N. P. Loomba (Eds.), *Health care administration: A managerial perspective.* Philadelphia: Lippincott, 1973, pp. 429–443.

United States Government. *The Budget of the United States Government, Fiscal Year 1981.* Washington, D.C.: U.S. Government Printing Office, 1981.

United States Government. *Statistical Abstract of the United States,* 1979. Washington, D.C.: U.S. Government Printing Office, 1979.

Vroom, V., & Yelton, P. *Leadership and decision-making.* Pittsburgh: University of Pittsburgh Press, 1973.

Williams, J. L. Health care costs: Why should we worry. *New England Journal of Human Services,* 1981, *1,* 31-37.

CHAPTER 2

Doke, L. A. & Risley, T. R. The organization of day care environments: Required vs. optional activities. *Journal of Applied Behavior Analysis,* 1972, *5,* 405-420.

Drucker, P. F. *Management: Tasks, responsibilities, and practice.* New York: Harper & Row, 1974.

Hall, R. V. *Managing behavior* (Part I). Lawrence, Kansas: H & H Enterprises, 1975.

Mager, R. F. *Goal analysis.* Belmont, California: Fearon Pitman, 1972.

Raia, A. P. *Managing by objectives.* Glenview, Illinois: Scott Foresman, 1974.

CHAPTER 3

Beckhard, R. Organizational issues in the team delivery of comprehensive health care. In I. K. Zola and J. B. McKinlay (Eds.), *Organizational issues in the delivery of health services.* New York: Prodist, 1974.

Butler, A. G., Jr. Project management: A study of organizational conflict. *Academy of Management Journal,* 1973, *16,* (1).

Drucker, P. F. *Management: Tasks, responsibilities, and practice.* New York: Harper & Row, 1974.

Drucker, P. F. *Managing in turbulent times.* New York: Harper & Row, 1980.

Gray, J. L. Matrix organization design as a vehicle for effective delivery of public health care and social services. *Management International Review,* 1974, *11,* 73-82.

Kouzes, J. M., & Mico, P. R. Domain theory: An introduction to organizational behavior in human service organizations. *Journal of Applied Behavioral Science,* 1979, *15,* 449-469.

Neuhauser, D. The hospital as a matrix organization. *Hospital Administration,* 1972, *17,* 8-25.

Wedel, K. R. Matrix design for human service organizations. *Administration in Mental Health,* 1976, *4,* 36-42.

CHAPTER 4

Bass, B., & Vaughn, J. *Training in industry: The management of learning.* Belmont, California: Wadsworth, 1966.

Christian, W. P. Programming quality assurance in residential rehabilitation settings: A model for administrative work performance standards. *Journal of Rehabilitation Administration,* 1981, *5,* 26-33.

Christian, W. P., Troy, P. J., Lipsker, L. E., Czyzewski, M. J., & Luce, S. C. *A comparison of two methods of staff orientation in a residential human service setting.* Paper presented at the Annual Convention of the Association for Behavior Analysis, Milwaukee, Wisconsin, May 1981.

Ellis, H. *The transfer of learning.* New York: MacMillan, 1965.
Hackman, R., & Lawler, E. Employee reactions to job characteristics. *Journal of Applied Psychology,* 1971, *55,* 259–286.
Mager, R. F. *Goal analysis.* Belmont, California: Fearon Pitman, 1972.
Quilitch, H. R. A comparison of three staff-management procedures. *Journal of Applied Behavior Analysis,* 1975, *8,* 59–66.

CHAPTER 5

Dunnette, M. (Ed.), *Work and nonwork in the year 2001.* Monterey, California: Brooks/Cole, 1973.
Jurgensen, C. Job preferences (what makes a job good or bad?). *Journal of Applied Psychology,* 1978, *65,* 267–276.
Lawler, E. Control systems in organizations. In M. Dunnette (Ed.), *Handbook of industrial and organizational psychology.* Chicago: Rand-McNally, 1975.
Morales v. *Turman* (364 F. Supp. 166 [E.D. Texas, 1973]).
Pomerleau, O., Bobrove, P., & Smith, R. Rewarding psychiatric aides for the behavioral improvement of assigned patients. *Journal of Applied Behavior Analysis,* 1973, *6,* 383–390.
Porter L., & Lawler, E. *Managerial attitudes and performance.* Homewood, Illinois: Dorsey Press, 1968.
Porter L., & Lawler, E., & Hackman, R. *Behavior in organizations.* New York: McGraw-Hill, 1975.
Risley, T. R., & Favell, J. E. Constructing a living environment in an institution. In L. A. Hamerlynck (Ed.), *Behavioral systems for the developmentally disabled: II. Institutional, clinic, and community environments.* New York: Brunner/Mazel, 1979, pp. 3–24.
Wyatt v. *Stickney* (344 F. Supp. 373 [M.D. Ala. 1972]).

CHAPTER 6

Abeles, F. A. How to prepare an effective scientific research proposal. *The Grantsmanship Center News,* 1982, *10,* 52–57.
Christian, W. P. How to obtain foundation grants for applied research and human service programming. *The Behavior Therapist,* 1982, *5,* 129–133.
Conrad, D. *Successful fund raising techniques.* San Francisco: Institute for Fund Raising, 1976.
Dermer, J. (Ed.) *America's most successful fund raising letters.* New York: Public Service Materials Research Center, 1976.
Doh, J. C. *Planning-program budgeting system in three federal agencies.* New York: Praeger, 1971.
Fisher, J. *How to manage a nonprofit organization.* Toronto, Ontario: Cumberland Press, 1978.
Hannah, G. T., and Risley, T. R. Experiments in a community mental health center: Increasing client payments for outpatient services. *Journal of Applied Behavior Analysis,* 1981, *14,* 141–157.
Hillman, H., & Abarbanel, K. *The art of winning foundation grants.* New York: Vanguard Press, 1975.
Hurst, J. C., Davidshofer, C. D., & Arps, W. Current perceptions and practices of charging fees in college and university counseling centers. *Journal of Counseling Psychology,* 1974, *21,* 532–535.
Joint Commission on Mental Health and Mental Illness: Report to Congress. Washington, D.C.: United States Government Printing Office, 1974.
Jones, R. L., & Trentin, H. C. *Budgeting: Key to planning and control.* New York: AMACOM, 1971.

Kansas Office of Mental Health/Retardation Services. Budget policy paper. Topeka, Kansas: Kansas Department of Human Services, 1981.

Kurzig, C. M. *Foundation fundamentals: A guide for grant seekers.* (Revised Ed.) New York: The Foundation Center, 1981.

Lewis, M. O., & Gerumsky, A. T. (Eds.) *The foundation directory* (8th Ed.) New York: The Foundation Center, 1981.

Mazade, N. A., Surles, R. C., & Akin, J. S. Fiscal resource development for state mental health agencies. *Administration in Mental Health,* 1976, *3,* 183–188.

McCaffery, J. Revenue budgeting: Dade County tries a decremental approach. *Public Administration Review,* 1981, *41,* 179–189.

Muchmore, L. *Kansas Department of Budget Instructions.* Topeka, Kansas: State of Kansas Printing Office, 1981.

Pyhrr, P. A. *Zero base budgeting.* Speech delivered at the International Conference of the Planning Executives Institute, New York, May 15, 1972.

Roback, H. B., Webb, W. W., & Strassberg, D. Personality difference between fee-paying and non-fee-paying patients. *Journal of Consulting and Counseling Psychology* 1974, *42,* 734–737.

Somerville, W. Where proposals fail: A foundation executive's basic list of what to do and not do when requesting funding. *The Grantsmanship Center News,* 1982, *10,* 24–25.

CHAPTER 7

Attkisson, C. C., Hargreaves, W. A., Horowitz, M. J., & Sorensen, J. E. (Eds.). *Evaluation of human service programs.* New York: Academic Press, 1978.

Broskowski, A., & Attkisson, C. C. *Information systems for health and human services.* New York: Human Sciences Press, 1981.

Christian, W. P., Clark, H. B., & Luke, D. E. Client rights in clinical counseling services for children. In G. T. Hannah, W. P. Christian & H. B. Clark (Eds.), *Preservation of client rights: A handbook for practitioners providing therapeutic, educational, and rehabilitative services.* New York: The Free Press, 1981, pp. 19–41.

Donaldson v. *O'Connor,* 493 F. 2d 507 (5th Cir. 1974).

Mace, M. The president and corporate planning. In *Harvard Business Review—On Management.* New York: Harper & Row, 1975, pp. 119–142.

Morales v. *Turman,* 364 F. Supp. 166 (Ed. Tex. 1973).

New York State Association for Retarded Children v. *Rockefeller,* 357 F. Supp. 752 (E.D.N.Y. 1973).

Pennsylvania Association for Retarded Children v. *Commonwealth of Pennsylvania,* 334 F. Supp. 1257 (E.D. Pa. 1971).

Risley, T. R., & Sheldon-Wildgen, J. Invited peer review: The AABT experience. *The Behavior Therapist,* 1980, *3,* 5–8.

Schulberg, H. C., Sheldon, A., & Baker, F. *Program evaluation in the health fields.* New York: Behavioral Publications, 1969.

Weiss, C. *Evaluation research: Methods of assessing program effectiveness.* Engelwood Cliffs, New Jersey: Prentice-Hall, 1972.

Zusman, J., & Wurster, C. R. (Eds.), *Program evaluation: Alcohol, drug abuse, and mental health services.* Lexington, Massachusetts: Heath, 1975.

CHAPTER 8

American Psychological Association. *Ethical Standards of Psychologists: 1977 Revision.* Washington, D.C.: American Psychological Association, 1977.

Association for Advancement of Behavior Therapy. *Ethical Issues for Human Services.* New York: Association for Advancement of Behavior Therapy, 1978.

Christian, W. P., Clark, H. B., & Luke, D. E. Client rights in clinical counseling services for children. In G. T. Hannah, W. P. Christian & H. B. Clark (Eds.), *Preservation of client rights: A handbook for practitioners providing therapeutic, educational, and rehabilitative services.* New York: The Free Press, 1981, pp. 19–41.

Favell, J. E., Favell, J. E., & Risley, T. R. A quality-assurance system for ensuring client rights in mental retardation facilities. In G. T. Hannah, W. P. Christian & H. B. Clark (Eds.), *Preservation of client rights: A handbook for practitioners providing therapeutic, educational, and rehabilitative services.* New York: The Free Press, 1981.

Griffith, R. D. An administrative perspective on guidelines for behavior modification: The creation of a legally safe environment. *The Behavior Therapist,* 1980, *3,* 5–7.

Hannah, G. T., Christian, W. P., & Clark, H. B. (Eds.). *Preservation of client rights: A handbook for practitioners providing therapeutic, educational, and rehabilitative services.* New York: The Free Press, 1981.

Joint Commission on Accreditation of Hospitals. *Standards for services of developmentally disabled individuals.* Chicago: Joint Commission on Accreditation of Hospitals, 1978.

Martin, R. Legal issues in preserving client rights. In G. T. Hannah, W. P. Christian & H. B. Clark (Eds.), *Preservation of client rights: A handbook for practitioners providing therapeutic, educational, and rehabilitative services.* New York: The Free Press, 1981.

Risley, T. R., & Sheldon-Wildgen, J. Suggested procedures for Human Rights Committees of potentially controversial treatment programs. *The Behavior Therapist,* 1980, *3,* 9–11.

Sheldon-Wildgen, J., & Risley, T. R. Balancing clients' rights: The establishment of human rights and peer review committees. In A. Bellack, M. Hersen & A. Kazdin (Eds.), *International handbook of behavior modification.* New York: Plenum Press, 1982.

Tarasoff v. *Regents of The University of California,* 17 Cal 3d 425, 131 Cal. Rptr. 14, 551, p2d 334, 83 ALR 3d 1166 (1974).

Wyatt v. *Stickney,* 325 F. Supp. 781, *aff'd on rehearing,* 344 F. Supp. 1341 (M.D. Ala. 1971), *aff'd on rehearing* 344 F. Supp. 363, *aff'd in separate decision,* 344 F. Supp. 387 (M.D. Ala. 1972), *aff'd sub nom,* Wyatt v. Aderhold, 503 F. 2d 1305 (5th cir. 1974).

CHAPTER 9

Kappel, F. *Vitality in business enterprise.* New York: McGraw-Hill, 1960.

Nowlen, P. M. Developing an effective board organization. In W. H. Silverman (Ed.), *Community mental health: A sourcebook for professionals and advisory board members.* New York: Praeger, 1981, pp. 34–43.

Robins, A. J., & Blackburn, C. Governing boards of mental health centers: Roles and training needs. *Administration in mental health,* 1974, *2,* 37–45.

Index

AUTHOR INDEX

Roback, H.B., 125, 285
Robins, A.J., 194, 286
Roemer, M.I., 7, 282

Schulberg, H.C., 280, 285
Schwartz, I.S., 280
Sheldon, A., 280, 285
Sheldon-Wildgen, J., 165, 185, 275–76, 281, 285, 286
Silverman, W.H., 286
Smith, R., 111, 284
Somerville, W., 131, 285
Sorensen, J.E., 280, 285
Stoessel, O.B., 281
Strassberg, D., 125, 285
Surles, R.C., 124, 285

Thompson, J.D., 279

Trentin, H.C., 136, 284
Troy, P.J., 78, 249, 283

Vaughn, J., 79, 283
Vroom, V., 9–10, 283

Webb, W.W., 125, 285
Wedel, K.R., 38–39, 283
Weiss, C., 280, 285
Williams, J.L., 2, 283
Wolf, M.M., 280
Woodward, J., 279
Wurster, C.R., 280, 285

Yelton, P., 9–10, 282

Zola, I.K., 283
Zusman, J., 280, 285

SUBJECT INDEX

Absenteeism, 6, 24, 50, 96
Accident reports, 75
Accountability, 4, 12, 26, 30, 40, 64, 68–70, 151–54, 176, 184, 190, 200, 203
Accounting, 9, 17, 62, 64, 67, 138, 167, 171
Achievement motivation, 9
Adaptive organizational structure, 40–42, 57, 68
Advisory boards, 27, 191–201
Advocacy, 8, 9, 112, 159, 176, 186, 189–90
Affirmative Action, 49, 61, 101, 120, 168
AIM (of effective management), 14, 34
American Association of Fund Raising Counsel, Inc., 128
American Civil Liberties Union, 176
American Medical Association, 66
American Psychiatric Association, 66, 165
American Psychological Association, 66, 177, 285
Analysis, 15, 34, 37, 70, 122, 131, 138, 141, 149
    of budgets, 149
    of data (results), 7, 28–29, 30–34, 57, 81, 91, 104, 120–22, 152, 154–56, 172, 175, 203, 207
    of goals, 19–21
    of job, 80–81, 83–84, 93
    key factor, 1
    of objectives, 203
    of tasks, 12
Anecdotal records of performance, 29, 88
Annual reports, 64–67, 129, 131, 165–66, 170–75, 193, 198–99, 207–8, 280
    flow chart for development of, 172–73
    format for, 170–74
    obtaining feedback concerning, 172–75, 207
    preparation and dissemination of, 172–75, 207
Apprentice training, 86

Assertive training, 87
Assessment, 16–17, 28, 62, 69–70, 88, 111, 152–57, 163, 178, 181, 197–98, 203
    baseline, 15, 28, 69, 101, 107, 109, 152–57, 164, 174, 207
    behavioral, 62, 80–81, 88
    of community needs, 21, 197–98
    follow-up, 62, 152–55, 205
    of interpersonal skills, 101
    medical, 62
    of patient's needs, 62, 69, 80, 157, 161, 163
    of performance evaluation, 109
    of pre-training, 81, 101
    of program needs, 16, 163, 203
    of resources, 16, 18, 203
    of staffing schedule, 97
Association for the Advancement of Behavior Therapy, 177, 276, 285
Audiovisual aids, 79, 83, 90, 180, 183, 190, 208
Audiovisual recording, 65, 81–82, 87–88, 101, 154
Audiovisual training, 81–82, 87–88
Authority, 8, 12, 35, 38, 41, 44, 55–57, 59, 67–68, 73, 100, 160, 192, 199, 203
Automatic recording, 29, 109

Baseline level of performance, 15, 28, 31–34, 69, 101, 107, 109, 152–57, 163–64, 174, 207
Behavior, 10–13, 26, 100, 114–16, 120, 125
    antecedents for, 11–13, 23, 203
    baseline level of, 15, 28, 31–34, 69, 101, 107, 109, 152–57, 163–64, 174, 207
    checklist, 88, 108, 115
    consequences for, 10–13, 23, 25, 108–13, 117, 119, 121, 124–25, 203, 206

Joint Commission for the Accreditation of Hospitals, 41, 47, 154, 185, 286
Joint Commission on Mental Health and Mental Illness, 124, 284

Key factor analysis, 1
Knowledge of results, 116, 122, 206

Latency recording, 109
Lawson Associates, Inc., 130
Leader effectiveness, 9
Learning, 79, 87, 90, 108
  trial and error, 87
Leave accrual, 50, 75, 113
Legal guidelines, 18–19, 23, 26, 28, 49, 54, 60, 62, 69–70, 73, 80, 95, 101–2, 105, 139, 157, 170, 202
Legal policy, 4, 14, 41, 47, 98, 166, 179
Legal safety, 176–90, 208–9
  assessing program status relative to, 178–79, 189
  criteria for, 177–79, 189
  strategies for ensuring, 179–90
Licensing and certification (of staff), 48, 60, 95, 167, 170
Local housing authority, 19

Maintenance of behavior change, 15, 25–26, 28, 31–34, 70, 80, 92–93, 101, 106–10, 204
Management by objective, 1, 2, 27
Management levels, 36, 38, 41
Management style, 9
Management theory, 1, 2
Manager effectiveness, 10, 13, 58, 202–9
Matrix organizational structure, 1, 39, 40–42
Measurement, 15, 29, 34, 37, 70
Medical review, 76
Medicare/Medicaid, 6, 19, 95
Medication control, 51
Meetings, 103–5
  promoting good behavior at, 105
  of treatment teams, 103–5
Mental health services, 3, 143–44
Middle management, 21, 26, 30, 36
Mission of program, 14–19, 34, 37, 41, 43, 47, 49, 56, 70, 84–85, 123, 154, 170, 201, 203
Modeling, 26, 82, 87–88, 100, 121
Morale, 9, 23, 91, 94, 97, 98–100, 110, 114, 120, 152–53, 155
Morales v. *Turman,* 95, 151, 284, 285
Motivation, 79, 87–88, 108, 112

National Institute of Mental Health, 281
Needs assessment, 4, 34
Negotiation, 71–73, 75, 96, 102–3, 121, 205
Newsletter, 171
New York Association for Retarded Children v. *Rockefeller,* 152, 285
Non-profit corporation, 129, 131, 150

Objective behavioral description, 59, 80
Objectives, 20–23

Observation and recording of performance (behavior), 26, 28–29, 34, 57, 80–81, 83, 88, 93
  automatic recording, 29, 109
  bias in, 108–9, 156
  direct measurement of permanent products, 29, 109
  duration recording, 29, 109
  event recording, 29, 109
  halo effect, 109
  interval recording, 29, 109
  latency recording, 29, 109
  leniency effect, 109
  methods of, 29, 109
  of patient behaviors, 115–16
  sources of data for, 111–12
  time sampling, 29, 109
Operational definition of behavior (performance), 20, 33, 47, 70, 80, 153, 188
Operational plan, 14–15, 81
Organizational behavior management, 24
Organizational development, 27
Organizational structure (design), 35–46, 203–4
  adaptive organizational structure, 40–42, 57, 68, 73, 172, 203
  of boards, 198–99, 201, 209
  charts of, 9, 37, 43–48, 54, 57, 103, 166, 168, 170, 203
  domains of, 36
  integrating function of, 53, 55–56
  malfunction of, 36, 47
  matrix design, 1, 39, 40–42, 203
  problems in, 36, 47, 203
  pyramidal (hierarchical) design, 1, 35, 38–46, 55, 203
  roles in, 35–36, 99
  systems of, 28–29, 203
  theory of, 7, 279
  unitization, 106
Orientation, 7, 12, 21–24, 27, 46, 48, 52–55, 58, 61, 66, 71, 73–78, 83, 92, 94, 96–97, 99–103, 105, 121, 167, 172, 201, 204, 208
  of board members, 198–201
  checklist for use in, 74–78, 92, 204
  group, 73–74
  on-the-job, 74, 78
  Orientation Checklist, 74–78, 92, 204
Output, 59, 69–70

Parent Advisory Board, 45, 65, 73
Parent involvement, 64–65, 67
Patient care teams, 39
Patient monitoring, 85, 115–16
Patient Status Report, 103, 115–16
Patient tracking system, 111, 115, 155–58, 175, 182, 207, 255
Peer review, 53, 57, 158–60, 164–69, 204–8, 265
  case consultation, 166, 207
  contracting for, 165–67, 175
  follow-up, 169

form for use in, 168
interdepartmental, 53, 57, 158, 175
peer review committees, 166, 169
performance standards for peer reviewers, 166–68
planning for, 166–68
preparing for, 165–66
procedural steps for, 169
program review, 166–169, 207
reviewee satisfaction, 169
written report, 169, 175
Pennsylvania Association for Retarded Children v. *Commonwealth of Pennsylvania,* 151–52, 285
Pension, 50
Performance appraisal, 94, 108–22, 158, 175, 206
for boards, 199–201
criteria for, 108–10
sources of data for, 111–12
strategies for, 110–22
Performance contracting, 58–73, 213–29
for consultants, 162–63
negotiation in, 71, 73, 75, 92, 101–2, 165–67, 172
for supervisors, 59, 101, 205
Performance evaluation, 8–9, 108–22, 204–6
Performance measures, 2, 10, 12, 17, 19, 29, 79, 98, 136
Performance standards, 58–73, 213–29
for administrative (supervisory) personnel, 67–68, 100–101, 156, 213–20
for board members, 195
for consultants, 162–63
coordinating function of, 68
format for, 59–60
for human service manager, 60–67
integrating function of, 67–69
for non-administrative personnel, 68–69, 221–29
for peer reviewers, 166–67
in program evaluation, 153
reinforcing function of, 67
revision of, 72–73
special projects, 88, 93, 108, 119
Permanent product data, 111, 115, 120, 153, 156, 199
Personalized system of instruction, 83–86, 91, 93, 108
Personalized training plan, 84–86
Personnel file, 32, 61, 72–73, 76–77, 91–92, 109, 113, 118
Personnel management, 6–9, 12, 14, 23, 26, 28, 60–61, 94–122, 152, 155, 167–68, 172, 203
absenteeism, 6, 24, 50, 96
affirmative action, 49, 61, 101, 168
benefits, 23, 50, 59, 61, 75, 99, 112–13, 137, 149, 168, 198
bonuses, 79, 98, 102, 110, 113, 119, 159, 164
budgeting for, 102

career development, 102, 112
codes of conduct, 73, 99, 119, 121
compensation (salary), 12, 23, 50, 59, 61, 75, 99, 112–13, 119, 137–38, 149, 168, 186
corrective action, 100, 120–22
corrective interview, 119–22, 206
demotion, 119–20
disciplinary action, 49, 100, 101, 113, 119–22, 160, 189
dress code, 49, 114
employment of the handicapped, 97, 101
entrance interview, 118
Equal Employment Opportunity, 49, 61, 101, 168
exit interview, 97, 118
firing, 49
grievance, 49, 97, 99, 110, 118, 188
hiring, 49, 68, 71, 73, 95, 97–98, 101, 121, 205
incentive systems, 102, 110, 113, 119–20, 122
leave accrual, 50, 75, 113
licensing and certification, 48, 60, 95, 167, 170
meetings, 103–6
monitoring performance, 98, 100, 103, 108, 111–13, 122, 168, 179, 189, 190
morale, 9, 23, 91, 94, 96, 98–100, 110, 114, 120, 152–53, 155
negotiation, 71–73
orientation, 58–78
peer pressure, 104
performance appraisal, 94, 108–22, 158, 175, 206
performance contracting, 58–73, 213–29
performance evaluation, 8–9, 108–22, 204–6
performance standards, 58–73, 213–29
personnel file, 32, 61, 72–73, 76–77, 91–92, 109, 113, 118
position (job) titles, 44–45, 59–60, 101
positive teaching interaction, 101
probationary status, 49
professional work force, 102, 121
promotion, 119
rating scales, 108, 114
recruitment, 8, 49, 61, 68, 71, 75, 97–98, 100–101, 106, 121, 152, 167, 198, 200, 205, 208–9
resignation, 49, 96, 98
retirement, 113
routines and checklists for, 102–3, 108, 111, 113–14, 121, 189
shift change, 50, 111–12, 115
staff development, 102
staffing pattern, 95
staff satisfaction, 16, 111, 116, 122
staff-to-patient ratio, 4, 16, 18, 95, 97, 106, 168, 170
substitute staffing, 96–98
supervision, 4, 7–9, 23, 41–42, 48, 52–53, 61, 70, 92–122, 155, 157, 167, 205